Road Warrior:

CONFESSIONS
OF
A MALE STRIPPER

Nick Molloy

Pen Press

First published in Great Britain by Pen Press

All paper used in the printing of this book has been made from
wood grown in managed, sustainable forests.

ISBN 9781906710521

Printed and bound in the UK
Pen Press is an imprint of Indepenpress Publishing Limited
25 Eastern Place
Brighton
BN2 1GJ

A catalogue record of this book is available from
the British Library

Cover design by Jacqueline Abromeit

To the Scottish Liberal Democrat, who worked for the RSPB, whom I met in a gay club after a performance in Bournemouth. You said I should write a book about my experiences that tackled all the prejudices. I can't remember your name, but this is for you.

Also, to Mike Baldwin, without whom this book never would have been.

Like a loser's reach – too slow and short to hit the peaks...

FOREWORD

I was advised to write this foreword by several friends who had read the text. Basically, they thought it didn't do me justice. A couple of them even expressed the view that I come across as negative about the stripping business. In the light of their comments and feedback, I feel it is necessary to state my position clearly. This is not to justify but merely to clarify. What follows is an honest appraisal of the male strip scene in the UK. The emphasis is placed on the word 'honest'.

Unfortunately, in a society now so steeped in hypocrisy there is little place any more for a candid man. In a domain where the truth has unpleasant consequences, it appears that the vast majority now bow to that hypocrisy. For example, one agent told me this book had the makings of a bestseller if only I was a little less candid. Apparently, the reader needed to love me. I must appear warm and cuddly. Furthermore, I was told virtually all autobiographical material these days is penned by a ghost writer with a healthy sprinkling of fiction to help the story sell to a naïve public. Nobody ever needed to know provided I was economical with the truth. Another agent said that I could be perceived as chauvinistic because of the candid way I have described the behaviour of women on hen nights. Apparently, I should cut out these potential offensive elements. In his defence, a female friend of mine did point out that there are very few references to me having female friends throughout the text.

I haven't written this book to try to win friends and influence people. I am highly opinionated but at the same time I am highly analytical. I form my opinions after much analysis and feel I could argue my position with the very best.

I am someone who has always found it hard to be in step with the mainstream. However, I am extremely passionate about my interests and many things about our modern society make me angry. A fair bit of that anger emerges in this book. I haven't set out to offend but some people may inadvertently feel that way. This book isn't designed to make me look good. I'm not a celebrity and the reader will therefore have little interest in what charities I give to or the sacrifices I make for my friends.

I have tried to give you a totally honest and uncompromising account of life in this offshoot of the sex industry. So honest, in fact, that you, the reader, may decide you don't really like me all that much at the end. I hope you are not too quick to judge. This book started as an anti-prejudicial project. Everything that follows did occur; none of it is fictional. All the characters exist, but the names have been changed to protect their true identities (and potentially prevent me being sued).

Nick Molloy – June 2008
nick@sexecute.eclipse.co.uk

PREFACE

I have one of the best jobs in the world. I live out a relatively stress-free existence. I'm my own boss, I get to travel, to see different places and I have plenty of spare time on my hands. On the downside, my salary is modest, but the job comes with plenty of 'minge' benefits. Short of being a highly paid professional athlete, I can't imagine any other job I would rather have.

Yet, given all the above, I am beginning to wonder whether becoming a professional male stripper has been worth the ride. I used to have stability in my life. A well-paid job had bought many home comforts. At the tender age of 25, a six-figure salary had bought a fast car and a house in Sussex (albeit mortgaged). My girlfriend had moved down from Scotland (we had been dating since we were 18). We were going great and the future looked bright. So bright I had to wear shades.

However, money has never really been my god. Fulfilment has always meant more to me. Deprived of what I believe was my true calling in life (as a professional athlete), my somewhat warped mind took an opportunity that came along to enter the small, but unconventional world of the artiste or performer. Finally, I would get paid and earn a living out of training my body.

There have been many highs and a few lows, but as I write, my life has been transformed and right now it seems to be disintegrating around me. The rock in my life, my girlfriend of 13 years, seems so alien to the character that I have become. That age-old philosophical question of whether we can be different people at different times in our life seems so topical right now. Have I become someone different? Have I actually taken on the persona of my stage character? Are Nick and Sexecute now one and the same?

I feel like I am currently in a terrible limbo state. My existence brings me so much pleasure, but it is also bringing me so much pain. The pleasure-pain principle is so intertwined as to be inseparable, at least for me.

I simply wasn't this emotional when I had my 'normal' job and the existence that went with it. Now I seem to ride an emotional roller coaster. Days, people, meetings, encounters, frissons; they all seem to blend into one another. The boundaries have become blurred and fantasy and reality sometimes seem frighteningly similar.

I have some difficult times ahead and for the first time in a long time, I feel frightened and alone. Maybe I should have stayed straight-laced after all. My girlfriend has just stated that she "can't fucking believe" me... I have a job I love, a girlfriend that loves me and permission to fuck other women. Yet still I'm not contented.

Without trying to appear conceited or arrogant, I often feel envious of stupid people. It appears that they derive so much pleasure from simplicity, yet I seem forever bitter and twisted. Whether this is a by-product of intellect, a dysfunctional childhood or even a product of my imagination, I'm not sure. I know that on paper I've got just about everything going for me, it just doesn't feel like it. Maybe I've fallen into the trap and I am somehow beginning to mould into a stereotype of something I abhor. The average profile of a male stripper is something I am keen to distance myself from. Yet maybe, somehow, it's closing in on me...

Chapter 1

The Formative Years

Taking my clothes off for a living could hardly be termed my calling in life. In fact, to this day, most of my friends who knew me prior to my strip career still can't believe it. Those that have ventured out with me to shows pinch themselves when they see me perform. They can't reconcile how the quiet, reserved person they knew as Nick somehow transforms into the cocky, gregarious, outgoing character on stage known as Sexecute.

Personally, I don't understand the difficulty they have in reconciliation. All my life people seem to have underestimated me and I seem to have been forever proving people wrong. I guess most people don't talk to someone in quite the same way if they think he could hit you, as opposed to someone who they think never would. I suffer from this. People don't think I'll strike and they are continually surprised when I do.

Quietness should never be interpreted as under-confidence. Quite the reverse in fact. If you are confident of something you should not need to brag about it. If you can deliver the goods, then just get on and deliver them. It is the people that lack confidence that feel the need to replace what they don't have in ability with a volley of verbal diatribe. This is aimed at displacing the listener and convincing them that the person before them can actually pull off what they claim they can. It has always dismayed me that people are so easily fooled. I often ask why are we so anaesthetised to the lies? Our whole society now seems predisposed to it.

I often recount the fairytale from childhood about the emperor and his new clothes. The one whereby the emperor was surrounded by yes men who constantly told him everything he wanted to hear. They did this so much so that when the emperor walked out into the street with no clothes on, everybody still told him that his outfit was great. It wasn't until a small child shouted out that the emperor had no clothes on that the reality hit home. I often feel like that small child. I'm sure I see the world for what it is. It just seems that so many others choose to see it another way. They wrap it up in cotton wool and package it up in complete divergence to the reality. The great opinion leader – television – excels in this area. Is it a great educational tool providing endless entertainment or the drug of the nation, breeding ignorance and feeding radiation? Our fascination with tabloidal news reporting would seem to suggest the latter.

By the age of 28, I had become one of the world's youngest cynics. Taking my clothes off for a living has become a form of therapy to me. In order that you might understand why this is, a brief overview of my background and what shaped me is required.

I was born in 1974 in what is known now as Greater Manchester. Both my parents heralded from Salford. Eight years prior to my arrival they had given birth to my sister; both of them were only 16 years of age. They were married at the tender age of 21 and my sister was a bridesmaid at their wedding. I was the planned pregnancy.

Both my parents were from a working-class background and just before I came along they had bought a small bungalow in an 'up and coming' (read downmarket) little village called Little Lever, near Bolton. Sometime after I was born, Little Lever achieved the dubious honour and hit the headlines for having the highest number of unplanned teenage pregnancies in the country.

The early years for my parents were something of a struggle. My mum worked from home making coats. My dad performed various odd jobs until he finally landed something semi-respectable working as a sales rep for a frozen food company.

In my early years, I was of course oblivious to their struggles or the obvious dysfunction that ruled our household. It is only when looking back at events that it is clear to me that all was not 'normal'.

My years from birth to the age of ten, whilst not the smoothest, were my happiest and most contented. I had plenty of friends, no responsibilities and my spare time was dedicated to the pursuit of what economists refer to as utility (happiness). Playing with my friends was the centre of my world and not much seemed to impinge on my happy-go-lucky existence. I was a confident, outgoing, driven child. If I was a youngster today, I believe I would be diagnosed as having Asperger's Syndrome (AS).

Asperger's is essentially a mild form of autism that can cause some learning difficulties. Psychologists debate over precise symptoms, but they include difficulties in the basic elements of social interaction, a failure to develop friendships or enjoy spontaneity, a pursuit of specific or narrow areas of interest and a tendency to use and interpret language very literally. Most individuals with Asperger's Syndrome can learn to cope with their differences, but may continue to need moral support and encouragement to maintain an independent life. Adults with Asperger's Syndrome have reached the highest levels of achievement in fields such as mathematics, physics and computer science and Hans Asperger described many of his young patients as 'little professors'. Indeed, researchers and people with Asperger's Syndrome have contributed to a shift in attitudes away from the notion that AS is a deviation from the norm that must be treated or cured, and towards the view that AS is a difference rather than a disability.

Anyway, I certainly had many of the symptoms and struggled with school at first. For example, to this day I can't hold a pen 'properly' (another symptom). However, I seemed to adapt pretty well and I had an uncanny ability at mental arithmetic. In the latter part of junior school, I was far too quick for the teachers and I was rivalling Carol Vorderman whenever I watched *Countdown*.

From the age of seven upwards, I was interacting much better and spent much of my time out of the house and with my friends. My dad was in training with his new job. This frequently meant that he went away on Monday morning to some far-flung place and didn't return until late on Friday evening. My mum simply wasn't interested in the things I was interested in: football, dinosaurs, game books; these were all at the centre of my world and those of my friends. I was walking the mile-long journey to school on my own and most nights after school I would play football. We would either hang around on the school fields and play or migrate to the field where Little Lever played their home matches. After football I would return home somewhat reluctantly and if allowed, return out again afterwards. My mum rarely allowed me to bring friends back to the house. If I wasn't permitted to venture back out, I felt imprisoned.

Football really was the centre of my world. I decided at an early age that I wanted to be a professional footballer. I was reasonably gifted as an athlete, being quick and able at most sports. Only my friend Stephen was better at sports in our year group at school.

My competitive urge seemed to take hold at an early age, yet I firmly believe we are as equally a product of our environment as well as our genetics. The men in my dad's side of the family are all competitive and prone to exaggeration. I was told constantly from an early age how successful they all were at sport and how they were always getting the better of people in nearly every situation. How much of an influence this had on my early development is hard to say, but it almost certainly played a part.

I decided early on that my narrow field of interest was going to be that of a professional footballer, no matter what the cost. I would train seven days a week, 52 weeks a year. I remember telling my dad when I was nine years of age that I would never smoke or drink because top sportsmen don't do that sort of thing. He smiled and said that I would change my mind when I got older. I remember clearly having a bet that I would not drink when I got older. The only thing I can't remember was whether there was money involved or not. I won a couple of bets against him where he gave me £10, so maybe it was for £10. He really ought to be paying up someday soon!

My friend and big rival, Stephen, began to play for clubs that could be described as being 'in the system'. I remember his dad being very humble and supportive towards both his sons, encouraging them to do what they wanted to do. Later in life Stephen discovered women and drink; he didn't have the necessary discipline to make it as a pro. However, he did go on to coach for Bury and Manchester City. His less talented older brother, however, did go on to make it as a professional footballer.

I remember being aged ten and Stephen telling me to come and join the club he was playing for. "But I have no way of getting there," I protested (it was several miles from our abode). His dad could take me, he said.

Yet, at the age of ten, my world was about to fall apart. My dad had been training for a couple of years to step into a new role at work. We had hardly seen him, except on the weekends, for some time. His company had been grooming him to run a frozen food distribution depot and an offer had finally come in for him to run a depot of his own. The snag would mean a permanent move for him and his family. I, of course, was never party to any negotiations. I think my dad talked things through with my mum, but the decision was a clear-cut one. Why would he have trained for all those years just to turn an opportunity down? Besides, it could lead onto bigger and better things for him, or so he thought. He accepted the role. The house in Little Lever was put up for sale and my parents began to scout for houses in South Wales.

My protests fell on deaf ears. They thought they were doing me a favour. Little Lever was, and still is, a shithole in the eyes of most people. It had its fair share of typical inner-city urban deprivation problems: teenage pregnancies, violence, drugs. My then teenage sister had gone off the rails at school, dating a succession of moronic Neanderthal-like boyfriends who were well known to the local police. I recall clearly a time when a gang of 20 or so marauding skinheads chased my friends and me off a football pitch. Needless to say, we didn't hang around to ask questions. We regularly used to run away from Meagan, the local teenage escapee from the mental asylum, on the way home from school. Yet these were all side issues in my life and I hardly considered them a major threat. All that mattered was football and my mates. All of that was about to change and change radically for the worse…

*

The screams were deafening. They always scream on a ladies' night. In fact you could probably dress up a chimp in a fireman's costume and they would still scream with the occasional shout of "get yer cock out".

However, there was something different about them on this night. This crowd was actually hysterical, or should I say suffering from hysteria. I can only liken it to some of the old black-and-white footage I remember watching of the Beatles. Small gangs of girls would scream incessantly and hysterically, apparently for no reason other than being in close proximity of a few Liverpudlians. The very same Liverpudlians could have walked the street unnoticed only a few years before, but now they had become blessed with the benefits of celebrity. The media had hyped them and peer groups demanded the worship of them. According to the media some girls were so overcome by their presence, that they actually fainted.

In all my time as a stripper, I can say that this level of hysteria is thankfully rare, so rare in fact that I had long ago concluded that the media had made up the story of the fainting girls just to shock and create headlines. After all, why would someone to be so overcome with emotion that they would physically pass out just because they sighted somebody they had read about/seen on television. As a story it is totally bizarre and completely outlandish.

Yet before my very eyes, on this warm Leicestershire night, the very same phenomenon I had dismissed as myth and make-believe was happening before my very eyes. As I had strode to the stage a woman had grabbed my arm and stroked it along its length whilst looking longingly into my eyes. Perhaps she was the catalyst for what was to follow. Perhaps what she had decided she wanted, they all wanted. Who knows?

Half way through the act I perform explosive one-handed press-ups whereupon I swap arms mid-air. I'm not a dancer. Dainty moves are not my forte; power moves are. It is designed as a dramatic gesture, but it never got this sort of response before. After a few explosive press-ups I pause for effect and look up slowly. The entire front row of women were swaying gently, unsteadily. Three of them at least looked close to fainting.

When I went walkabouts into the crowd (totally naked), I was pawed at like a god. Usually some jealous, bitter, ugly or superior type has a few crude expletives to expunge in my general direction. This is the price that is paid for not attending to every single woman in the room combined with a form of self-loathing on their part that requires a frustrational outlet for their ire. The stripper is often that outlet. On this occasion, however, mass hysteria had taken over and they all worshipped the very ground on which I walked. I could apparently do no wrong.

I finished the act, picked up the box into which I had erotically disrobed my garments and made my way for the exit door (at the back of the hall and through the expectant throng). A slim, twenty-something brunette barged some of her fellow hysterics out of the way and made a mad charge in my direction. She jumped on my back and wrapped her hands around my neck. She gushed sweet nothings into my ear,

"Shag me – I'll wait for you out the back, we can do it against the wall."

"Later," I replied, desperate to escape the madness and discover the pheromone they had all seemingly been poisoned with. If I could bottle its effect, I'd be a millionaire…

The next day I was late arriving at Blackpool. I had telephoned ahead to notify the club of my traffic problems. As I walked through the door the DJ recognised me and announced over the tannoy, "Ladies and gentlemen, the stripper has entered the building." A cheer erupted amongst the gathered throng and a sea of bodies parted like the biblical red sea. A couple of slaps on the back later mixed with a cry of "get in there, son" and I had reached the sanctity of my dressing room. A wry smile crossed my face and I couldn't help but think how my new life beat the hell out of wearing a suit and working for a living.

*

My parents settled on a place called Llantwit Major, a picturesque little village on the South Wales coast. It was about 20 miles from

Cardiff with very little in between. Llantwit was very different to Little Lever. Although they were similar in overall size, Little Lever was part of a huge conurbation that stretched for miles, and a total population that exceeded two million people. By way of contrast, Llantwit Major had about 10,000 people and was surrounded by fields and the sea. I can visit there today and it always seems quite nice; a place of almost idyllic tranquillity. In 1984 it became my hell on earth and remained so until 1992.

On December 2nd 1984, I left Little Lever in the back of a car. It might as well have been a prison van transporting me to jail to begin my sentence. I remember clearly my last day at school. I felt strangely emotional as a line of my friends were waving goodbye at me as I walked away across the school field. I also remember not feeling very well a couple of days prior and the teacher had said something about maybe it was because I didn't want to move. It could have been upsetting me a little, he hypothesized.

Two months before leaving Little Lever, my mum had finally succumbed to the pet pressure. For years I had wanted a dog and never been allowed one. So had my dad. With the imminent trauma of the oncoming move was the timing a coincidence? Without Jasper, my Rottweiler, the Llantwit years may have been too much.

My parents sold their house in Little Lever and moved into a bigger house in Llantwit Major. Real estate wasn't worth much in Little Lever then and I don't suppose it's worth much now either. Property prices in Llantwit are hardly the most expensive when compared to many locales, yet when compared to Little Lever they are decidedly upmarket. My parents took on a far bigger mortgage and again times became difficult for them financially.

The area was noticeably more affluent and my mother adopted a distinct 'keep up with the Jones" attitude. Suddenly, I was allowed to bring friends into the house without asking because all the other mothers in the street allowed their offspring this freedom. I guess Llantwit just didn't have the same number of uptight, pregnant, teenage single mothers that Little Lever had. The tension in the parents wasn't quite as evident.

Initially, things didn't seem too horrific. The new children at my school were polite and cordial. They, after all, had been taught much better manners than their Little Lever counterparts. However, their initial niceties could not hide their falsehoods. I was horrified to note that nobody really seemed to like football. My new classmates seemed to label football as a 'girly game' whereas rugby union was the 'manly game'. To this day I despise the union code. Rugby league I have a lot of time for. My opinion on rugby union, however, has never changed. Rugby league is a working-class game played by professional athletes, where the ball stays in plays for over 60 minutes of the average game. To me, rugby union is an upper-class game played by beer swilling rodheads, where the ball stays in play for approximately only a quarter of the game (20 minutes). Although this may be considered an extreme view and certainly won't be a popular one in England, the facts support themselves. Just look at what has happened whenever rugby league teams have met rugby union teams. The first time a league team was allowed in a flagship union contest, the Middlesex Sevens, the league team won it when playing under union rules! The league teams were not allowed entry again for several years after this embarrassment. Having stolen all the best players from league, the union authorities thought that the time was ripe to prove union's superiority. The league team won it again!

Aside from the debate over whether rugby union is a sport for non-athletes, my point was that I wasn't even remotely interested in rugby union. I wanted to play football; my dream was to be a footballer.

I joined the local town team, but things didn't go well for a number of reasons. Firstly, the team already had a striker and the 'coach' was unwilling to try me in that position. Furthermore, he hadn't heard of wingers. Due to my propensity to put myself in positions and situations that most people are unwilling to consider, they instead preferred me in the role of goalkeeper, particularly given that it was a weak area for the team. The coach was willing to try me in every position except up front (where pace hurts the most). Perhaps, most importantly, I wasn't exactly settling in with my new team-mates. As an Englishman in a

Welsh team, the tension was sometimes evident and the anti-English jibes used to hang over me like a terrible odour.

It wasn't long before I decided I was wasting my time (even at the age of 11 I was very decisive) and told the coach I wouldn't be coming to his sessions anymore. His reaction was to visit my house and try and use my mother as a battering ram in an attempt to persuade me to return to training, even promising that he would play me up front in future. A mixture of stubborn pride and ominous foreboding made me stick to my guns and I told him I wouldn't be coming back to play for them. After attempting to change my mind for about an hour, he left the house – defeated. The verbal abuse soon began from my mother about how I had been so rude to him and how it was wrong to talk back like I had.

This was perhaps the turning point when things really went downhill for me. My former team-mates used to come up to me in the school yard and tell me how they were better off without me and that they didn't need me anyway. The anti-English jibes began in earnest and it was not simply confined to my fellow pupils. I distinctly remember once being lectured by a teacher on how the Welsh weren't like "you English".

My reaction to all this English baiting was to react in the worst way possible and return fire in equal measure. I became anti-Welsh and would mock my Welsh comrades on the subject of their unfortunate place of birth. I fully realise now that this was the wrong thing to do. I have nothing against Wales or its people. Indeed, since visiting as a stripper, Wales has left me with some very fond memories.

Yet I never saw it that way when I was young. If my parents had moved to Cardiff, things would probably have been very different. Cardiff is a big, cosmopolitan city with a lot more tolerance to groups and situations. Instead, they moved to Llantwit Major, a small country retreat with a very parochial feel to it. Issues were made of small things and I paid the price.

I began to retreat into myself, but I wasn't going to go down without making a fight of it first. I sought out another football team who was based about six miles away. I attended one training session, and order to attend that one training session, I was picked up by one of the coaches on the team. He very graciously drove to Llantwit to pick me up and drove me back again at the end of it. However, without transport to their training ground I was unable to attend their training sessions. I was unable to drive at 12 years old and I was essentially defeated by logistics.

I complained bitterly, repeatedly and loudly about how I didn't like my new world. My parents just repeated the same old tired line about how I hadn't given it enough time and how everything would be alright in the end. I remember complaining that the school didn't even have a football team until you reached the final year (and then albeit sporadically). I will never forget the comment that came from my sister. With venom that would have made many a drag queen proud, she stated, "It won't matter by then because you will be no good anyway." If words could kill, then they were them.

I retreated completely into myself. My footballing ambitions had been wiped out by forces seemingly out of my control. I had no close friends. They were all Welsh and seemed to hate English people. I went from being a very confident kid to completely lacking in self-belief. Jasper, the pet Rottweiler, became my rock. Every day we would go off together on our solitary walks where I would tell him all about my despair and dismay and how I longed to return to Little Lever. The long summer holidays would pass by without any visitations from other people. Jasper and I would walk and muse about the problems of life and how to fix them.

My school work seemed to suffer also. Call me paranoid, but I am convinced that teachers sensed my alienation from the rest of the class and played/preyed upon the fact. If there was something that nobody in the class understood, I was always the one to be asked the question. Invariably, I would be shouted at for not having listened the first time. In the first year of comprehensive school, I was demoted from the top maths class because I got all the answers right in the exam. No, you didn't read that wrong. I was extremely gifted at mental arithmetic. I could compute the answers faster than someone with a calculator and didn't need to show the workings. Because I hadn't shown the workings the teacher marked my answers wrong even though they were right. When I pointed out the paradox, she accused me of cheating! To quote her: "I can't work those sums out in my head therefore you can't work them out in your head." I responded by pointing out that I had in fact worked them out in my head and I must therefore be better at sums than her. I was immediately sent from the room and told to stare at the wall for an hour. I wasn't very big at the age of 12. I only weighed about five stone and so I did as I was told.

I ceased to make the effort at school and was happy to drop down the classes in the various subjects where they graded on ability. My school reports were laden with comments about how my ability far outweighed my performance. However, my current association with societal misfits was already beginning to manifest itself. I found that those in the lower classes were less judgemental and egotistical. They often possessed learning difficulties of their own and as a result were also to some degree 'outcasts'. I remember another time in a games class whereby I jogged the 1500m giving encouragement to another 'outcast' who was struggling. The teacher gave me detention.

I also remember another time when I couldn't do games because I had broken my leg (playing chess ironically). The games teacher didn't seem to buy my excuse despite the fact that I had a huge plaster on my leg and I was walking around on crutches. Apparently, I needed a sick note and I didn't have one. Another shouting session ensued.

I hated secondary school and I guess my experience is not too much out of the ordinary. I am sure many people share my sentiments. After all, are schools not simply training grounds for the workplace? You get up in the morning, attend school, get told what to do all day, get given work to take home with you and you are shouted at even when you are right. You learn the essential lesson that you are but one little irrelevant cog in a much bigger wheel. I would also argue that it is a precursor to the slave nation principle. That is, it teaches you to work very hard for little or no reward. This in turn prepares you for the world of work, where every employer seeks employees that will work very hard for as little remuneration as possible.

I didn't like this form of indoctrination and I have never accepted it to this day. I always have and always will be my own person. I have never conformed just because somebody else did or because somebody else wanted me to. At school they labelled me 'Tracksuit Man' because I only ever wore tracksuits outside of school. For some reason this seemed to offend my school colleagues who reasoned that I should instead wear more fashionable garments. I, on the other hand, still live true to the motto "form follows function". That is, if an accessory doesn't have a functional reason to exist then it shouldn't exist. Therefore, if we take the example of the tracksuits, I took and still take the view that tracksuits are comfortable and practical. Therefore, I like to wear tracksuits. Everyone else seems to take the view that they are not pretty to the eye and should therefore not be worn. I, however, care little for such unpractical views and don't care one iota what other people think of my apparent nonchalance on the subject. If you don't like tracksuits don't wear them. However, don't tell me not to wear them because you will get short shrift.

This stubborn refusal of mine to accept regularity and bend to societal norms did not aid my general sense of well-being during this period. The whole world seemed to be against me. The only one who listened sympathetically was Jasper. I used to cry myself to sleep at night. The last time I remember crying in front of my parents I was 11 years old. After that, I confined it to my pillow at night. I remember once coming home at lunchtime (the house was near the school). I had been rowing with the maths teacher again and I let myself in with the key as usual. I was feeling frustrated and helpless after losing yet another unfair fight. I couldn't possibly win the argument even though I was clearly correct. The tears had been welling up in my eyes on the walk home and the minute I stepped through the door Jasper came to greet me, wagging his stump as usual. I sank to the floor in despair, threw my arms around him and the tears came in floods. Jasper seemed perplexed, concerned almost by my reaction to his greeting. At least he seemed to care.

During the Easter holidays I would sometimes go and visit my grandparents in Salford. My wise old grandfather (on my dad's side) was the one family member that I could seemingly relate to.

When I told him how much I hated living in Llantwit, he seemed to sense my pain. He also used to drive me to Little Lever and leave me there for the day, picking me up in the evening. I could at least attempt to go and visit some of my old friends.

It wasn't as if my parents weren't frequent visitors to the North. They used to regularly go and visit their parents on the weekends (every few months or so). I used to ask my mum to take me to Little Lever every visit, but there was often an excuse. There was never enough time and she even said outright once, with apparent disgust, "What do you want to go there for?" I had been clearly talking to deaf ears for some time.

Football had gone from my life and I had become freakishly insular in my outlook. I still had sporting ambitions and my attention began to turn to more individual sports. Boxing had always been a favourite of mine, even when football was king. I remember hitting someone in the playground and after that incident people used to ask me, Nick, will you come and Sugar Ray Leonard so and so. (I hit him with a bolo punch.) Marvin Hagler was my god. I remember watching Alan Minter butcher Vito Antuofermo when I was five years old. I took an instant dislike to Alan Minter. When Marvin Hagler destroyed Minter for the world Middleweight crown in 1980, he instantly became my favourite.

As my situation became more and more desperate, my thoughts shifted from wanting to be a professional footballer to wanting to be a professional boxer. However, my mother would again interfere with my ambitions.

When I am into something I don't do it by halves. I am in it to win it. I began to do my usual thing with boxing. It became an obsession. I persuaded my parents to take me out a subscription to boxing news. I read it cover to cover each week. My boxing knowledge became encyclopaedic, almost unhealthy. I first said I wanted to join a boxing club when I was 11, but my mother told me I wasn't allowed. I pushed a lot harder when aged 14 and 15. This time she threatened to throw me out of the house if I ever went to a boxing gym! It is quite possible that logistics would have again intervened to thwart my plan, but my plan was KO'd even before I could enter the ring. The best I could manage was a bit of shadow-boxing, in my bedroom mirror. I watched the tapes and tried to imitate those I admired. However, I did this with a very hollow feeling. Slowly all my confidence ebbed away.

The only 'sport' I was allowed to play/compete in was chess. Personally, I view chess as a game not a sport. My definition of sport states that athletic endeavour must be involved to classify it as a sport. This rules out activities such as golf, snooker, and darts. They are classified as games. Sports such as cricket have always been a bit borderline for me as to whether they should be classified as a game or a sport. Anyway, in my final year at primary school I won the annual chess competition without knowing all the rules of the game.

As all my other activities were eroded I joined the local chess club, where I temporarily found some solace. I was never a great player, I just saw it as a bit of fun. However, chess taught me a lot, particularly in defeat. One error can undermine a couple of hours of concentrated good work to the point of collapse. I lost count of the number of times I snatched defeat from the jaws of victory. Chess teaches you to lose. What I mean by that is that it teaches you to lose with dignity, but also to take much from the defeat. You are able to go away, play the game over again and analyse where you went wrong. Taken correctly, defeat makes you stronger and more capable the next time. These are very valuable life lessons. Furthermore, in a similar way to boxing, it demands so much control from its protagonists. When you make a bad move, you cannot simply pick up the board and throw the pieces away (or even at your opponent). That would be to concede defeat. Instead, you must coolly regroup yourself mentally and devise a strategy that can counteract your mistake. This demands a high level of restraint and self-control. When applied to real world situations these are extremely valuable lessons.

When I first joined the club I was the leading junior player and I was soon asked to play for the senior team. By the age of 14, I captained the second senior team and soon formed a third team for my legion of up and coming youngsters, which I also captained. I sometimes used to play up to eight people at once, but I stress

I was not a great player. To the average man in the street I may seem like a world-beater, but in reality I was just a reasonable club player. I became friendly with a guy called DK (he was called DK because there were four David Evans in his class at school and the distinguishing initials stuck). DK was a good player, he went to the Chess Olympics with the Welsh team and is officially ranked as an expert in the game. In all the games I ever played against him, I have only ever beaten him twice.

Chess club was also a social outlet for me. I was more friendly with men three, four and even five times my age than I was with any of my classmates at school. One of them, Terry, used to pick me up and we used to go and play an extra night each week at another club some 15 miles away. However, it seemed to me that my mother also attempted to interfere with my chess. She knew that I was playing for the team and she knew that on match nights I had to be there for certain times. Yet, when I would point this out and state that I would need to eat early, it didn't go down too well.

I never have been a very good cook. In fact, I am appalling to this very day. I was never shown how to, I don't derive pleasure from it and have no inclination towards it. However, I've got to eat. My diet is especially important to me nowadays. Back then it was less so. Yet I still needed to eat. In the end, I managed to get my mum to tell me how to make rice. On chess nights I used to make myself some boiled rice and eat it on its own. It was very boring, but at least I would arrive to the matches on time!

I continued to play chess until I left for university. It is one of my few pleasant memories from my time in Llantwit Major. Yet it was only ever going to plug a gap for me. Often, after finishing chess, I would like to go for a run. I would pound the streets of Llantwit Major, punching imaginary opponents in my boxing fantasy. After all that mental stimulation, the release of the physical energy was unusually satisfying and it was particularly pleasant on a warm summer evening.

*

"Some of them can even take traffic cones, you know."

My location was Bristol. I had just performed at a gay fetish club night called Deviant. I'd secured the gig by walking into a gay club in Bristol and asking if they hired strippers. The reply was negative, but the friendly grey-haired gentleman standing at the bar said he was interested in hiring my services for his club night.

Rob is a good guy; I like him. He's a kindred spirit; a fellow nonconformist who doesn't sit comfortably in the society we live in. Apart from the leather get-up he wears, he could easily pass for a cuddly old granddad – someone more akin to a pipe and slippers rather than hard-core gay sex club impresario.

Anyway, I had performed at Deviant once before, but a stripper is frankly too tame for this crowd. I had returned at Rob's bequest. He wanted to hire me as a model, albeit an unusual one. Three hundred pounds demanded that I was naked, had to be tied up and pretend to be whipped, beaten and stretched in an underground dungeon by vicious skinhead masters, who wore copious amounts of leather. It was actually quite fun and very professional. I was earning over twice the average strip fee and wasn't mutilating my genitals as I normally would. Instead, I was being photographed by an overwhelmingly friendly, caring bunch of people who kept asking me if the ropes binding my hands were uncomfortable.

Whereas I was being paid to be photographed, there were plenty of others present who were undergoing the same treatment just for the sheer hell of it. Some had all four limbs bound to a cross. Others were tied over a specially constructed bench, being spanked with paddles. Others still were being stretched on a medieval-looking rack!

In the corner were the slings. Bald, leather-bound granddads wearing chaps with their arses hanging out seemed to abound in this area. Some were in the sling with their feet in stirrups, whilst another leather-clad man was thrusting his entire fist deep into the anal cavity of what I can only describe as the victim.

Whilst I was staring in a sort of horrified wonderment, thinking to myself 'I bet that hurts', Rob approached and told me of the traffic cones. How far in the traffic cones go, I never actually established.

I slept on Rob's couch that night as I was bound for Cardiff the next day. Before we could sit down and chat the night away, however, Rob had to lock up his 'slave'. His slave was a young guy barely out of his teens. A regular on club nights, he had to do as Rob told him. In the spare room there was a steel cage about four foot square. The slave spent the night locked up in there.

After securing the subservient deviant member, Rob and I chatted the night away on the ills of conformity. What wonderfully liberal minded people my new profession was introducing me to.

*

My torment probably peaked around the age of 14. I'm not sure whether I adapted to my lonely existence, began the development of extensive coping mechanisms, or if I began to see the light at the end of the tunnel (escape from home). Things began to improve a little. My daily routine, that of going to school, coming home and reflecting whilst out walking Jasper, then generally sulking until crying myself to sleep changed little. However, a couple of minor changes gave me some focus and re-direction. I was able to choose some of my subjects at school and drop some of the ones I didn't like. A couple of new ones became available that weren't available before (such as business studies and media studies). Other subjects actually took on a real and more serious edge. History, for example, ceased to be a juvenile pastime where we were required to draw pictures of invasions. It became interpretive and investigative for the first time.

Media studies was largely viewed as a Mickey Mouse subject by those that took it and even more so by those that didn't take it. That is a shame, because it taught me more than other subjects during my stint in academia, with history probably coming a close second. Media studies was taught by a character who was known to all and sundry as 'Caveman'. This could be ascribed to his scraggly appearance and dodgy beard. He also had a carefree attitude. His real love and primary calling was as an art teacher; media studies was an aside. He would come in, give a lecture and then leave us to our own devices for a month until the next section of the course was due. Most used the free time as just that. Caveman, however, was always available to those that sought his council (me, myself and I). The key thing that media studies and history taught me was to question things. Most people take things at face value. It is a sad indictment on our current society that straight teeth in your mouth are now more important than the words that come out of them. Both subjects emphasised that everything we hear, everything that we are told, is probably not as it seems.

My parents were keen for me to do well at school if not at sport. It was probably about the only thing they really encouraged me in. As a result, I managed, under the pretence of media studies, to get my parents to change their daily paper from the Daily Mirror to The Independent. The minute I left home it was exchanged for the Daily Express.

After my acceptance slowly and reluctantly began to set in about football (and was still setting in about boxing), I was allowed a cheap set of weights from Argos and began to tentatively weight train (aged 14). My body responded well to my discipline and weight training gave me an individual sporting focus. It was a sort of adaptation to my original goals. Lifting weights in my room was something I could do on my own and nobody took it away from me. Of course that didn't stop my mum from trying. She complained almost non-stop about my new activity. She would walk into my room and go into the cupboard whilst whining incessantly about the barbell in the way of the door. She would complain constantly about the noise I supposedly made whilst training upstairs. Even training in isolation brought its guilt trip problems!

It wasn't long before I could clean and jerk (lift a weight above your head as the Olympic lifters do) my own weight. Most grown men struggle with such a feat, yet as a scrawny teenager I was already there. I was one of the smaller boys in my class at school. My new physique became the envy of many and it also began to change people's perceptions. I hadn't grown that much particularly, but I have small joints (the shape of a classic body-builder) and the perception was, and still is, that I was bigger than I am. I was starting to realise some of my strength potential. All the guys at school began to challenge me to strength contests. I was able to resist all-comers despite being heavily outweighed. Yet despite the challenges I was still unable to make close friends. I was still an outcast, albeit one to be respected.

My body began to undergo changes at the usual age. Fine pubic hair began to grow when I was 13, going on 14. At 14 I had my first wet dream. My parents were never the most comfortable talking about the birds and the bees. In fact, they were distinctly uncomfortable. I recall a conversation when I was about 12 or 13. Both of them sat there in the kitchen, my dad leading the conversation with interjections from my mum. I just sat there nodding. No new information was offered that I hadn't already garnered from the popular media. Certainly, I was poorly prepared for the perils of puberty.

The popular media had taught me the basic principles of sexual intercourse. The man inserts his penis into the woman's vagina. Beyond that I knew very little. Because I had no friends, I had not benefited from their experiences. That is, either from those with sexual experience, or from those with more liberated and informative parents.

I hadn't even conceptualized the reasoning behind erections. My dick was hard about half of my waking existence. If I had been aware of its function, I might have been embarrassed that is was erect so often. However, it was normal to me. Indeed, when I was 18, after going out with my girlfriend for three months, she commented that she had never actually seen me soft!

My first wet dream was an unusually low-key event, particularly given that I didn't really understand what had happened. I remember waking up with a huge sticky mess in my underwear and a wet patch in the bed. I guess my coping mechanisms were becoming well established by then. I just calmly went to the bathroom and cleaned myself up.

Repeat occurrences of the incident every few days allayed my initial concerns that something was wrong. Furthermore, I was beginning to remember some of the dreams and they were always pleasant. A couple of times I distinctly remember having that orgasmic feeling whilst in my sleep, brought on by some random sexual encounter played out in my head. I would wake up to the sticky mess, but the pleasant memories made up for it. I didn't have any material that I could research to find out what was happening to me and I had no friends to consult either. Despite this, the regularity of the occurrence and the obvious changes occurring within my body reassured me that it was just a sign of a newfound maturity.

The other obvious change after the onset of wet dreams was my state of arousal. I had always had fantasies since an early age. I distinctly remember when only six years old being 'turned on' (in a six-year-old sort of way) by a girl grabbing my genitalia in the playground and threatening (in a playful way) to pull them off. I had gone to bed at night from an early age and played out fantasy situations of a sexual nature in my mind. Those sexual fantasies merely matured as I got older. They went from a doctors and nurses type scenario to actually wanting to poke and prod with the nether regions. At that age my fantasies were still in their infancy.

After becoming sexually reproductive, however, the fantasies took on a new overtone. It became apparent that simply rubbing up and down against the duvet brought a pleasant sensation, one that simply wasn't that good before.

My first masturbatory experience stuck close to the pleasure-pain principle. It was simultaneously both great and frightening. I knew nothing about masturbation or the techniques (the likes of which had never been mentioned in our household). I just knew that playing with my dick was extremely pleasurable. One night I was lying awake unable to get to sleep; in my head a fantasy situation was being played out with a girl that attended my class at school. I had adopted a method of rubbing my dick between both my hands as if trying to keep it warm. The sensation of pleasure continued to heighten until every muscle and sinew in my body tensed, my dick stiffened and I thought I had just pissed myself. I couldn't quite believe it, 14 years old and I had just pissed myself! When I turned on the light, I realised that I hadn't. The liquid that had come forth was not urine, but a white, messy, sticky fluid. I mopped it up with my underwear and putting two and two together, realised that the ejaculate bore a close resemblance to the sticky mess I was waking up to every few days in my underwear.

However, I still knew nothing about what was going on in my body. Indeed, I didn't masturbate again for a good couple of months after the first incident. The second time I was feeling braver and more prepared. Several sheets of Kleenex lay by the bed and the light was on so that I could witness and study the event. After I realised that there was nothing to be scared of and that the experience was wholly pleasurable, I became (and indeed still am) a 'wankaholic'. Indeed, as you will see one day I became a professional at it.

Yet I only found out about the internal workings of my body by reading biology books and I only became familiar with the term 'cumming' at university when I was 18. My newfound friends were somewhat perplexed by my apparent naivety, so much so, they thought I was joking. I let them think I was. Being a virtual social outcast (VSO) had deprived me of some of the very important lessons that kids often learn from their peers. It was certainly a subject my parents did not broach, presumably because they did not feel comfortable doing so.

The subject of girls during my years in Llantwit Major is a very sore point. When I left Little Lever I was a confident, outgoing kid (I had even kissed a girl behind the bike sheds). Since becoming a VSO I had been denuded of my confidence. I lacked completely the social skills required to mingle, fit in and integrate with groups. I had become an isolationist, even though deep down I didn't want to be. I also used to take things very literally and had an unfortunate habit of repeating something my dad had once said: "There are three types of women – stupid, very stupid and incredibly stupid." Needless to say, this didn't go down terribly well. How much of this was me reacting to my pain, like a wounded animal, and how much of it was down to Asperger's-type behaviour, I'm not sure.

The truth is that I wanted to be loved and accepted just like everybody else. However, I wasn't prepared to compromise who I was just to do that (nothing's changed). I was not prepared to do or say things just so I could fit somebody else's view of normality.

What you see is what you get and if you don't like it, I guess that's just tough. People can be cruel, especially children and youngsters. I guess I felt the brunt of that and the resultant herding mentality. I made a conscious decision that I wouldn't change myself to fit a stereotype or behavioural norm. I began to view my stay in Llantwit as a prison sentence that simply had to be served. As with all life's journeys, however, it is so much harder when you do it alone. I still had Jasper. I felt he was the only one that truly loved me back. He didn't demand anything of me particularly – just walks and food – and he didn't continually upset or disappoint me.

There were several girls at school that I had the hots for. Alas, I didn't know where to start. Firstly, I lacked the confidence or know-how to approach them and chat them up. Secondly, it appeared to me that the school was full of people who exhibited juvenile and moronic behaviour. At the age of 15-16, most of my school colleagues began to drink alcohol socially at a club in the town. I was dragged down to this place once (and once only, I might add). With hindsight it was a most amusing scenario. A plethora of 16-year-old boys sat around the edges of this club on chairs, unable to order drinks with a complete lack of knowledge of what to do or how to behave. They all (with one exception) put on the bravado that they were in fact 'manly' by attending the said establishment and acted as though they were 'it'. Personally I found the whole scenario very uncomfortable. I don't and didn't want to drink alcohol. Neither did I wish to have my eardrums perforated by the music and neither did I want to use a megaphone just to speak to the person next to me! I didn't see the function of being there and when I pointed this out to the two people who had dragged me there, they had no evidence to the contrary. I didn't go again (in adult life I have also learnt that nightclubs are awful pick-up joints).

I got four 'A' grades and four 'B' grades at GCSE and continued with A Levels. The entire sixth form years served to re-emphasise my VSO status. Some school colleagues began to have relationships with their peers. I, in the meantime, continued to look towards my release date and little past it. It seemed to me that so many of my school colleagues were riddled with arrogance. Llantwit was distinctly middle class with higher aspirations. This bordered on snobbishness and I felt this was very well represented by the inhabitants of the sixth year.

We were older now and some of our more childish disagreements from yesteryear were put to one side. However, I just didn't belong in this group of people. Looking towards my escape at the end of sixth year, I desperately hoped that university would be my saviour – a fresh start with more like-minded individuals. I began counting down the days.

I longed for a girlfriend; someone to extol the pleasures of the flesh with and someone to confide in apart from the dog. However, Miss Llantwit didn't seem to exist. My two years in sixth form passed much as the previous six had. However, this was not the case for the majority of my school colleagues. Each passing Monday they would return to the common room and tell tales of their further drunken exploits from the weekend before.

When I was 14-15 I played badminton with a couple of guys in my year who nearly became friends. However, a year later they were more interested in getting drunk and proving their 'manliness' by downing pints. They even said they did not like the taste of the liquor. How they were able to afford the expensive drinks they did not like, I don't know. I guess they borrowed the money from their parents. When I would point out the apparent logicality of their actions, they had no defence. They merely said that men drink.

I was invited to a couple of parties in sixth year (as was the whole sixth form). I even attended one! However, it was more of the same: people getting drunk, a distinct lack of intelligent conversation and no girlfriend material. Maybe she was out there and I missed her or lacked the social skills to go and get her. Yet, from where I stood, all I could see was mindless, stuck-up, drunken girls completely lacking in personality. I refused to go to any more of such events. They just used to depress me.

Naturally, such isolation leads one to question oneself: Is it me? Is there something wrong with me? Is everybody else right and I'm the one in the wrong? I certainly didn't make things easy for myself in Llantwit. I didn't try very hard to adapt and fit in. A couple of incidents from memory, however, supported my assertion that my isolation wasn't all my fault. I maintain that the people and/or culture of Llantwit was very middle to upper class and isolationist. During the brief time I played football for the under-12 team, one of the matches was against Grangetown (a rough suburb of Cardiff). At the end of the game (which we won), a couple of their players offered to swap shirts. Our players looked upon the offer like they had just been given a vial of the bubonic plague and told to down it in one! I swapped shirts and was rebuked for doing so.

This alienation/isolationist practice was repeated in a different way when I was in the sixth year. As part of our geography A level we had to spend a week away at a study centre. We were there with another group of sixth years from a Cardiff school. I instantly got on with many of the Cardiff students. I also fancied one of the Cardiff girls. If I had any confidence, and maybe a method of transport, I would have asked her out. However, at that stage I completely lacked the confidence to do so. Anyway, the Llantwit students kept themselves to themselves and didn't mix with the Cardiff students at all. A bus delivered us back to Llantwit at the end of the week and I was saying several goodbyes, but I was the only Llantwitian doing so. Although not openly rebuked, my mixing with the Cardiff crowd was clearly frowned upon by my other classmates. It only added fuel to my theory that all would have been well if my parents had moved to Cardiff instead of a tiny provincial town.

I remember the above week well. It was also the time I was first introduced to Roachford. *Top of the Pops* came on the TV in the evening and I heard what I can only describe as an inspirational track. I acquired the album, and the track 'Get Ready' became my gospel: *"How long can the walls of the past remain. How long can a mountain be too high to climb. Nothing don't last forever. Everything changes in time. Get ready for the dawning. How long is too late to change. Just how much do you care if tomorrow is still the same."* It was as if Andrew Roachford had written the track about me, for me. I couldn't stop listening to it. It was like a connection, as if there was somebody out there who actually understood. It still inspires me to this day.

My failing to acquire a girlfriend had not gone unnoticed at home. My mother used to constantly bitch at me because I was the only person in the entire sixth form who hadn't attended the said party the previous week (having a son who was an outcast probably caused the other wives to talk). Also, she used to go on about how so and so's mother had told her that so and so brought home a new girlfriend the other week. I'm not sure whether making me privy to such information was designed to make me go and acquire a token girlfriend or possibly just to make me feel depressed and inadequate. Needless to say, it did the latter.

Furthermore, my grandmother (on my mum's side) would ask finger-pointed questions about whether I found anyone in my class attractive. It wasn't long after that when my mum told me that my grandmother had been telling everybody in the family that I must be gay due to my lack of girlfriend. I now have countless numbers of gay friends and it irks me even more with hindsight, that both my mum and grandmother tried to attach stigma to how they were labelling me. They didn't refer to me as gay, they instead suggested that I might be 'queer' as if something might be insidiously wrong with me.

Throughout this entire time, no-one sought to comfort me and even find out whether I had an opinion on the subject. I could have had a secret girlfriend for all they knew. What if I was gay? I can't help but think that if I was gay, I would have been that stain on the family name, the social stigmata who brought shame on many. Many people now assume that I am gay. I take it as a compliment. However, back then, the accusation cut through me like a sharp spear. All I wanted was a girl whom I could love and vice versa. Yet, as usual, those who should have been the closest people to me seemed not to understand or even show any interest in me. My isolation felt complete and I couldn't wait to leave home.

I began to apply for university places. I had this wonderful idea (albeit very naïve) at the time that advertising would be the industry for me. I wanted to be an advertising copywriter (the guy that writes and comes up with the witty strap-lines for advertisements). I figured that it would be creative; I liked the idea of not wearing suits and at the time advertising executives were getting rich. Like many things in hindsight, it seemed like a good plan at the time.

Not knowing any better, a degree in marketing seemed a good solution. Naïvely, I thought such a course would teach me the skills of and lead me into my chosen profession. Marketing courses were largely the domain of the new universities or old polytechnics. In our new, wonderful, politically correct climate, polytechnics had been wiped out and everybody was put on an imaginary equal footing. Of the old universities at the time, only two had specialist marketing courses: Lancaster and Stirling. Since I was allowed to apply to five old universities, I applied to three others in history, as I was predicted to get a straight A at A Level and it was my favourite subject. It encouraged analysis and deep thought. Furthermore, thinking outside of the box was rewarded and encouraged. Essentially it was my sort of subject.

I sat a MENSA IQ test, thinking it would look good on the application form. I scored 153, apparently placing me in the top 1% of all scores. For the first time in a long time, I had a sense of optimism about the future. Any thoughts of working in the sex industry were completely alien to me…

*

Well there I was, working for and about to be featured in a mainstream glossy magazine. Maybe I should have felt that I had finally made the big time, but I'd been a cynic for more years than I cared to remember. The day that the mainstream media begin reporting fairly, logically and truthfully, I'll drink a bottle of undiluted baby oil. Therefore, there simply had to be a catch.

Since my incarnation as a willy wiggler, I had received many phone calls from TV companies and their minions. Populated by the public school jet set, my dealings with them did nothing to allay my increasing sense of dismay with the world. I looked into working in the media before leaving university. However, unless you are willing to initially work for dog biscuits it seemed a pointless affair. No wonder it remains the domain of the public school/Oxbridge clique.

People from ordinary backgrounds couldn't afford to eat whilst they gained their experience. Wealthy parentage is a big step up into all professions, some more than others...

The researchers (those that make the initial telephone calls) from the various TV programmes typically seem to have heads filled with air. Similarly, they all seem to have had their ears surgically removed. They either react incredulously or don't seem to hear the fact that you would want to be paid to appear on their TV programme. Mummy and Daddy may well be funding their dabble with the media, but some of us still need to eat.

The Trisha Show used to be a regular caller, but two of their researchers had heart attacks when I asked for payment. They don't call me anymore because they keep having to find new researchers. *The Graham Norton Show* wanted me to come and get my dick out for nothing. When I enquired about payment, they talked about the possibility of travel expenses. The budget for the show is huge, probably millions and they are trying to pull stunts like this!

It is a similar story on the modelling circuit. I once did a charity catwalk event appearing alongside a guy off *Big Brother* called Kemal. When the cameras were rolling he played the character off *Big Brother*; when the cameras were turned off he blended into the crowd. Dozens of so-called models were present on this day, preening themselves, putting on their make-up (including the men) and generally trying to look beautiful. I talked to well over a dozen of them. All were regulars on the catwalk. All had posh accents. None of them had ever got paid for modelling, but they all lived in hope.

Yet here I was about to model and get paid by FHM (a major high street glossy men's magazine). The story was that I was to be pitched head to head against a porn movie and female stripper in a contest to see who could turn on a panel of 'FHM High Street Honeys' the most. A guy with an infrared camera was going to point his device at the girls to see if blood was flowing to any parts of their bodies that we couldn't visually see with the eyes. That way, we would know if they were getting turned on. I was told I would only be needed for an hour or so at most. However, in true journalistic 'wanting everything for nothing' style, I was actually there most of the day.

First the truth: The four 'honeys' claimed not to be turned on at all by the porn movie (at least not whilst all those strangers were watching). Mr Infrared and I seemed far more amused by the images flickering from the screens. The female stripper had more success, but the girls were actually terrified of being perceived as lesbians. They partook in a little pole dancing lesson but remained very distant. They warmed to Sexecute far more. Possibly this was because he was the last item of the day and their inhibitions had lessened slightly. Also he was a male stripper, something the honeys would find more socially acceptable to be aroused by (compared to the other competitors). They were also being encouraged to be more demonstrative by the photographer, because frankly they had been a bit of a damp squib for most of the day. Comments were passed by the crew on how I was the first one to bring them to life a little.

Mr Infrared had been a complete waste of money. He was actually some sort of plumber and his camera was actually used for detecting damaged pipes in walls. I was even directed to slap one of the honeys on the tits and remove my hand slowly, hoping to bring about some infrared effect, but still nothing showed up.

Now for the write up. Terry Christian alluded in his book to how it was a waste of time ever meeting a journalist for an interview because they had a pre-script that they had to stick to. That is, they had already written the story and meeting the personalities from within the story was just a journalistic formality. Sometimes they needed a photograph to go with it, but in any case, they were going to write the story how they perceived their readership wanted to see it. So it was in this case.

The porn film was written off as a limited success. The male stripper wasn't shown in the magazine, and his write-up was lukewarm. The female stripper, however, had her image displayed clearly and the write-up said that the honeys were basically gagging for her (not hiding behind the couch which was closer to the truth). Lots of specially constructed infrared images, all coloured in on a computer, were present to back up the mendacity. I should have guessed really. They spent the best part of the afternoon trying to coax the honeys into liking the female stripper and arranging suitable photographic angles. I was given about 20 minutes at the end of the day with one take. The message of the article was, of course, take your girlfriend to a lap-dancing club immediately. They are all gagging for a lesbian threesome. I repeat, why are we so anaesthetised to the lies?

Chapter 2

Character Rebuild

I got the necessary grades and was packaged off to Stirling to begin my new life as a wannabee marketer. Scottish degrees last four years (instead of the usual three) and given the vagaries of the Scottish degree system I was unable to study any marketing until the third year of my course! I had a broad choice of courses for the first two years, studying a wide variety including business studies, history, psychology and philosophy.

My excitement was evident when the day came for me to leave Llantwit Major to go to Stirling for the first time. My thoughts abounded with optimism and the possibilities that a fresh start may bring. Exploration, women, debauchery and new friends all filled my thoughts. I was sorry to leave Jasper behind, but I wasn't going to miss much else. I am sure my parents meant everything for the best, but moving away from Little Lever had seen my world fall apart. University was my new beginning.

I was guaranteed a room on campus for the first year and the future once again had a rosy tinge. Any thoughts of trepidation at the prospect of living alone and away from home for the first time were non-existent. I had served my sentence and I wanted to escape.

Things didn't get off to the best of starts when, upon arriving in Stirling, I was informed that they had an accommodation crisis. For the first time in their relatively new 25-year history, they had been unable to provide all first years with a place on campus (the government in their infinite wisdom had set new targets for students to be placed in higher education irrespective of competency and more students had enrolled than ever before). As a result, my first night at Stirling was spent sharing a room in a hotel with Matt. This was a blessing in disguise, one of those rare times where fate gave me a disguised hand. Matt became a great friend and remains so to this day.

Neither of us were particularly happy about being homeless without a place on campus. We would just have to wait patiently for the natural attrition rate of the first two weeks to take its toll and for a room to become available. The first few weeks of university are often the hardest for 'normal' people. By normal, I mean people who come from perfectly functional homes and backgrounds. They are, after all, separated from their friends and loved ones for the first time and this takes its toll on some. People drop out and return to their haven of comfort with their parents. Being a child of dysfunction, I merely had to sit and wait for the 'weak' normal ones to die off (in the case of the suicidal quite literally). Sure enough, it happened after we had been homeless for about a fortnight.

In the meantime, Matt and I managed as best we could living out of our small hotel room. We were both conscious that we were missing out somewhat on social introductions to potential new-found friends and societies. We used to prowl the halls of residences at night searching for suitably populated kitchens where we could mingle and hopefully find a kettle where we could boil some water for our pot noodles. Neither of us had a clue about cooking and even if we did, we lacked the facilities to cook. Our diet was shocking! It consisted largely of cereal, pot noodles and chocolate bars! The first time we went to the laundrette was an experience. We had to be accompanied by an 'expert' who knew how to work the machines!

It was this night stalking of the residence kitchens that led to an encounter with my much maligned, and for some reason still ultra tolerant of my dysfunctional ways, girlfriend. However, catching the fish was like landing a white shark with a tiny fishing net. Zoe was reading a book when we entered the kitchen. She had dark curly hair with brilliant blue eyes. I just sat and stared; I even forgot about my pot noodle. Matt noticed my attention was diverted and began chatting to the strange woman, who in turn began chatting to me. I didn't understand a word she said! A South Ayrshire accent with local colloquialisms ensured communication would be difficult.

Accents have always been and still are a big turn-on to me in a girl. Scottish accents are amongst my favourites, but they take a little adjusting to if you aren't used to them. I can tolerate most accents on girls as long as they are relatively soft. Scottish speak, however, has many of its own words. At first it sounds like a completely different language!

When Matt and I finally secured our campus rooms, Zoe began to make a habit of coming over and 'waking' me up in the morning. Unknown to her, I had set the alarm half an hour before so that I would be bright and alert for her arrival (whilst still pretending to be sleepy of course). I had already declared my intentions openly, stating that I really liked her and hoped things would lead to more. She wasn't so forward. Instead, she played what I would recognise in future to be a typically female game. By placing all my cards on the table, I had unwittingly handed her all the power and she was able to exploit and use my weakness (albeit I think this was unintentional on her part). She possessed those typical female insecurities and doubts that seem so intrinsic when their thoughts turn to men. Zoe is unlike any other woman I have ever met, yet still she played a game that seemed almost instinctive.

One night after I'd known her for about five weeks and after our friends had left the room, things got a little steamier. Our first real kiss (our technique left a lot to be desired) was followed by some fumbling around in the dark, albeit limited. Every time my hands began to wander, her hands put them back where they began.

By the time I wandered back over to my residence some time later, I had a permanent grin on my face. The feeling of intimacy was so intense, so real, it is difficult to convey the words of how I felt. For me the feelings went far beyond a sexual one. Maybe it was because I had told her so much about myself, things that I had never told anyone else before. Up until then, nobody had seemed interested in the real me before and I wanted to believe that I had found her. It was my first time; the physical had become mixed up with the emotional.

I am sure, dear reader, that you can imagine my horror when the following day she denied any such goings on and blanked me in public. It wasn't until we were alone again that she acknowledged anything had happened and we experienced a repeat performance. However, the emotional roller coaster ride was just beginning. To my continual and immense frustration, Zoe was exhibiting two personas. There was the public one where we were just good friends and the private one where we were a little bit more.

I firmly and truly believe today that men and women can't be friends without the sex part getting in the way (expect where they find each other mutually unattractive). So it proved to be the case in this very first instance. I was trapped. I wanted her more than anything I had ever wanted before. Yet the acceptance followed by immediate rejection pattern was tearing me up inside.

Fortunately, my newfound friend, Matt, proved to be a very sympathetic ear. I told him everything and he continued the pretence in front of Zoe that he knew nothing. If I hadn't been able to confide in him, I'd have probably gone insane. I hung out with Matt most of the time. Several of our classes overlapped and we always used to eat together in the evening (remember we couldn't cook so we used to eat at a cheap, subsidised student bar). We became close.

Generally, my life felt a whole lot better. My confidence was slowly starting to return after the seven-year pounding it took whilst I was 'incarcerated'. I had made some good friends, something that had been missing for a long time. I had something to look forward to, finally. However, the situation with Zoe was making my life a misery. I wanted it so badly, I'd have done anything to get it. This meant I became a glutton for punishment and absorbed the ongoing mental torture as best I could.

Eventually, things came to a head; I said that I was unwilling to let the current situation continue. Either we formally announced and acknowledged our relationship or I didn't want to see her again. She wanted us to remain friends. I said it would be impossible for me to do so. It would just be too painful for me. It felt like a business negotiation. Effectively, she had been presented with the take away close. Buy now and commit, or the offer will disappear for good.

She took the offer, albeit reluctantly. It was if I had forced her hand and she considered having me as a boyfriend a lesser evil to losing my friendship. I know it sounds ridiculous. She says now that she was scared. If she committed to a relationship, she knew it would be a very serious thing for her and she feared that I would then have the power to hurt her. She later said that her behaviour at the time was stupid. However, there is no doubt that she resented me and my actions (the take away close) for some time afterwards. She would never allow any form of public affection (apparently this was unfair to our other friends). Essentially, the public status quo remained; it was just that a very poorly kept secret had now been formally announced.

With the formal announcement, the bedroom antics intensified. Waking up lying next to her naked form in the morning produced a huge adrenaline surge, followed by an immense feeling of inner calm. It was like the final piece of the jigsaw falling into place. I could go off and attend my day's classes whilst being at peace with the world.

We played around with each other's bodies for weeks. She was never as comfortable as I was about the whole nudity and lights on thing. I remember making her wank me off for the first time (lights on). I knew that as a biologist, part of her would be studying me like a lab rabbit. The very thought of me as her submissive test subject turned me on even more and she stared intently at my cock as she rubbed it up and down. I was too embarrassed to let myself go then; I also knew that she would disapprove. I wanted the whole building to know what was going on, I really wanted to have sex with her on the kitchen floor whilst everybody in her corridor watched us. Still, the whole sex thing was new to me and the thought of her, with my dick in her hand, was more than enough to get me hard at the very thought of it. Indeed, Zoe has since said that she didn't actually see my dick soft until about three months after first seeing me naked.

Even in those early days, my thoughts were always very exhibitionistic. I wanted everybody to know and preferably to see our sex life and the kinkier the better. Zoe was considerably more tempered. We once did it outside where nobody was ever going to see us, but that was as far as it went. When we stayed at her mum's I used to fantasise about her sister walking in on us.

However, all of these thoughts remained firmly ensconced in the world of fantasy. Zoe's conservatism was a very heavy counterweight to my sexual extremities.

*

I held out my hand and said, "Hi, I'm Nick from the stripped down fabric company."

'Corporate' strips, as I called them, are some of the most fun. Strippers are regularly asked to turn up in and surprise people in a variety of different uniforms. However, when a guy turns up in a white naval uniform or a fireman's outfit, on the day that it just so happens to be somebody's birthday, the victim can usually recognise the stripper a mile away. Even when the police officer arrives to request that the noise be kept down from the party, it's usually just too coincidental. If somebody is getting married or it's their birthday, then a police officer would turn up to take his clothes off – wouldn't he?

With that said, the police officer probably has the highest success rate of non-suspicion amongst victims compared to other traditional stripper uniforms. I attended one party on a Saturday night and when one of the guests proclaimed that there was a policeman walking down the stairs, one of the girls rushed to the toilet and began flushing away her recreational drugs! She was gutted when she found out I was a stripper.

Corporate ones, however, have 100% success rate. They never suspect. I turn up in a suit at the company premises during the working day. Done properly, I will arrive at a pre-arranged meeting either posing as a buyer or a potential client. The victim listens attentively as I explain what a nightmare my journey was and how hot the train was with all those sweaty bodies crammed into cattle class. As I am explaining about the heat, somebody cues the music and Nelly's 'It's getting hot in here' springs into life. I then proclaim that it's so hot I am going to have to take my clothes off!

Another method is to swap business cards. As I slide my male stripper card over the table, the victim usually does a double, sometimes triple take. As they stare at my Cheshire cat grin the music begins…

In this particular instance, I was a fabric salesman and the victim clearly had a complete disdain for that particular breed. The stripped down fabric company line went straight over her head and she was getting quite tetchy with me. I had to insist on her feeling my revolutionary new fabric.

"Funnily enough, this fabric has proved very popular with male strippers," I said with a certain amount of smug satisfaction.

Finally the penny dropped. I'll never forget her face. It looked like she had just stared into the eyes of Medusa. There was a pause for about two seconds before she turned and ran. Maurice Greene would have been proud with her start, but her colleagues had obviously anticipated her move and two burly chaps with beards rugby tackled her before she could reach the sanctity of the door. She was dragged kicking and screaming back to the centre of the room and placed on a chair where all could see me eventually wave my cock in her face.

The corporate ones produce a lot of job satisfaction. They are the wind-ups that always come good. Once, I even performed in a sixth form college, posing as a visiting teacher. I expected to receive snide comments from jealous pubescent boys (that would have been the reaction at my school). However, I was pleasantly surprised to receive a rousing cheer from all and sundry, almost restoring my faith in human nature.

I have sprung similar surprises where I have posed as a friend of a guest at private parties, mingling in my suit before delivering the coup de grace. That brief look of surprise that comes just before the look of horror always makes me smile.

*

The remaining university years passed fairly uneventfully and effectively completed my rebirth. With my confidence fully returned, my real persona was starting to break out into the world. I finally had somebody I truly loved whom I could call my girlfriend. If I believed in marriage I would probably have proposed. However, I believe ceremonies to obtain pieces of paper are both expensive and outdated. This is my pure logic coming through again and fortunately for me, Zoe has always thought the same. That ticking time bomb of when should we tie the knot was never going to be a problem for us.

In the early years of our relationship, it was clear that I was the one who wanted it more. I suppose I needed it more, maybe because I was more vulnerable. To come from an environment where I had felt so misunderstood I guess I craved someone who understood my foibles and with whom I could communicate satisfactorily. I obviously craved sex and there was probably an element, if I am honest, of proving my family wrong. They had concluded I was gay even though they had missed what I thought was self-evident; namely I didn't fit into the culture of the small town in which I had been entrapped. Ergo, there was nobody there for me. By meeting Zoe so soon after leaving home, it sent a message back to those who sought to label me. It told them that maybe Llantwit had been a bad move for me after all.

As the summer approached to end my first year at Stirling, I refused to go back home to Llantwit. Instead, I got a job as a kitchen porter at the Manchester branch of Harry Ramsden's. I ended up working alone on the nightshift (about 50p an hour extra). I had obviously become accustomed to isolation, as I actually preferred it to the day shift. If the truth be told, I hadn't escaped my anti-social nature.

I gave my nana and granddad some rent from my meagre pay and stayed with them. I am thoroughly glad I did. I had always enjoyed the company of my granddad; the one member of the family who seemed to accept me for who I was. I was fascinated by his endless stories from the wartime and others chronicling his obvious non-conformity. We also used to watch endless boxing tapes together.

It was the most substantial amount of time I ever spent with him and also the last amount of quality time I would ever spend with him. He became ill not long after and went into a slow decline until he eventually pegged out on the day the twin towers were hit by the planes. By that time, his full mental capacity had long since left him.

My granddad was also very sympathetic to my need to visit and look up my old friends from Little Lever. I had renewed confidence and independence now. I decided, despite my mother's protestations, that I would reconnect with my old friends. However, I was in for a bit of a shock. I may have been trapped in a time capsule where nothing had changed, but as I was to discover, I was alone in this. I visited my old primary school and was recognised by the remaining teachers (much to my delight). Through them I hooked up with Rachel (daughter of one of the teachers and my first ever real crush) and through a younger cousin of one of the people in the class, I got a number for Elen. The three of us tracked down a few others from our primary days. It was great to see them, but it made me realise that things had moved on. There was nothing left for me in Little Lever any more.

I tracked down my old friend and sports rival, Stephen, plus a few others. Some former friends had been detained at her majesty's pleasure. Rachel looked divine, but we never kept in touch. She had a boyfriend and I had a girlfriend. Maybe we would have done if things were different.

Elen and Stephen used to be really good mates, but it was obvious that we were not friends anymore. We had no connection, nothing in common. When I had left Little Lever, they had continued with their maturation. By contrast, I had remained trapped in time, clinging to old memories. It was a harsh lesson for me, but a very important and valuable one. It enabled me to bury the ghosts and move on. I am only in contact with one person now from my Little Lever days. Mat used to live next door. His dad was best man at my mum and dad's wedding. Apparently, my dad and his dad were best mates. When we moved away they lost all contact. I think their sons may well have been best mates. However, we are now mates, separated by distance and missing time. Still, whenever I meet up with Mat, I have a really good time, catching up and reminiscing about old times.

When I returned to university for the second year, Zoe would still often appear cold, resentful and distant towards me over the way that our relationship had begun. I could never command her full attention and I often felt I would never be as special to her as she was to me. Still, with the girl in my life, the rest of it began to settle down.

I became a model student. I was top of the class in both history and philosophy scoring straight firsts. When the marketing course finally began, it was unfortunately a huge disappointment, taught by either pure academics, or people who had failed in industry. My grades initially dropped because I was thinking too much out of the box when tackling issues and questions. It took me over a semester to realise that my approach of questioning everything wasn't welcome. Indeed, the complete opposite. The teaching of marketing at university was like the teaching of a GCSE subject. Copy the theories out of a book, regurgitate them in an exam and get good grades. When I asked repeated questions about creativity and the methods of running a business, the lecturers were devoid of answers. In fact, they were openly hostile to my line of questioning – patently unable to answer me when I asked how I could improve. This was contrary to any of the subjects which were classically academic (eg history).

In the history department, the doors were always open if students had questions or wanted to discuss how they could improve their grades. Once, I was very disappointed to only receive an average grade discussing the impact of Thatcherism. I naturally took my tutor to task, but he was able to counteract my points and made me realise where I had failed to actually answer the question. With regards to marketing, I eventually realised the way forward was to dumb down and just copy from the course text book. For my final year I didn't attend any lectures and only the minimum of the required tutorials. I still came away with a 2:1.

I knew at the time that my marketing degree was practically useless. Its only worth was the value it created in the mind of a naïve employer. With hindsight, I realised the whole marketing/

business degree was even worse than I had given it credit for. It had totally failed to prepare its students for the world of work, except for the role of an employee who has no thoughts of their own. The entrepreneurs must have gone to a different school. I left university knowing nothing at all about the sales process or its methods and techniques. Indeed, some marketing lecturers mentioned sales like it was a dirty word! The art of negotiating was never mentioned, I didn't know how to do books or accounts. Instead we were encouraged to read academic texts on how to construct theoretical business models (something I have never used), as opposed to a practical business plan or projection. Tom Peters' *In Search of Excellence* was a course text. This was a book detailing why selected companies were deemed excellent. Peters had already had to write a follow-up book on why many of his "excellent" companies had failed not long after he wrote the first tome! Were his selections and resultant inclusions of such obvious failures merely irony, or did it point to a deeper level of stupidity?

During my first year at university the number of people who had applied to do marketing was only just in double figures. By the time I graduated, the number of graduates was in treble figures! A huge number of students had swapped from their originally intended courses to sit a marketing degree. Why? Because, it was easier than their originally intended degree. They were literally giving marketing degrees away. Any monkey who could copy out of a book could have got one. However, as usual my view was not popular. There were less than ten of us on the course that expressed such a view. The rest revelled in the fact that they had time to party all the way to graduation without having to do any hard work or put much thought into it.

I didn't want to attend my graduation day. I considered it an indictment of our university system, an authority spewing forth an effluent of undeserved, worthless degrees. I attended only for my parents, mainly my dad. It was a rare moment where he was able to show that he was proud of me. I had achieved something he had wanted to do himself, but due to circumstances he had been unable to achieve it. I guess it was an archetypal example of the parent finally fulfilling an unachieved ambition through the offspring.

The Scottish degree system enabled me to continue taking history courses until my very final semester. They became my antidote to the marketing classes – intellectual thought with detailed probing and investigation. I actually looked forward to the four-hour tutorials! I continued to get top marks in the history courses and enjoyed them far more than my 'chosen' subject. In my final year, I was offered the opportunity to pursue a PhD in history. However, Doctor Sexecute never really appealed to me. I have never fancied the life of an academic and anyway I wanted to earn some money and have some financial independence. Living another three years close to the breadline just so I could call myself Doctor, was not at all desirable. Furthermore, even if I were a doctor by qualification, I would never actually want to be referred to as such. I have never believed in titles (primarily because they are inherited). Even those titles that are earned seem pretentious in their usage.

My final year's dissertation had been on the marketing of professional football and on the back of it I decided to try and get into that line of work. My advertising dream hadn't quite worked out. I discovered that creatives come in pairs (copywriter and artist). They were also meant to work for free for a while to prove themselves! I got down to the final 50 at Saatchi and Saatchi (from over 2000) and on a final shortlist at JWT for the positions of account executive and media buyer respectively. However, I had never coveted either position particularly. My lack of enthusiasm probably showed. Also, it appeared to be an incestuous business. A large proportion of people I met at the interviews had relatives in the industry and the interviewers kept asking which family members worked in advertising. It all made me feel a little uneasy.

My dissertation probably went far beyond what was actually required for a bachelor degree. Questionnaires were sent out to over 150 football clubs here and abroad. On a limited budget I visited the commercial managers at five professional clubs (starting in London and making my way north). I spoke to several more on the phone. A couple of professional clubs even bought my dissertation from me upon completion (including Olympiakos in Greece). I still had sporting ambitions and one day I would make my living from training my body…

I had just gone completely arse over tit on stage in front of dozens of people. There was some spilt drink on the floor and this had proved my undoing. The pain from my ankle, where I had gone over, was excruciating and I could feel the blood in my dick rapidly draining out to other parts of my body. What an interesting week this was turning out to be.

On the Sunday I had performed the longest strip I had ever done. The gentleman concerned had opted for something different at his private party. He didn't want a strip show as such, more of a stealthily stripping waiter. I served drinks and chatted to his guests. Every 30 minutes or so I removed a garment until I was serving in nothing more than a stars and stripes g-string (he was American). It was a very well-to-do affair and one inebriated, posh, older lady nearly fell over and injured herself upon seeing me in the g-string. I have become friendly with the booker since then, so I classify it as another day of enrichment.

A couple of days later I made my way northwards to begin another tour of the Northern gay venues. I generally did a different venue each night for about a week. During that time I would hopefully climb a peak or two in the Lake District and visit some friends; both old and new.

The cultural difference between the Northern and Southern clubs was always quite striking. The Northern audiences tended to be more amiable, whereas the staff in the clubs were often less so. Having just driven nearly 200 miles to get there, one would be lucky if you were offered a drink and the changing areas were typically appalling. On my visit to Bar NY in Doncaster I was changing in what looked like a doss-house toilet. It had a room attached to it, but I was instructed that the strippers "weren't allowed in there".

The act went well and I went downstairs for my customary drink of water afterwards. I chatted to various people for about an hour and went upstairs to retrieve my gear. I found the slightly inebriated manager of the said venue on his hands and knees over my kit bag. He had been rummaging through its contents and had found my g-string. I caught him sniffing the g-string quite merrily. He seemed quite embarrassed and I didn't know what to say. I guess in a weird kind of way it was a backhanded compliment, so I just said "thanks for your interest", packed it away again and was on my way.

Anyway, I was flat out on my back in Downtown, a club in Wakefield. It was one of he grottiest, dirtiest places imaginable. If you were unlucky the changing area was a step between the kitchen and the back bar. If you were lucky the back bar was closed. I knew it must have looked bad by the horrified look on the bouncer's face and the way she (yes she) was mouthing "are you alright" at me in my prone position.

I grimaced and nodded at the same time, fighting to my feet. I couldn't put any weight through the ankle and had to lean heavily onto my good leg. I somehow limped through the remaining half of the act. The pain must have been quite bad because it had overcome the effect of the elastic bands and my dick had reverted back to its normal flaccid size. When I limped back out later, all I could hear was "he didn't have a very big one". Nobody said "didn't he do well considering he couldn't actually walk".

I left Downtown feeling more than a little disgruntled and hopped back to my car. The feedback from the accelerator and the resultant pain was too much for my damaged ankle (the right one). I had to drive from Wakefield to Sheffield using my left foot exclusively. It was just as well it was late at night with little traffic and that I encountered no police cars. My progress was a little erratic.

The next morning I couldn't stand on the ankle at all, let alone walk. The application of ice to the ankle was like the application of electrodes to the testicles (shocking). I was certain I had broken it again. The symptoms were identical to when I had done it before.

I was staying with Dave and John, the agents who arranged the tour. They have always been extremely gracious hosts and Dave drove me to the hospital to get an x-ray. Initially, it was diagnosed as a break because of the shadow on the bone in the x-ray. I was sent away in plaster and told to come back the next day. When I returned the plaster was ripped off, but I was told to keep the crutches. A specialist had studied the x-ray. The shadow on the bone was due to the previous break. I had merely torn all the ligaments in the ankle. I should be mobile again within a few weeks, I was told.

I actually returned to the stage little more than a week later with a bit of a limp. However, it made me realise how frail and unstable my new income was. Hurriedly, I joined Equity, the performers' union. As part of the joining fee they included insurance. If I was to break my leg or worse, then maybe I could at least have some money coming in during my convalescence.

*

At university I had rekindled my interest in sport. My long-term knee problem had finally righted itself after years of torment. The standard prescription for my ailment was to put both legs in plaster to help precipitate an early cure. However, the doctors I visited seemed disinterested, for some reason, in referring me for such treatment. They preferred nature to take its course. A broken ankle acquired playing chess (I know, it sounds ridiculous) when I was 14 meant that one leg was in plaster for several weeks. Needless to say it seemed to cure the knee problem in the right leg. I'm sure the left knee would have healed similarly if this simple course of action had been taken. Instead, I suffered with the pain for years.

I began gingerly by visiting the cinder track at the university, which was usually in a state of flood for 300 of the 400 metres of surface. On only my third visit, I was clocked at 11.9 for the 100m. I was particularly encouraged, as only the year before there had been a one-off competition whereby every club in the football league had entered their fastest player into a 100m-sprint challenge. Only three out of the 92 entrants succeeded in going under 12 seconds.

I joined the university track team and found I had only one rival in the sprints (the standard was hardly high). Although I didn't take sport terribly seriously at university (there was a complete lack of facilities or encouragement in individual events), it was a decent re-introduction for me. I acquired a decent training partner in my Spanish friend, Roberto, and we engaged in various weight training and sprint programmes together. We made our own way to some inter-university track meets and also took part in the Scottish bench press championships (I came second in my weight class).

My rediscovery of sport and my incorrect assertions about advertising had taken me in a new direction with a view to the working world. On the back of my dissertation, I decided I would attempt to find work in the world of sport on the commercial side. I approached countless numbers of football clubs and alleged sports marketing agencies. Unfortunately for me, timing is everything and I didn't have it. I had an amazing 'interview' at Leeds United whereby the interviewer clearly knew nothing about the emerging commercial nature of football and the use of club images as brands. I mentioned something about the young supporters being the future consumers and he said they should be at home in bed not watching football! Needless to say, I wouldn't be working there. Manchester City invited me to a game and a meeting with their commercial manager to tell me about the chicken and the egg. As I had no formal sales experience he couldn't offer me a position, but how does one get experience without being offered a position? He recommended that I come back in a year with some experience. I suggested that he might not be able to afford me then as I might be earning a lot more than the £15,000 per annum he was talking about. He said that was a chance he would have to take. I did phone him after a year but asked him to match the £40,000 I was then earning. Needless to say, he choked.

Alan Pascoe Associates (then a sports marketing company run by the former track athlete with many connections in UK athletics) offered me a job on the proviso that I begin work for free. I politely asked what I was meant to eat and where was I meant to live in the interim period before they began to pay me for my services. I was met with the answer that several other people were willing to work for free to break into sport. It was a similar story at TWI. I told both of them that I wasn't a registered charity, nor a robot. I starve if you don't feed me and I need money to buy food. Needless to say, that was not particularly well received. That was when I first started to realise that the best positions in firms seem to be acquired by the well-to-do. They, after all, have the contacts and the rich parentage to see them through the early years when the remuneration is insufficient to live on. The rest of us just get regular jobs.

I began applying for those regular jobs. These were the jobs I simply had no interest in or passion for, but, I needed money to buy my independence and to begin having my own life. Three interviews on and I was offered a job working for an IT contract recruitment firm in central London. I would receive a £13,000 basic + commission. The same day they made their offer, I had an interview with another recruitment consultant interviewing for his client in St Albans. I'll never forget the meeting. I explained to him that I was going to take the offer I had on the table unless he could offer me something better. He explained he wasn't in a position to do that but suggested we have a chat anyway. We did, which became very informal and at the end of the hour we thanked each other for being candid and taking the time. He wished me luck with the other position and said something very prophetic: "I think you'll go one of two ways, Nick – either you will be incredibly successful at what you choose to do, or you will reject the whole thing and go and live in a field in the middle of nowhere." Interestingly, he didn't raise the possibility of both scenarios occurring…

*

I was just starting to prepare myself to go on stage. It was a Thursday night and I was at a gay venue I play regularly in Kings Cross. Central Station is now one of my favourites because there is always something weird and wonderful going on in the basement. To the uninitiated, however, it could be deeply intimidating.

Mark, the manager, appeared in my upstairs landing changing area and spoke in his soft dulcet Irish tone, "Nick, there's going to be a slight delay. We have had a problem with the dogs, they've been fighting."

I knew there was a small bull terrier type dog that lived somewhere on the premises, but I had never seen the plural version.

"I thought you only had one dog?" I asked curiously.

"Not the canine version, I mean the human dogs in the basement. They are all now licking their wounds."

The Dog Pound, as Mark duly informed me, was a regular event at Central Station. The clientele was split into owners and dogs. The owners would literally walk the dogs on leads and the dogs would bark, growl and do as their owners told them… mostly. On this particular night, a fight had broken out between the dogs (on all fours) and some dogs had been bitten. The delay was so that their wounds could be tended to.

The Dog Pound was not the only unusual club night that had taken place at Central Station, as Mark was all too willing to divulge. The baby club involved numerous grown adult men who would come and dress in nappies and pretend to be helpless babies. 'Mothers' would tend to the babies, often scolding them for soiling their nappies. On other nights there was naked oil wrestling. Spurt was a wanking club and weirdest of all was the night that Mark recoiled with horror, when plastic sheeting had to be put down to contain all the bodily ablutions. I certainly didn't envy him in the clean-up operation.

Personally, up close, I have seen the CP (Corporal Punishment) club, the buff club and the filming of a lesbian porn film – all within the walls of Central Station. In fact, male strip shows are a relatively tame and civilised affair in that particular part of Kings Cross.

With its tolerant and liberal attitude to life, it remains one of my favourite venues on the circuit and I have met and made many friends within its walls. Long may it live and prosper.

*

I took the job at Passive Resources. The bank graciously lent me £3000 so that I could buy some suits, hand over the required two-months deposit to rent a flat and survive the first month until I got paid. I asked my boss to be where he lived and he replied Croydon. Not knowing the London area at all, I decided that would be a decent a place as any to live and rented a less than salubrious flat near East Croydon station. The owner of the flat I wanted wouldn't accept me as a tenant, presumably because I was too young. There were very few properties within my price range, so I was left with the one bedroom flat that had no central heating and mould growing on the walls.

I won't ever forget my first week at work. It was an incredible period of ups and downs. I had been unable to secure the flat until the end of my first week and Passive were keen for me to start. They put me up in a hotel for the first week just off Tottenham Court Road. I boarded a train, on a Sunday evening bound for Hemel Hempstead where I would spend my first day on a company introduction course. That train journey was where I read for the first time *Jonathan Livingstone Seagull* by Bach. It is a short story about a seagull who simply didn't fit in with his flock. He was always striving for more, but was continually told that his behaviour wasn't normal or befitting a seagull. Eventually he became a total outcast but found his own way to achieve what he wanted from life. I found it to be an incredibly moving tale, probably because I related to it through many parts of my own life. Also, I guess it was a period where I was feeling incredibly alone and vulnerable again. I didn't want to be doing the job I was about to take, nor was I relishing the countless hours of struggle or debt. Still, it had to be done to progress.

The first week was hellish and introduced me to what was to come. Passive was the market leader in their sector, but had been milking a cash cow for too long. The market was changing and Passive hadn't adapted. I was to be part of a crack team that had to secure new business. This meant constant cold calling in an attempt to build relationships and win business. The rejection was persistent and constant. It was something I wasn't totally unfamiliar with.

At the end of the first week, I moved into the flat overlooking the train tracks. Despite it being a real dive, the feeling I had when I stepped through the door for the first time is one that I will probably never experience again (I have felt it once more since, which I will come back to). An incredible feeling of power and self-satisfaction came over me as I walked around the near-empty rooms. This hovel was my space. I wasn't sharing it with other students who would leave the kitchen in a mess but have an equal right to do so. I wouldn't have my mother telling me that I must turn the light out because I was wasting electricity. I could do what I wanted, when I wanted without comeback or retribution for the first time in my life. That feeling will be hard to top.

Zoe joined me a week after moving in. At the time, she was unclear whether she was going to join me or remain in Scotland. I hadn't seen her for months. I had made it clear that I was unwilling to remain in Scotland. Both myself and Matt had similar sentiments about working north of the border. Nationalism up there was rife and this often over-spilt into openly aggressive anti-Englishness. After fours years we had both had enough of the snide comments and references to the battle of Bannockburn. The so-called intellectuals at university even resorted to writing snide comments on library walls asking for rematches of famous battles. I used to clash constantly with Scottish nationalists, particularly in history tutorials, where I would draw out the comparisons between modern Scottish nationalists and the early days of Benito Mussolini's fascism. I would invariably win the argument and gain another enemy. It became so bad that one tutor, who I got on particularly well with, banned any such talk in his tutorials. The last Scottish nationalist stormed out of his class in a bluster after inviting me to step outside. I accepted but he stormed off telling me to "grow up".

Anyway, I wasn't prepared to stay and work in Scotland. The national mood was such that I couldn't bear every third of fourth person that I met. When I met her, Zoe had always been very patriotic and resistant to living in England. It nearly became a deal breaker. Anyway, I was the first of us to begin work in earnest. She was yet to find a placement in biomedical science and followed me to London in search of something in that field.

For the first few months we were losing money. Zoe took a job at British Gas in a call centre whilst she applied for suitable jobs. I wasn't earning commission. The cost of living far exceeded my basic and her meagre wage. I had to take out an overdraft in addition to my loan.

I spent many a long hour in work trying to get to grips with my new world. I really was thrown in at the deep end and had to learn fast. My marketing degree was woefully inadequate for the real world of business-to-business sales. The constant threat of the axe hung over us all. Another graduate in the team was the first to get the chop after only four weeks. I formed a very good relationship with Chris, one of the guys in the new business team. He was a fair bit older than me, at 34 to my 22. However, he had many years of experience in sales and was not afraid to pass on the benefits of that experience. A healthy banter also arose between us and certain other members of the team. In fact, as we got to know each other better, the banter became absolutely vicious, each of us taking delight in the apparent misfortune of the others. Nothing or no-one was sacred when it came to the barracking.

After about two months I went for an interview with a sports marketing company as I thought my days with Passive might be numbered. I didn't get the job and it was probably a blessing in disguise. Things started to turn and I began to make my first placements. Greg, my boss, was fairly young. He was simultaneously both unable and unwilling to pass on the fruits of his industry knowledge. I was learning by making errors (a good, but long and hard way to learn) and picking up general sales techniques from Chris. However, once I got through the initial period things began going very well for me. In fact, much better than for everyone else (Chris excepted).

By the end of my first year I had earned just under £35,000. At this point I applied for another job in sport (managing a fitness club), but clashed with the regional manager. Again, I think this was a blessing in disguise. By the end of my second year at Passive, I earned £78,000. I was their most successful salesman at this point and was appointed sales manager. In my third year, I earned £120,000 and was their most successful sales manager. Many changes had occurred by the third year. New business had become the most successful and rapidly expanding sector of the company. Chris had been appointed divisional manger. However, the new business division had won few friends, myself in particular. At the time, Passive was listed on the FTSE 250. It was a very corporate company with a corporate image and corporate values. Successful new business people, by contrast, fit a completely different profile. By their very nature they have to be outgoing, aggressive, relentless, be inquisitive to the point of almost being argumentative and this combined with a thickness of skin that would make a rhinoceros proud. They don't make good yes men and arse licking doesn't come all that naturally to them.

Passive had a love-hate relationship with the new business team and particularly me. They loved the money we were generating, but they hated our individualistic outlook. Team players belonged in the corporate side of the company. New business wanted driven, money-hungry individuals. As a sales manager, I began to cultivate clones of myself. My cloning worked well for the third year. I earned far in excess of anyone else and speaking meritocratically, should have been set for better things. However, we do not live in a meritocracy and petty jealousies are often the order of the day.

Certain senior personnel within the company took offence to my success and attitude. They thought I had an attitude problem. My results suggested they had a perception problem. Anyway, they proceeded to attempt to renegotiate my contract without my consent. If I were to tell you the precise details of what ensued, the publishers of this book would be having kittens at the prospect of litigation. Needless to say, I didn't agree to the contractual change and it cost Passive £40,000 in court.

After the court case I wrote a three-page letter to Passive extending the olive branch of friendship and suggesting that they make me a member of their board. It contained numerous references to frozen food (one of the directors came from that industry). It thanked the directors for attending my leaving do (the court) and went on to mention such gems as how easy it was for all the lollies in the freezer to become deflated and defrosted and how hiring people from Birdseye could stop the rot. Most of the killer one-liners came from my then ex-boss, Chris. He had turned up to testify at the tribunal. We were faxing each other back and forth before the final draft. One fax came through from him and I immediately called him up on the telephone. We were both laughing out loud before uttering even a hello. Anyway, I faxed the final draft to all their offices. Obviously, I didn't receive a reply, but it was extremely satisfying. Also, I proved about 20 people wrong who said that I couldn't take on a massive PLC in court and win.

Chris was still friendly with a then ex-Passive director who had left acrimoniously. He told him about the final faxing episode and chuckled, "The evil bastard, I bet they rue the day they ever met him. Of course, he'll never work in the industry again."

"Paul, I don't think he wants to work in the industry again. I think he's got bigger plans," replied Chris laconically…

*

Normally Aberystwyth would be way too far to consider going to for a strip job. However, I'd had a top tip from a mate that Scotland was the hot place of the moment to buy property and I'd agreed to go and have a look with him. When the agent phoned and offered me the job in Aberystwyth, I'd agreed on the basis that it was sort of on the way back. Sort of…

Besides, when I was at school all the Welsh nationalists had trotted off quite merrily to Aberystwyth University. I guess I was kind of curious whether all the rumours about the place were true. Did the hills really have eyes? Would we be gang raped by marauding hillbillies? Would we be burned at the stake for speaking with an English accent? Those sort or rumours.

I should have really studied the map before agreeing to go to the place. It was a long drive even when already being half way there. However, it was a nice day, the scenery was pleasant and I had good company. All was well.

It was starting to go dark when we pulled into what looked like a pleasant seaside town. No hillbillies, no burning stakes. All looked good.

I rendezvoused with the booker. This was no large ladies' night, but a private affair in a pub for about 12 females. My mate was hoping that nookie would come after the night's proceedings, but it didn't look promising. He has a particular fetish about age. He likes them young. Only one of them looked under 35 and she had two noses and three ears. Furthermore, I could smell trouble with this lot from 200 paces. My plan was to get the money, perform and run.

I succeeded in the first two objectives and as I was leaving the stage the chants began for my mate to strip as well (as often happens). When I returned five minutes later, after getting changed, he was being held in the middle of the room with his trousers around his ankles. He was struggling to free himself (unsuccessfully) whilst his captors pointed at his nether regions and sneered. It reminded me of something that might have occurred at Abu Ghraib. If a gang of men had done this to a woman, it would have constituted a serious sexual assault. When women do it to a man, it is strangely classified as a bit of fun.

I gathered up my costume and packaged it away ready to execute the final bit of my plan. That is, the run bit. The females were insistent that I stay around and talk to them for a while. I would normally do this anyway, but the atmosphere was tense and I engaged them a little hesitantly. Then one of them insisted I dance with her. One of my golden unbreakable rules is that I don't dance. I can't dance, I don't like dancing and I think anybody that does it looks like... well... not good. I only really admire break dancers because I can appreciate the athleticism.

Anyway, I politely declined to dance, five times, before she exploded.

"I can tell you're fucking English," she spat.

Almost simultaneously the mother of the one with two noses and three ears exploded at my mate, accusing him of trying to molest his daughter. How rich, I thought, given what they did to him only ten minutes earlier.

"Time to go," I shouted.

"Yes," he shouted back.

We made a hurried exit to streams of abuse. We were lucky not to get covered in phlegm. We hadn't eaten in hours and we agreed on a pit stop at a fish and chip shop before leaving Aberystwyth. We entered such an abode. The customer was speaking to the vendor. We began discussing our order. Our English accents were obviously offensive because the customer and vendor then began speaking in Welsh. We looked at each other and ran for the car. I'm sure I saw a burning stake as we were driving away.

On the way home another motorist failed to stop on a roundabout and ploughed straight into my car, causing my car to roll over and skid down the road on its roof. The very next day I was to fly to Tanzania to climb Kilimanjaro. My resultant injuries completely ruined the trip. I'm never going back to Aberystwyth...

*

Having won the court case, I was then free to move on to my next project. The behaviour of the Passive people had left me in no hurry to return to recruitment. I still had sporting ambitions. Indeed, I had been thinking for some time about becoming a football agent. After all, they performed essentially the same role as a recruitment consultant; they just did it for much bigger sums. I had been attempting to find out what I could about the industry, although there was very little written about it and what was written was for the American market only.

Whilst fighting the court case I had been given the phone number for an agent in motor racing and after my initial call we met to discuss things. He was very receptive to my ambitions. He openly said that he didn't have much of a head for business, but he had all the contacts in the motor racing world. He suggested that with his experience and contacts in the motor racing world and my drive for the business side, we would make an ideal partnership.

I had a few grand in the bank that I had just won and I was keen not to have to go back to recruitment. I also wanted to do something in sport. I had never viewed motor racing as a sport (more of a pastime), but viewed it as an opportunity to make money. The amounts that the drivers in Formula One were making (and their agents) were astronomical. Thus, I saw pound signs and decided to give it a go. Initially, my money would bankroll the project. I could write a book on this entire project! However, I'll condense matters: Basically, I secured another £300,000 in funding from an eccentric millionaire. This was after I had hired one sales guy working out of my spare bedroom and several failed visits to venture capitalists. I took exception to being asked what my father did and what school I went to by the venture capitalists. The old school tie brigade was still very much in force.

The £300,000 was used to secure the drives for three drivers who the motor racing agent recommended. I didn't question his judgement (an error). That was his area, after all. Yet I had reservations about two of the drivers, because they seemed to lack the requisite drive and determination to succeed. Adam, the third guy, had it in abundance. The other two drivers were placed in Formula Ford (the passion of the eccentric millionaire), but the main thrust was behind Adam in Formula 3. I hired some basic office space and recruited three sales staff to have an all-out blitz on obtaining sponsorship sales for the cars.

It turned out to be much harder than any of us ever expected. We were all so naïve to the politics of motor racing. I, like most people, had casually watched these events on television and assumed that merit ruled the day. I assumed that the top drivers were hired by the top teams. I assumed that companies sponsored the top teams to obtain maximum exposure. That, however, is far too logical.

As we found out to our cost, teams hire drivers who can afford to pay, irrespective of their ability. Companies sponsor the teams on the basis of personal connections and involvements. I attended a motor sport sponsorship conference and was horrified as I sat through a talk by the head of the sponsorship team at Shell Petroleum. She emphasised continually the emotion of being involved with Ferrari. Not once during the talk did she mention anything about return on investment or what sponsoring Ferrari did for Shell. I was starting to spot the danger signs, but at this stage the full scale of the problem had not yet hit home.

Our initial sales strategy began by targeting all the companies that had ever 'sponsored' a racing car. We had dozens of car magazines and began by calling all the names on the sides of the vehicles. Our pitch was, "If we could offer twice the exposure at half the price, would you be interested?" In any line of business, the answer would have to be yes. To our amazement, the answer was a resounding no in all cases. Yes, *all* cases. The reason given was always the same. They stated that they were only involved with the driver because he was the son/nephew/cousin etc of a board member or client. There was never any legitimate business reason for the deal. We were therefore unable to compete on a business footing.

I had to change the strategy. We achieved a modicum of success by selling the car on a race-by-race basis to businesses local to a particular racing circuit. For example, we would pitch to companies based in Kent when the next race was at Brands Hatch. The biggest sponsorship deal we closed was worth £20,000 for one race to be held at the British Grand Prix at Silverstone. Adam had a special Hotwheels suit made, his entire car was decked in Hotwheels colours and they even hired three Page 3 girls to drape over him everywhere he went. Adam was racing in a section called the scholarship class. Basically, it was half the budget of the full-scale Formula Three championship because they were using the old cars from previous years (we couldn't afford the £400,000 for a full Formula Three drive). The Hotwheels sponsorship was a real coup for us. Current F1 drivers Takuma Sato and Anthony Davidson were not too happy on the day because Adam was getting all the attention with his Page 3 girls! However, the following Monday we had lost all hope of getting any repeat business from the arrangement. Several Formula Three teams had telephoned Hotwheels offering them the same arrangement next year for free! We just couldn't compete with that. The difference was that we needed the cash whereas every other team didn't. Every other driver was sponsored by his father's company. Nobody in the paddock was having to raise the finances for their drive from an outside source.

Essentially we were involved in a massive rich kids' playground. The full scale of the fraud that is motor racing was brought home to me. Adam seemed to be the real deal. We are great mates to this day. Many people, including several so-called experts, seemed to acknowledge his ability as a driver during the F3 season.

Prior to the start of the season, I had also struck a deal with a TV production company and they agreed to make a fly-on-the-wall documentary chronicling the exploits of the driver and the backing team. The documentary ended with us attending a meeting with Williams Formula One. Jonathan Williams, the alleged talent scout, wanted to talk about the possibility of Adam testing their Formula One car. The Williams management wouldn't allow the cameras into the building. Things concluded with me emerging from the meeting and telling the camera that we had just been offered a Formula One drive if we would be willing to pay for the privilege, the same as how every other driver began in Formula One.

Motor racing truly is a pastime without merit. As Chris (my ex boss) once said, the F1 world championship is best likened to the 'lets all race around my garden pond world title'. That is to say, its permissible entrants are limited. I have long maintained that if motor racing were open to all, the likes of Michael Schumacher would not even make the grid of Formula One. If, for example, every Olympic 100m athlete had to pay £5 million in order to enter, the chances are that the Olympic 100m champion would be a plus 12 second runner. It doesn't take a genius to do the maths and work out how many would be excluded.

Needless to say, the whole project died a death. Adam's talent was recognised by him being given a 'paid' drive in the German Porsche championship the following year. The drive was offered by the team at the back of the grid the previous year and his drive was to be funded by a rich kid team-mate. His payment was his expenses and a couple of hundred quid per race. We drove to Germany in my car to sign the contract. I was entitled to 30% of anything he earned but I told him to keep everything.

I lost all my hard won Passive money on this project and most of the savings I had in the bank. It was a very bitter pill to swallow, particularly as in many ways we had achieved so much – 43 separate sponsors had come on board from scratch (albeit mostly small sponsors) and interest had been garnered in a relatively unknown driver from Formula One teams. I even managed to get Passive to sponsor us for £3000. I went back into their offices in a disguise. Accompanied by a TV crew, I successfully pitched the idea to a group marketing director. They would have been horrified had the documentary actually aired!

Yet, it was all for nought. I was hopeful that the documentary would bring some money back. We called it the Ghetto Kid (because in motor racing terms Adam was from the ghetto). However, we were unable to sell the programme. Despite the numerous contacts that the production company had in television and despite although those that viewed the programme commenting on the excellent story and production, it remains on the shelf to this day. Its content was just too controversial and revealing about how Formula One really works for any of the major networks to show it.

I lost my shirt on this project and it seemed that I was standing there again as the lone fall guy. I'd put my money up and so had the eccentric millionaire. However, he could afford to lose his money. He made more in interest every year than what he lost. I had just taken a huge right hand square on the chin and was seeing stars.

I was now facing the terrifying prospect of returning to work in an arena I couldn't stand. Furthermore, if I was being realistic I would have to retrace my steps and take a role lower down than I would like. That is, in all likelihood, I would have to start at the beginning again. Quite frankly, I'd have been willing to do just about any reasonably viable alternative...

*

I had received a call from a Frenchman in London one Sunday afternoon. He wanted to know if I performed private shows. That is, shows for one. I have been asked this many times over the years and the answer will always remain the same. Namely, as long as the fee is paid, then of course I do.

It is nearly always men who ask for private shows. I can count on one hand the number of times I have been asked by women to perform private shows. You can then further divide by a quarter the number that actually meant it. A few dozen men have asked, however, and they always mean it. Some people think I'm mad for doing these.

"What if he had a gun?" they ask.

"What if she had a gun?" I counter.

Weirdos are fairly common in my world but most of them can be screened out in the initial telephone call. If I'm really suspicious I ask them to supply all their personal details in writing or pay a deposit. This kills off the Peter Sutcliffes pretty quickly.

In fact, I have made a few genuine friends through one-to-one shows. In that sense they have enriched my life. Some people will book you time and time again (say three to four times a year), others once only. Others still believe that they will get a little more than a strip show if they repeat book. They really shouldn't think this as they have been told otherwise upfront. Still, it sometimes takes then two to three attempts before they realise what I told them initially holds true. You then never hear from them again. Some of the guys that book one-to-ones are incredibly wealthy. Others just have regular jobs and have maybe seen me on stage somewhere and want to hire me for themselves – like a personal treat.

Most of the guys I have seen have also hired prostitutes/escorts in the past and wanted to try something a little but different. It is true that most of these bookers are hoping that strips might eventually lead to sex. I've always said I'd do anything for a million, but nobody has ever made such an outrageous offer. Demi Moore is therefore safe in her role for the time being.

It isn't as if some of these guys couldn't afford to make the offer. Some of them most definitely could. I've been to some places that are positively palatial. One place was the top floor penthouse (on three floors) in a block of flats near Mayfair. I estimated its value at about ten million quid. The guy later told me it was worth 12 million. Similarly, a mansion in Hampstead I was once called to must have pushed it close for total value. I have also attended countless others where the guys have been millionaires (or thereabouts) without being stupidly rich. To be fair, most of the bookers are quite wealthy by most people's standards.

Anyway, as I was saying, I'd been booked by the French guy for the very same evening in Earls Court, London. I arrived and was warmly greeted by him and ushered into his spacious flat. He paid me up front and then asked me if I was OK with two 'escorts' also performing for him at the same time. I replied in the affirmative and we sat down to await their arrival.

Whilst we were waiting he asked if I was also an escort. I replied in the negative, which seemed to disappoint him. Eventually these two young antipodean guys arrived, looking like they had just finished surfing. The French guy really didn't know what he wanted. He got the two surfers to drop their trousers and start wanking either side of him whilst I was still sitting politely on the other side of the room.

"Would you like me to perform now," I asked inquisitively.

He stared at me in a drug-fuelled haze and simply said, "No, I think I just want sex. Perhaps it would be better if you just went."

I'd been paid to sit in an armchair for thirty minutes. It was the easiest payday I think I've ever had. I bade my farewells to the wanking surfers, collected my belongings and left.

*

I still had a couple of thousand in savings. I decided to take one final look at being a football agent. What I found in that industry, however, horrified me even more than motor racing. Firstly, I made the mistake of offering to work for free in order to gain entry and to acquire some experience. When I first graduated, everybody in sport had made it a prerequisite to work for free in order to enter the industry so I was following that same logic. Several agents were willing to see me on that basis, but once they met me they couldn't get me out of their offices quick enough! I made the mistake of not dumbing down. Instead I came across as a bit of a live wire who might well be able to enhance their business, but crucially, also steal it.

I decided the only route was to go it alone and this created many problems. Firstly, the Football Association officially require you to put down £100,000 as a bond to register as an agent. Hundreds don't bother and nothing is done to enforce it. Others (such as well thought of ex-players) are hurriedly ushered through the system and licensed. The only agent I found to be helpful was an ex-England player who was getting out of the agent game. He laid it out quite simply and plainly for me when I met him – don't bother. He stated that it would be impossible for me to make it as an agent because the industry is so corrupt and incestuous. Without highly established contacts and a hefty bank balance it would be impossible to even begin to consider it, he contended. After all, ran his argument, he knew everybody in football and he hadn't been able to make it work the way he would like. I asked him to elaborate further and he did.

He gave me a theoretical example. Let's say I had a player who was very good and I approached club A, who happened to be very interested in my player. They would approach their preferred Agent J who in turn would make an approach to my player. My player would be asked if he would like to play for A (he would presumably reply in the affirmative) and would then be told that the deal could be done but he would have to sign with Agent J and ditch his current agent (me). I protested and said I would sue the player for breach of contract if he reneged on the deal. My informant (Paul) said that would be admirable but the incestuous nature of football would mean that no player would ever sign with me again. Furthermore, if my player didn't sign with Agent J then Club A would refuse to deal with me and would not sign the player. Inevitably, Agent J would therefore get his man (unless my player was incredibly loyal and a lifelong friend).

Agent J would then invoice club A for his cut in brokering the resultant transfer. However, Mr D, an official of Club A, would then arrange for his son to invoice Agent J for 'consultancy' services involved in the deal. Thus, a slice of the pie made its way back to Mr D, the official at Club A. In the picture Paul painted, everybody in this very small industry wins except outsiders and new entrants. Furthermore, club officials (such as managers/chairmen) who broker transfer deals were incentivized to purchase players that were less than ideal for their team. That way they could sell them on again after a season and legitimately buy their replacement because 'the deal hadn't quite worked out'. Those officials then directly benefit from the sale of the failed player and the purchase of his replacement. This certainly explained some of the more perplexing/unnecessary purchases by major teams over the years.

I again suggested an antidote to this scenario. I would simply approach other premiership teams. The news wasn't great. Paul went through every team I could mention and named the inside contact who brokered the transfer and his son/nephew/family member who acted as a consultant for the preferred agent with whom that club dealt. If Paul was to be believed, it was to be a forlorn task.

Nevertheless, not to be deterred so easily, I shook hands with Paul and thanked him for his insight. Six months later, I phoned him up and said I wish I had taken his initial advice (don't bother). Everything he had said had turned out to be correct. During that time I attempted a number of things to gain entry. I tried partnering with scouts (to quote one "this game is like being in the masons"), offered my services as a sprint coach to clubs and tried touting around a couple of junior players to clubs. Whilst conducting the latter I will never forget the conversation I had with the head scout of Swindon Town. He stated that they are unwilling to look at players who are not recommended to them. I said, "I am recommending this particular player." He said that I wasn't one of his sources. I countered by stating that if my player was the next Pele, how would he ever know if he wasn't prepared to watch players in his role as the scout? He went quiet and then muttered something about if I wasn't prepared to play the same as the others then that's just the way it was... I was beginning to understand what Paul had meant. The Swindon scout was not alone in his outlook (just more blatant) and when I finally secured the player in question – a trial with a conference team – he didn't show up!

Eventually, my head began to hurt from banging it against a brick wall too many times. My money reserves were near depleted and anyway I had begun carving out a career elsewhere and that career looked far more interesting...

*

"OK, Ashley, start wanking him now until he cumms... and cut."

I suppose I was on a porn set, at least it was sort of porn. I had been approached by an agent about being one of the victims in something known as CFNM. To the uninitiated, that stands for Clothed Female Nude Male. It is an emerging genre of fetish, in which men are sexually humiliated by women. The women retain their dignity throughout the proceedings.

In line with the rest of the porn world, the stories are corny and unbelievable and the acting is appalling. Strictly speaking, it isn't porn as we know it because there is no penetrative sex. A CFNM woman wouldn't stoop that low. From my point of view it was porn without the risks. I had been offered the chance to do porn before but had declined on the basis of risk. So what if everybody was tested? The sex was unsafe and viruses like HIV can lie dormant and undetected in an initial test.

My first venture into CFNM had been less interesting than I had hoped. The director had hired a farmhouse in deepest Sussex for his requirements. The setting must have eaten too much into his budget because he couldn't afford any women that would actually touch any of the men. As a result the storylines had to be adapted and the men had to wank themselves off as the women watched, pointing and laughing.

As someone whose sexual fantasy is to be gang raped by at least five women, it was all a little tame and disappointing. In between takes, I got chatting to some of the girls. A couple of them were porn actresses. This was child's play to them. They obviously would have been willing to do just about anything; they just hadn't been paid enough on the day.

The one that had interested me most was Ashley. After all, she had piercing blue eyes and curly brown hair. She reminded me of Zoe. I got her number hoping to meet up with her sometime outside of a CFNM film set. However, she had deliberately given me a false number. OK she wasn't interested. I could handle that. It's not a problem. The sly method of saying no was a problem. It got my back up at least. What's so difficult about being honest?

This time the setting was different. The director had spunked less of his budget on setting and more on actresses. He had hired somebody's flat in Bromley (albeit a nice modern flat). The actresses had been hired this time on the basis that they were going to get their hands grubby (literally).

Ashley was again one of the motley crew. In the morning I had played out a quite ridiculous storyline whereby I was getting frisky with my 'girlfriend', but before we could really get down to it her mother came home. So that we wouldn't be found out, I then had to climb naked over a balcony and hang down over a mezzanine floor only for an estate agent and her client to walk in the room whilst I was dangling. In my helpless position they giggled and wanked me off whilst I protested. My 'girlfriend' was most helpful during the wanking. She played with her fanny, out of the shot of the camera, to help me along.

As I was having to do two shoots that day (interpret the word shoot as you see fit), I was to be filmed first and last so that I had the maximum 'recovery time'. The second scene was almost as ridiculous as the first. I was ordered to strip by my mum because my sister's friends wanted to examine a naked male body. I would then be called a "dirty boy" by my mother whilst the sister and friends giggled and played with my cock. Ashley was 'made' (read contracted) to wank me off. This felt like sweet vengeance after she had given me a false phone number previously. Whilst she was doing the deed, my head was full of fantasy. Most of it was along the lines of 'serves you right for lying, bitch'. It was a most satisfying orgasm. Most guys would actually pay for this and I was actually getting paid. It sure beat the hell out of working for a living.

Chapter 3

It all Started with a Sauna...

I rang the door bell again. Still no answer. It was May 2002 and things hadn't been going my way these last couple of years. Forced to take my original employer to court at my own expense, I then saw nearly all my savings evaporate in a high-octane experiment that went wrong. I wasted a further six months investigating the football business and now I had travelled two hours to get to Balham, South London for a pre-arranged meeting with this trainer of strippers and he wasn't in! What had I done to piss the gods off?

I staggered back from the building straining my eyes to see if there was any sign of life. It was a warm May day and I was hot and bothered from the tube journey. I tried calling his number from my mobile, but there was no answer so I turned begrudgingly to head back towards the tube station. As I did so, a big black guy wearing an expensive and very gay looking string vest was helping an elderly gentleman along the road, a man I was later to know as the Rock of Ages.

The elderly gentleman introduced himself as Michael and his helper was Paul. He bade me enter his flat. Those in the know often assume that it was Michael who helped me start my career as a stripper, but in truth, we have to delve further back than that to an encounter a couple of years previously in a sauna.

The sauna encounter is not as seedy as it initially might sound. At the time I was an aspiring track sprinter. Years of constant training on the track and power training in the gym, combined with a careful diet, had brought my body fat level down to just above six percent. I was every bit the professional in attitude, training six days a week (sometimes twice a day). I researched and implemented the latest training theories and pushed myself to the limit in order to be the best I could possibly be. Eventually I posted times of 22.4 for the 200m and 49.7 for the 400m. They call the 400m the man killer with good reason. Even when you are trained to the hilt it is still going to really hurt and quite possibly end with you crawling onto the grass so that you can throw up. I was told that breaking 50 seconds for the 400m puts you around the top 100 mark in the UK. This only left me to lament further about what might have been. If I could make it into the higher end in something as hard as the 400m, what might I have done in football?

However, genetically there existed far more gifted athletes than me and also I didn't use the drugs. Contrary to what may be banded about in the popularist media, virtually all athletes (most sportspeople) use performance-enhancing drugs. It isn't possible to succeed at the highest level without them. Urine tests are easily passed and the authorities will always sweep things under the carpet for the betterment of the sport. I carefully considered the possibility of joining the 'steroid brigade' but concluded that although I would improve markedly, I almost certainly lacked the genetics to take me to the very top. I would have probably been a top 20 athlete as opposed to a top 100 athlete. Essentially I would still have been nothing more than an also ran, just a more up market one. Top 20 athletes don't earn a living from the sport and the long-term side effects from steroid usage can be quite harmful.

After training, I regularly used to go to the sauna to try and ease those aching muscles (if I woke up in the morning and wasn't sore I wondered what was wrong). It was one bank holiday Monday, after a hard session in the gym, that I went to the sauna and first met John. I was sitting there stretched out minding my own business when this guy asked me if I was a model. I said no, only to be informed that given my physique I should be. John introduced himself and said he was a photographer. He also added that yes he was gay, but that wasn't the reasoning behind his line of enquiry.

Curious, I asked him for more detail. John explained that he was only an amateur photographer, but he had his own studio and his main area of interest was photographing artistic male nudes. Furthermore, models got paid. That got my attention, so I asked him how much and how often. The answer wasn't quite what I had hoped. Photographers will typically pay the model a fee (circa £100). If the photographer is an amateur, the images would just be for his private collection. If the photographer is a professional, he will then seek to sell them for publication. The model should be asked to sign a model release and can expect to be paid a more princely sum – maybe as much as £125-£150. I enquired how often one can expect this kind of work. John replied that the magazines may publish the same model about twice a year, so in essence not that often.

I explained to John that I had a very well paid job and that £100 here and there didn't especially appeal to me at that particular moment in time. That was when John said that if I was more interested in the money I should consider being a stripper as they worked much more often. He knew someone who trained strippers and could give me his phone number if I was interested. Strippers could expect a similar fee to models, but could also expect to work a few times a week. I reiterated my first point that I was earning a lot more than that and between training for the track and my job I had no spare time. Thus, part-time was not an option and full time simply wasn't lucrative enough. John expressed his understanding and gave me a card saying that if I ever changed my mind, he'd be glad to take my photo.

In truth, my time at work with Passive was nearing its end; political games had abounded for months and the situation was stressful. When we parted company, my lawyer made it plain to me that my mitigated loss in court would be far higher if I "was unable to find suitable similar employment". I therefore sat on my hands and prepared for the court war. My training suffered terribly during this period. I guess the situation was more stressful than I gave it credit for. It was during this period in late 2000 that I dug out John's card and gave him a call. I did so as much as out of curiosity as anything else. We arranged to meet and he took some nude photos of me; in return he provided me with a set of large glossy prints. The shoot was the night before the court case and although John wanted to shoot some more, I soon became embroiled in motor racing and football projects. They kept me occupied for a further 18 months or so.

After the motor racing had failed, my money reserves were depleted and I was at a very low ebb. I again called John and asked him about the possibility of modelling for pay. Suddenly, £100 for a couple of hours' work looked far better than it had a couple of years before. Deep down, I knew ultimately that I would have to return to the 'real world' – the world of work that I so truly despised. The reality of acting like a drone for the betterment of the great corporate monolith, in return for some coloured pieces of paper as remuneration beckoned. I still have nightmares about the thought of it to this day and getting paid for showing my body was a way of delaying the inevitable. Also, modelling didn't really feel like work – it was too easy.

John gave me four telephone numbers of people he knew who booked models. He also gave me a number of a company that made gay porn films (I told him I wouldn't be interested). Just as he finished his list, he remembered another number. He said I might as well have the number of Mike Baldwin. "If you are interested, he trains strippers. I'm sure he'd love to see you."

I began by telephoning the people who booked models. A couple were outdated (one wrong number, the other one said he didn't hire models anymore) but two of them requested that I e-mail them a photo. I did this and received an immediate response. One wanted to book me instantly for a paid session and the other said he would like to meet me with a view to taking 'test shots'. Their response was in stark contrast to more mainstream modelling agencies. As an experiment, I spent two days contacting over 50 'modelling agencies' by telephone and on the request of some of them, a further follow up e-mail with attached images was also sent. Some showed 'interest' but their 'interest' was of little use. They either wanted to charge a fee in order to join their books, wanted to arrange for a portfolio to be done with their photographer (at my expense) or some simply said they don't scout new faces. Only one asked to see me in person and he was to close down soon afterwards. Either way, all the terms favoured them. Acceptance of their terms would have meant they win and I lose. None of them were willing to guarantee any work. That is, they were a waste of time.

On the face of it, the companies that were marketing themselves as mainstream modelling agencies seemed to be reliant on aspirant models who were naïve and gullible enough to pay fees for the 'services' of the modelling agencies. In our now very much established 24-hour reality TV, celebrity obsessed society there will no doubt be an endless supply of young celebrity wannabees who believe that the modelling agency will actually look after them and find them work on a regular basis. I would wager that the majority of the income from most agencies comes from hopefuls as opposed to finding assignments for their models and taking a commission. I keep bumping into an ever-increasing number of these young hopefuls.

Thus it was that in March 2002 I boarded the train to Brighton and arrived for my first paid photo shoot. Richard and Barry were a gay couple that ran one of those high street photo development franchises. They had converted the room above the shop into a studio. I was asked to pose naked with various props and towards the end of the shoot some shots were taken with an erection. The whole thing lasted a couple of hours; they even bought me something to eat afterwards. I boarded the train back to Crawley £100 richer and it was probably the most stress free £100 I had ever earned.

I few similar sessions followed. I posed for a group at the London Camera Club and a few of their individual members booked me privately. Each time I posed for somebody I asked if they knew any other photographers who booked models and so my contact list began to grow, as did my portfolio of photos. Initially, I was doing a photo shoot every week or two. Because I was a new model and I appeared to be reasonably popular, the photographers were quite keen to shoot me (with their cameras, not a gun). I began to contact some magazines to see what their level of interest was. Esme, from a magazine called *For Women*, met me one day and we did some shoots outside. She was quite taken by one of the images I had sent her and asked if I would take her there. The shot was taken by an old boy called Pierre Gibbons. He probably took the best photos of any photographer I worked with. The image shows what looks like an infinite number of huge archways stretching into the distance, and nestled in one of them, quite subtly, is a naked model. That was the image that so interested Esme.

Sure enough, I took Esme to the location and we shot some film. I also took her to another amazing outdoor location in Sussex. Shoreham cement works takes some believing. Set back off the road, this enormous works site has huge warehouses (one of them flooded), filled to the brim with rusting and decaying industrial machinery. As you reached the quarry at the back, the noise from the road disappears and only the crows can be heard. It was like a scene from some post apocalyptic earth where civilisation has been wiped out. Whilst exploring the site, I found a small office where a newspaper lay on a desk, undisturbed for 12 years. I later did some digging and the date of the paper corresponded with the date of the site closure.

Anyway, Esme took some photos at Shoreham too and these became my first published images. I actually got fleeced, because I only got £100 and the images appeared across a few issues. However, I was young and naïve back then. Also, the images shot were a little amateurish. The tone of *For Women* is probably more *Readers Wives* than *Playgirl*, although it was probably the closest thing Britain had to *Playgirl*.

I registered with a couple of agencies who supplied naked male models and a couple of their assignments proved to be a bit different. At the time I was being offered a fair amount of porn work, both gay and straight. However, I always turned it down. I had a girlfriend that I was loyal and faithful to and furthermore, I would have been forever fearful of what one might catch. However, I always stressed that I would be happy to shoot anything in the singular.

One of the agencies to which I belonged was run by a guy called Scott (Scott is actually a pseudonym because he has a job as an actor and he doesn't want one role ever to be associated with the other). Scott's agency didn't find me much work because most of their assignments were for gay porn (early after registering with them, they asked if I was willing to appear in a film getting shagged up the arse by a girl with a strap-on. I politely declined at the time. However, one of the assignments they sent me to was a private photographer in Oxford. John was an elderly gentleman who wrote for one of the broadsheets as their tennis correspondent. His favourite hobby, as he called it, was to shoot naked young men in various states of undress around his house.

I posed for John on several occasions. Every time the formula was the same. There was never anything untoward. He was extremely polite and after the shoot, he would always cook me dinner. He was also very keen to show me some of the photos he had taken of other models.

I always talked to John afterwards for some time and I'm guessing I probably did so in a way that few of his other models did. I was always enquiring about life and the nature of his work. I remember another photographer friend of mine, Mark Glenn, told me that he met him once. Funnily enough, Mark wanted to talk to him about tennis, whereas John only wanted to show him pictures of models.

John was often jetting around the world covering various tennis tournaments and it was plain that he led a double life. On the one hand there was his conservative, almost haughty profession, where he was revered in the highest regard. On the other hand there was what most people would consider his sordid 'hobby'. He had managed for years to keep the two lives completely separate and although I didn't know him for long enough, I would imagine he did so at considerable angst and grief to himself. He probably came from an era and an environment where his hobby simply 'wasn't tennis' and he was forced to hide it for most of his life.

I would have liked to have got to know John better; he seemed a really nice, sweet old man, no doubt with many tortured demons waiting to burst forth from his closet. Unfortunately, he died whilst I was imprisoned in Dubai (more later). The last time I saw him, he was in failing health and he told me that he literally had a walk-in cupboard the size of a small room overflowing with the photos of the models he had taken over the years. Whether they sat there on the shelf or whether they were a constant source of amusement to him, I'll never know. He told me that upon his death, his most trusted friend had been instructed to enter the house and destroy all the material. The friend, I believe, was a former model of his.

I understand that several models turned up at his funeral. I was on a mailing list of his and the most trusted friend emailed a small number of people about his health, as he was nearing the end. My Dubai e-mail was on this list. Apparently, the models' appearance caused some embarrassment and consternation amongst certain parts of the family. Also, John's wishes hadn't quite gone according to plan. His sister had apparently reached the house first before the trusted friend. She found his store of photos and his hobby was unintentionally revealed. The trusted friend was apparently left the house in the will. However, he evidently wasn't the only one with a key. Rest in peace, John.

After I had been posing for cameras for about a month or two, there remained one number that I was yet to call. I was quite enjoying my 'work' as a model. It was certainly very easy and relaxed compared to what had gone before. However, I also knew that unless I could find enough Johns – that is, people who would book me on a regular basis – I knew I could never sustain a living doing it.

Thus, with a mixture of hesitant trepidation and wondrous curiosity I phoned the man who trained strippers to see how the land lay. There was no hard sell; the voice at the other end simply invited me to come and see him in his Balham abode. A couple of days later I was heading into London…

*

I was on the way to Merthyr Tydfil in the Welsh Valleys with another stripper, Toni Boredano. I was hopeful it would be a good evening. Welsh girls had a reputation amongst strippers as being 'up for it'. Furthermore, I liked Toni. He was one of the few strippers I have met that I feel I can safely turn my back on. That is to say, he won't stick a knife in it.

This, however, was in sharp contrast to the night before. I took a job that even the agent was dubious about. He had taken a call from people who in his words "sound dodgy". They had paid the deposit but he was still unsure. He said he'd leave it up to me as to whether I wanted to do the job. I phoned the booker who was a man with an Irish accent called Mary. He wanted me to arrive as a policeman and tell the female victim that there had been a mix up at the court. I had to take her back to jail (she was apparently to be released that morning)! I guessed that they were pikeys (travellers). I knew from my experience down the boxing gym that they were a strange bunch. They could be fiercely loyal and respectful but also prone to thievery. My tracksuit top went missing down the gym and one of the boxing coaches simply said, "Don't leave anything lying around these pikey kids – they'll have it." Twenty minutes later he was trying to tell me what nice people they were. I didn't share his sentiments. I found them incredibly cliquish and unwelcoming to outsiders. I therefore approached this job with caution.

Stimulation X had once told me of a similar job he had attended whereby the police were dragging somebody from the house as he arrived. He understandably declined to enter the said abode and perform. The pikeys wanted to string him up!

To be fair the job was OK. Aunty Mary was a man dressed as a woman. The victim thought I was a real copper given that she had just been released from the slammer and I kept the strip pretty tame. I collected my money, delivered the 'congratulations on getting out of jail' card and made my goodbyes. There were a couple of pikey brats who wanted to cause mischief on my exit (the brats were numerous and had all been thrown outside for the performance), but that was all. I struggled most of all with the broad Irish accents.

Toni and I went on in Merthyr to a storming reception. It was a stark and welcome contrast to the night before. Afterwards we both went 'fishing'. I was having more luck than him and pulled him aside.

"I think I've netted us some fish. Two sisters, but we may have to do the friend as well to sign off the deal."

"No problem, let's go," came back the reply.

We made our way back to one of the sister's houses. I was driving and somewhere between the venue and the house, Toni managed to steal the one I thought I had bagged. No matter, we could swap afterwards, I thought. Toni was quick out of the blocks and persuaded his chosen sister to swallow well and early. In the meantime, I was having problems breaking down the defences of the other one upstairs. Firstly, she wanted the mate to get some action as well. I had agreed to this, but the mate was comatose at this point having drunk about three times as much as anybody else in the club that night.

Having overcome this hurdle, and egged on by the other sister, she finally succumbed. Toni said afterwards that he thought we were going to come through the ceiling! We then set to work on turning the bout into a tag team affair. That is, you tag and swap partners. However, this was a step too far, even for the 'up for it' Welsh valley girls. I once shared a girl with another stripper after a show over the bonnet of my car down a dark country lane. Sharing is rare. Still, Toni and I had a satisfied glow about us as we made our way back to London that night.

*

The stripper trainer wasn't quite how I imagined. With his grey beard and bald head, he was more reminiscent of Father Christmas than a mentor of sex gods. He shuffled up the stairs, puffing and panting as he went. He explained that he was now diabetic and had recently lost a couple of toes, so he now had difficulty walking. The guy in the gay string vest introduced himself as Paul, also known as Eclipse. He was a stripper from up North and was staying with the mentor for a few days whilst he performed a few shows in the South of England.

We shuffled to the top floor flat and I was ushered into a cosy living room with a sofa older than Santa himself (who was in his late 60s). Father Christmas bade me sit down and introduced himself formally as Michael. Although he was now retired he had spent his life working in television as a costumier and designer, but his main hobby going back more years than he could remember had been helping start male strippers on the circuit. Given that, he asked how he could help.

I detailed the chain of events leading to our encounter, expressed my curiosity in future possibilities and asked if he could tell me everything I would need to know to make an informed decision as to whether stripping would be something I might be interested in. I had two pre-conceived major concerns that I was happy for him to denude me of. Firstly, my background had been power sports. As a result I am not especially flexible, certainly wasn't a dainty mover and surely all strippers had to be excellent dancers? Secondly, most of the performances presumably took place in clubs. My experience of clubs had resulted in a (some would say bigoted) view, that they were all full of drunk moronic types looking to cause trouble. Although I had never started a fight in my life, I had finished a few and surely taking my clothes off in a club was inviting someone to light the match that would blow up the dynamite store?

Michael listened carefully and did indeed respond with a double denuding. Firstly, strippers do not need to be professional dancers; in fact the vast majority of them had no formal dance training. Secondly, most strippers begin plying their trade on the gay scene and then once they have established a name for themselves, they might be invited onto the hen night circuit. Michael said that gay clubs enjoyed the luxury of experiencing hardly any trouble at all. The people in them had come to admire and adore the stripper, not to start a fight with him. The hen night scene was exclusively for women, non-performing men would be barred entry. Similarly the women were there specifically to view the strippers and the only trouble arose from those that had had a little too much to drink and anyhow, they were handled easily enough. Stripping was not usually done in front of a straight mixed audience, so reassuringly the potential for trouble and flare-ups was greatly reduced. "So then," he said, "there is nothing to worry about."

Michael asked if I would take my top off and show him my physique. I duly obliged and his eyes lit up. "Oh yes, the boys down Bromptons would love you."

Putting my top back on, I surmised that I might be interested. "How then should I go about getting started?" I asked. Michael pulled himself upright in his chair and adopted a more business-like manner. Apparently I would need to go away and do a few things and then come back to him. Firstly, I should choose five music tracks that I liked which would form the essence of my music. I would then need to think of a theme that would be the essence of the act. Most strippers have well worn themes such as cowboys, firemen or the officer and gentleman outfit from the Richard Gere movie. Once I had the theme, Michael could then help me design the costume to fit the theme. I would then have to work out a routine that would be between 15-17 minutes long (the typical length of an act). Once that was done, I could begin contacting venues with regards to getting work. Michael said that most venues paid about £90 in cash for a show.

Michael suggested I go away and think about things. Before I left I asked about my physique, explaining that I was still an athlete. This meant that I would always be ripped (defined) but that I tended to have a lean and mean look as opposed to a 'gym queen' or 'muscle Mary' type look. I had noted that Eclipse looked more like a gym queen than an athlete, assisted in his look, I suspected, by a few anabolic injections as well as his protein powders. At the time I was only about 140lbs. Although, given my light bone structure, I tended to look about 20lb heavier, I was concerned I might be considered too small. Michael again allayed any fears I had and assured me that if I could put things together, the audiences would like me just fine. As a parting shot he also mentioned something about teaching me to tie off (a technique to make your dick look bigger), but said we could get to that on a later date.

As I boarded the train back home I was surprised to find my mind racing at the possibilities. I actually quite liked the sound of everything we had discussed. Michael had mentioned that venues regularly re-book the strippers they like and he also said that there were several guys who practiced it as their full time profession. It sounded so much easier than working for a living. This possibility galvanised me into action.

Chapter 4

Giving Birth to an Alter Ego

I went to bed that night with my mind racing and woke up with a start some hours later, sitting bolt upright in bed. It was still pitch black outside, but I had just seen the light. I couldn't dance, but I could box. The footwork of a boxer is often compared to that of a dancer's and some boxers are often referred to as dancers in their style. I considered it unlikely that any of the other strippers would have chosen a boxer as their theme and furthermore, it had always been my fantasy to be a boxer. Coming out to loud music and flashing lights dressed as a boxer may go someway to living out that dream that never became reality.

I telephoned Michael with my revelation the next day and he was thrilled with the idea, adding fuel to my rapidly growing fire. When I was pouring all my money away during the motor racing project, one of the sponsors that we brought on board was Title, the sports equipment manufacturer, specialising in boxing. I phoned Stan, the managing director and said I needed some boxing shorts, a satin gown and some boxing boots, preferably returns. Half an hour later he had dug around in the returns cupboard and dispatched the whole lot for only £60. The gown had somebody else's name emblazoned on the back, but that could be removed. I chose five tracks, with an emphasis on *Rocky* themes, and worked out some very rough choreography for an act. I then went to revisit Michael.

When I arrived in Balham, Michael was alone this time. I had put my chosen five tracks onto a tape and having listened to them there was no objection from the guru. I then talked him through my 'choreography' and he suggested I try and run through the moves there and then in his living room. He put the tape into his music player and I went through my 'moves'. To my surprise, there was very little critique from Michael and there were many cries of "Excellent". Either I was a born natural or Michael wasn't being completely honest with me. He did suggest a few minor things, the most major of these being a shower scene with a sponge and soapy water. I was later to discover that this was a Michael speciality. He also said that in his view, you get your dick out right towards the end of the act and not for very long.

We discussed a stage name and I suggested Marvelous Marvin (spelt deliberately with one L) after one of my boxing idols, Marvelous Marvin Hagler. Michael suggested simply the singular word 'Marvelous'. So it was that Marvelous was born.

Another essential item in the armoury of any aspiring stripper is a set of publicity photographs. As a member of the London Camera Club, Michael offered to take the images for me and we could then choose the best one and have it reproduced in multiples. Some pretty good images resulted and I chose one with me sitting on a chair naked with a pair of boxing gloves covering the crown jewels. I then sought about getting 500 copies made on card, sized A4. However, the high street printers were charging astronomical price so I tried the one Michael referred me to, somewhere "up North". We sent away the original image and I duly received a large box back of the images. To be honest the reproductions were pretty poor and didn't do Michael's original photograph any justice at all. However, I now had some publicity material, which I could send out to prospective venues.

On another visit Michael told me about the art of 'tying off'. He gave me an elastic band and told me to wrap it around my finger three times. I then needed to get a pretty stiff erection and stretch the three-times-wrapped-over elastic band over the head of the penis, allowing it to constrict again at the base. This prevents the blood flowing back out of the penis and means that it will remain in an enlarged state throughout the duration of the act. Please don't be confused by this description, the elastic band does not maintain a normal erection. Instead, the penis goes limp and to the uninitiated eye, has a somewhat flaccid appearance (although if you look closely it appears more erect, just pointing down instead of up). Nor does tying off maintain the full erect size (certainly not for me and other strippers seem to concur). However, about 80% of the erect size will be maintained and this looks impressive, especially to those who are not aware of the 'secret formula'. This obviously looks especially impressive if the owner of the member is already endowed well above the average.

However, please let me shatter the first myth about stripping – namely that all strippers have huge dicks. They do not. Tying off allows Mr Average entry to the party. That said, there are only a couple of strippers I have come across with a dick that might be described as below average in size. Several are much larger than average, most probably around average. I have been complimented on the size of my cock a number of times, women particularly offering crude remarks such as "there's Mr Big Dick" after a performance. It brings a wry smile to my face every time. If only they knew. Sometimes punters will notice the elastic band, quite often they don't. On the gay scene most of the punters are aware of the technique. On the hen scene most are not.

As I became more experienced it became clear that Michael had his own formula to stripping. He had given every stripper the same tricks and techniques in their routines. However, tying off is a very individual thing. Some strippers use a single elastic band as Michael suggested. Others use several elastic bands. Some tie it around the base of their cock, others wrap it around their balls as well. Others still use a material called bias binding (available from haberdashery shops). Some others use women's tights. I have tried both bias binding and women's tights in the comfort of my own home. This means that you can tie it as tight as you feel comfortable, but I didn't feel at all comfortable. Bias binding particularly is very difficult to get off and numerous strippers have cut their dicks trying to free themselves. I am also aware of a couple of instances where venue owners were asked to pull on the dicks of the tied-up stripper to facilitate the release from the bias binding. Personally, I prefer elastic bands. Through experimentation, I now use one narrow one and a slightly thicker one simultaneously. It works for me and I also find the removal of elastic bands far simpler than other materials.

To answer the question you are probably all wondering, the answer is an emphatic 'yes'. It does hurt. It can pinch slightly when you first put it on and the longer you leave it on the worse it feels. Your dick turns bluer and gets number and number by the minute. It is not overly painful whilst performing (unless you have tied it too tight – bias binding beware). Most pain is felt when the time comes to cut it off and especially as you unravel the band. Imagine someone twisting your nipples aggressively. Then as the final constriction is removed, the pain flows away and you can breathe again.

I was nearly ready and now just required the music cutting and splicing into one long track. I scoured the yellow pages for somebody that could do this but came up short. I was presumably not looking in the right section and again asked Michael where the other strippers procured such a facility. He told me that a stripper he knew owed him a favour and was able to produce his own discs. He would call him and let me know if he could help.

In due course Michael called me to tell me that the favour had been procured. I was soon on the way to Brighton to meet Mr Multiface.

*

Mr Multiface agreed to meet me at the station and by way of mobile communication, we were able to find each other without difficulty. "You must be Marvelous," a voice bellowed from a clapped-out old banger. Mr Multiface shoutedly explained that his old diesel helped him cover the many miles required of his profession as cheaply as possible.

This was in stark contrast to my ride. I was still driving the Impreza Turbo I had purchased brand new for cash, nearly three years before. It was arguably the best £22,000 I had ever spent. I researched every car on the marketplace before buying and discovered that there was a four-door saloon that could genuinely eat a Ferrari for just over 20 grand. I found it hard to believe at first, but after being scared witless on a test drive, I was an immediate convert and ordered one.

It took six months to arrive from Japan and I had to go and pick it up in Norwich. I had been taunting my friends mercilessly for months about the supercar I had ordered (they didn't know what it was, few people did at the time). As I began driving it back from Norwich with only seven miles on the clock and looking at that big wing in the rear view mirror, a smile spread across my face and I again got that amazing feeling of independence for only the second time (the first being when I moved into my own flat for the first time).

I tormented friends for months. They didn't believe the capability of the car, although they became instant converts once they got in it. It provided me with hours and hours of entertainment, never broke down and was amazingly comfortable on long journeys. However, it wasn't the cheapest car to run. My insurance premium for the first year was in excess of £2000 and petrol consumption was high. It once did a mere eight to the gallon (although not with me driving, I might add – the culprit was Adam, my racing driver friend) and even on the motorway it only did around 25 to the gallon taking it fairly easy. Servicing was regular and relatively expensive compared to an average family saloon. It was therefore not the most suitable car in which to eke out a stripping career.

Mr Multiface didn't so much talk to me, but more shout at me in showbiz speak. It was as if his stage persona and the real him had been intrinsically linked; they had metamorphosed into one.

He drove me to his parents' rather large and expensive lair in Brighton. In his bedroom he very graciously mixed my music for me like a professional DJ, suggesting alterations to me as we went (such as cutting out the quiet sections). Posters adorned the room, invariably with Multiface in them, pictured with two or three other stripped-to-the-waist young men. I was analysing his physique, as I am often prone to do. He seemed to be holding a lot of water, no doubt a side effect of steroid usage. He was short, considerably shorter than me (at 5 ft 9 I'm not that tall), but he was quite stocky. Looking at the photos he looked like his physique had seen better days, but that could simply have been down to steroidal cycles.

I tried to engage him in conversation about the brave new world I was entering, but he was pretty unforthcoming, dismissing most questions with bellows and theatrical gestures. He enquired whether I had abs underneath my jumper. "Yes," I said and for the one and only time he dropped the stage persona and said that in that case I wouldn't have anything to worry about.

Mr Multiface completed the work on my music for me in between taking phone calls for a new venture he was starting called the Aphrodite occasion (naturally he had reverted back to the stage persona by now). Apparently it was a ladies' night he was promoting in partnership with a drag queen. Mummy was floating the initial capital required, as apparently it involved hiring the venue for a number of weeks and link-ups with catering companies. Looking around I was fairly confident Mummy could afford it and it wasn't too much of a surprise when I was later told that Mr Multiface was a failed public schoolboy actor.

Michael had told me to get a copy of the music on mini-disc, as well as CD. Apparently, an increasing number of venues were using mini-disc. This turned out to be completely fallacious. Instead, a couple of drag queens were only able to play mini-discs on their PA systems and were insistent that strippers bring mini-disc.

Mr Multiface was unable to assist with the mini-disc and the yellow pages again bore no fruit. I didn't and still don't know anyone with a mini-disc player or recorder, so Michael this time sent me to see one of the afore mentioned drag queens. I spoke to Sissy Bells on the phone to arrange the meeting. He came across as one of those stereotypical, gay Larry Grayson types, camp voice and all. The meeting was set and the next night I was driving into Kent.

Michael was also keen for me to meet Sissy Bells because he apparently organised a lot of ladies' nights and was on the lookout for some good new strippers. I was met at the door by a gruff Scotsman, called Jason (Sissy's partner). When Bells finally came down the stairs after making me wait for about ten minutes, he continued to fill/play the Larry Grayson role with bells on. A drag queen may well be a man who dresses up as a woman, but Bells also fitted the description of drama queen.

There were a disturbing number of similar personality traits between him and Mr Multiface, they were just different in the way they manifested themselves. Both clearly felt the need to be the centre of attention in the room they were in. Multiface tended to do this by making himself louder than those around him, Bells by dramatic hand gestures and head movements. I concluded that both of them were actually quite insecure, this was palpably demonstrated in their need to be the centre of attention. They were wanting to feel loved and adored by those around them. I wondered if this was a by-product of them acting on the stage. Or were they acting? Did the man create the character or was the character simply an extension of the man? It was too early for me to tell. Although I was yet to have any reason to suspect, I guessed that both Bells and Multiface would have a tendency to be somewhat mendacious when it suited them. The fragility of their egos probably meant that a few porkies at the expense of their fellow performers boosted their own self-esteem when they needed it.

Bells and Jason were quite clearly gay. At that time, I was only just starting to come into contact with the gay world, mainly through working with various photographers. Bells fitted the stereotype of a camp, effeminate man. Jason was the opposite. I wondered whether this was an example of the Arthur and Martha type of gay couple I had been told about (where one plays the woman in the relationship).

At the time, it didn't seem obvious to me that all drag queens must be gay. Taking things at face value, I had heard and assumed through the popularist media (therefore it is probably not to be trusted), that various men from all facets of society had fetishes that caused them to dress up in women's clothes, quite often the clothes of their wives. To date, I'm yet to meet a performing drag queen that isn't gay. I once did a show in deepest Essex, where the pub was full of men dressed very badly as women (some with beards) and a couple had female partners with them. However, talking to them after the show, they admitted to me that they were bisexual.

All this isn't to say that there are no straight drag queens out there, I'm sure there are one or two, but they are very thin on the ground. I could go on now for a whole book length about gender identity, but I'll keep it brief. What was interesting about my meeting with Sissy Bells was how it made me think about stereotyping. When I was younger, I was always a staunch advocate against stereotyping, primarily because I don't fit one. There hasn't been a box built yet that you could put me in. Experience has made me change my view on stereotyping. I now believe that the majority of most population groups have behaviour traits that do fit a stereotype. However, we must be careful not to characterise everybody in the same way and tar everybody with the same brush just because they belong to a certain clan. We should only be able to stereotype somebody after we have enough information to make an informed decision. Anything else would be prejudicial and that is simply unacceptable. Prejudice is one of my pet hates and in my role as a stripper, I often get to see people at their most raw. Their prejudices are frequently revealed and heightened, much of it directed directly at me.

Anyway, I found Bells a little difficult to handle. He fired short, snappy questions at me in much the same way as an overzealous teacher attempts to exert their superiority on a schoolboy. In many ways it was like I was interviewing for a position in his company. He would also make continual camp, sexual references and innuendo throughout his diatribe. I rarely get flustered to the stage where I would show it to anybody and Bells certainly wasn't going to achieve that. I took an instant dislike to him. By contrast, I quite liked Jason.

When Bells realised that his abrasive manner wasn't going to upset me he recoiled a little and relaxed more in my presence. He and Jason began bitching about other drag queens and Jason said that if I stuck with them they would look after me. To this date, I'm not really sure what was meant by that. I think they were trying to put me off working for other drag queens. They were also stressing how important it was to be reliable and this was the first inkling I got that strippers were not the most punctual or trustworthy bunch of people. Eventually, Bells took me upstairs and cut the music for me before sending me on my way. As I left he said he'd be in touch with some work soon.

Chapter 5

My First Time

It wasn't long before Michael had arranged my first show. It was to be in a gay bar in west London called Bromptons, a staunch favourite on the gay scene. They had four strippers on stage every Sunday night and a further one in the middle of the week. Michael knew the staff well at Bromptons and he'd put in a good word, so they agreed to try me out.

The day before I was due to make my debut I received a call from a guy who said he had acquired my number from Michael. He wanted me to strip that evening somewhere in Kent. I actually declined the offer (very politely), which didn't go down too well with him. I should have learned at that point that a stripper never declines work. Instead, he 'is busy' with other work. I have found out since that bookers do bear grudges and one sure fire way to trigger it is to turn down one of their jobs.

I hardly ever turn work away now, but if I do I know how to do it the correct way. I primarily declined the job because it was the night of the Tyson-Lewis fight. I had ordered it on pay per view and a couple of track mates of mine were coming round for what was sure to be an entertaining evening. Also, I had never done a show before and wasn't quite sure what to expect or even how the evenings went. I wanted to get the first one under my belt under Michael's watchful eye.

The next evening I made my way to Bromptons on the train. The thought of driving through London traffic without knowing where I was going was enough to give me nightmares. Although I still detest the London traffic, I now travel to every show by car (the new GPS systems are a big help).

I found the venue no problem, wandered inside and introduced myself as the stripper. "You'll be Michael's new guy," came back the reply. "Follow me, I'll take you to him." I was led through a fairly dark nightclub, down a few steps where Michael greeted me and introduced me to a couple of other fairly old guys. They were positioned near the front of the house, just in front of a large, brightly lit, elevated stage. It had an elevated walkway extending a few feet out from the stage and I wondered whether this was for modelling purposes.

Michael shuffled his way forward tugging my arm, leading me to the dressing room, next to the stage. We walked through a door into a small area full of bric-a-brac and immediately next to this was the dressing room. Any delusions of grandeur I might have had were instantly shattered then. The dressing room was a 6 x 3 ft room consisting of a small sink and dresser next to the sink. There was a rather grubby looking adjoining toilet. As far as dressing rooms go, this was not such a bad one, as I was soon to discover.

I began to lay out my costume when a gentleman entered and asked me for my music. He then said I was to be on stage in 30 minutes. One of the most common things people say to me after shows is "I don't know how you do that". When you press them further, what they mean is that they couldn't do it because they would be too embarrassed. This usually leads onto the question of whether I ever get nervous before shows. I never do and this reply is nearly always followed by "what about the first time?" The answer remains the same, which is often met with incredulity.

Well here I was at the first show and I swear to you I wasn't nervous. If we could measure nerves on a scale then sure, I was more nervous the first time than I am today. However, I would use the term uncertain rather than nervous. I always draw the comparison with running 400m or stepping into a boxing ring, both of which make me very nervous. If someone is coming at you trying to knock your head off, that's scary because you might get hurt. When I used to be told by the coach that I would be running the 400m on Saturday, I had to steady myself by holding onto the nearest immovable object and sit down to regain my composure! It terrified me. It isn't possible to sprint 400m all the way. If you are very fit, for the first 35 seconds or so you will use up all the reserves in your anaerobic phospocreatine system before your aerobic gycolosis system takes over. Your muscles start to disobey your brain's orders as they fill with lactic acid, your lungs feel like they are about to explode and you feel dizzy/sick. As you come into the home straight it is like being in one of those nightmares where you are being chased by monsters. Even though you are trying to run away your legs are like leaden weights. I remember once leading into the home straight only to be passed by virtually the whole field before the line. I always imagined everybody in the stands pointing and laughing until their sides hurt. I'm laughing at this as I write, it certainly looked hilarious when it happened to my mates! One guy even collapsed exhausted before crossing the line. It just didn't feel funny when it happened to be you on the receiving end. I liken the 400m to having a safe near-death experience. Even when you win, it feels like hell.

The point I am trying to make it that after running 400m for so long, very few other things scare me or make me nervous. I never did completely get over my fear of the 400m, primarily because I knew no matter what I did, it would be torturous (unless I jogged it of course). When competing in some other sports I have had no nerves. Powerlifting for example, is not frightening. It is one short burst of effort, but no real pain. When I ran the 200m it was very different to the 400m. It would hurt a little bit towards the end, but nowhere near like the 400m. Whenever I have competed in anything, the adrenalin kicks in as the competition draws close. This certainly keeps you alert and a little on edge, but not necessarily so that it consumes you completely reducing you to a useless bag of nerves. This is how it tends to be with stripping. Twenty minutes before I go on stage I sometimes feel that little adrenalin rush. I find that there is more adrenalin if I am about to try out a new routine or resurrect something I haven't done for a while. That is, I am stepping slightly further out of the reaches of my comfort zone. However, I have never felt anything worse than running a 200m before I am about to go on stage and that means I am well within my comfort zone.

That first time was certainly my most uncomfortable. It was like I was preparing for a 200m. There was more adrenalin than there would be today, an air of apprehension and uncertainty. I was, after all, stepping completely into the unknown. I put on the boxing boots first as they took so long to lace up. Everything else followed fairly quickly. The most difficult and time consuming bit was the process of tying off. Michael left me in peace to have a wank in private. Not that it mattered or matters. I have become completely blasé about wanking in front of people. I do after all tell people that I am now a *professional* wanker. By that stage I had been doing it for the photographers so it made little difference now that I was doing it for stripping.

I tied off a little too soon in my eagerness to be ready (I now leave tying off to the very last minute possible), put on the rest of my costume and waited eagerly for the music to start. It wasn't long before Eye of the Tiger began booming out of the speakers and I stepped through the stage door into the bright, glaring lights.

To tell the truth, I remember very little of that first performance. Of course, I was concentrating on my routine, on what I had to do next and listening intently to the music for my cues. I emerged onto the stage and began shadow boxing with my back to the audience. When I turned around and threw back the hood from my gown I could just about make out the hazy faces in the audience. The lights were gleaming down on me and it was difficult to see beyond them. If I stepped towards the front of the stage and beyond the intense glare of the lights, I could see the faces staring vividly, intently, dissecting my every move.

When I am on stage today, I am aware of everything that is going on around me. Events might as well be taking place in slow motion. My mind can just as easily be elsewhere; I could be thinking about tomorrow's training session or my forthcoming tactics to pull the girl I have just spied in the audience. That first time, however, I was a mirror of concentration and it probably showed. I don't even remember bringing my 'victims' onto stage.

Most strippers will invariably choose 'victims' from the audience and pull them up onto stage. The victims' exposure varies from light embarrassment to severe humiliation to acts of a more sexual nature. Personally, I have always erred towards the former. It just seems more respectful towards somebody I in all likelihood don't actually know personally.

I do remember exiting the stage to rapturous applause from a highly appreciative audience. As much as they were very polite and welcoming I couldn't help but feeling that their appreciation was more of the 'good effort' kind as opposed to the 'great show' type.

I hadn't done a particularly good job of tying off. It would take me more than a few attempts to actually get it right. A couple of people actually said as much afterwards. One in particular said that the fact my dick wasn't as big as it might have been was actually turning him on!

Whilst I was packing my costume away, a tall lanky dark-haired gent burst into the dressing area. He handed me a clipboard with a pen and bade me to fill in a few details such as my name and address. Upon completion he handed me £90 in cash. I was now a professional stripper.

I emerged from the 'dressing room' and wandered over to Michael for feedback. The reports were promising, he said. Everybody seemed to have liked me and "you were just so cool and relaxed out there, especially considering it was your first time".

A few of the slightly lecherous old men made their way over and seemed very keen to talk to me. I was and always am happy to chat to people after shows. The venues pay my wages and it only seems reasonable that I am pleasant and accommodating towards their customers. Nevertheless, that first time, their chosen topics of conversation were a little alien to me. As mentioned, one punter was very keen to tell me how turned on he had been because I hadn't tied off all that well. At the time I just stared at him blankly. How was I meant to react – was I meant to thank him on a veiled compliment? Another seemed content to bore me with stories of other stripping performances. I listened as intently as I could, feigning enthusiasm beyond my actual interest (I was trying to be polite). To this day I have little interest in the performance of other male strippers. It can be useful to watch them both to assess the competition and garner ideas. Yet as a pastime, its entertainment value has always been lost on me. Therefore, listening to the ravings of an incessant strip fan wasn't really my idea of a great night out!

Then there was Bonny. A tall, bald Scottish guy came over and began talking with no introduction. His opening topic of conversation was how he had been dragged onto stage by a stripper the other week and how he had been made to get his dick out on stage. He then went on to say how if it had been erect, it would have been much bigger than the stripper's in question. Again I ask – how is one meant to react when confronted with such... well... strangeness? I gave him a sort of knowing 'oh' by nodding my head. He then had a habit of ceasing to talk and staring intently at me without uttering a word, our faces only a couple of feet apart. I tried to engage him in a normal conversation, but he soon resorted back to his intense staring. I retreated to the sanctuary that was by Michael's side and soon made my exit. I was followed by one punter back to the tube station. I was naturally a little suspicious of the attention, but I guess I should have really been saying hello to the world of celebrity (albeit in a minor way).

To the people who go out of their way to attend strip shows the stripper is an idol, a celebrity. I was as much a subject of fascination to them as, say, Marvelous Marvin Hagler is to me. If I was ever to meet Marvin, sure I'd want to talk to him. I once met Chris Eubank on a train going back to Brighton. I approached him and struck up a conversation. He gathered quickly that I wasn't just your average fan in the street. I began to grill him about training methods and techniques and his experiences in boxing. Did he really avoid Roy Jones? Did he train on the track? What did he do to condition his abs for the constant rain of blows? Did he really dislike Nigel Benn? Had he planned his image so people would hate him but therefore want to watch him lose (thereby getting more viewers and therefore more money)? etc. My line of questioning was perhaps a little forthright and intrusive. He could have told me to take a running jump or answer politely. To his credit, he chose the latter.

I am continually bombarded with questions from people after shows, but obviously they are all stripping related. The favourite in gay venues relates to my sexual orientation. Other favourites are how did I get into stripping? Does my family know? Does my partner mind, etc. Like Eubank did with me, I always try to politely answer the questions.

That first night in Bromptons, however, was a little unusual. Perhaps it was because Michael had already told them all about me, but they spoke to me as if they already knew me. It was as if I was performing for the umpteenth time and I was meeting old friends. It also struck me that night that I was more than just a stripper or a performer. I was a sexual object, something to be adored and admired for the pleasure of the viewing audience.

This, of course, is to be expected. I was putting myself on a pedestal of sexuality. It was only natural to expect that people would go home and wank over my image and what they imagined they could get up to with me.

What I wasn't prepared for was the forthrightness of the audience that night. Virtually every approach to me after the show had a sexual connotation, yet without ever asking the question directly. Although I was in my late 20s, the general consensus was that I could have been in my teens/early 20s. Most of the approaches were from men in their late 40s or early 50s. Assuming I was gay, would I really want to go and have a sexual liaison with them? Wouldn't I go and have one with someone my own age? As a stripper (and therefore presumably fairly attractive), couldn't I rightfully take my pick of the younger, better looking ones? Also, how were they ever going to pull me if they didn't actually ask?

It was all a bit strange, but nonetheless an interesting experience. The audience had essentially been welcoming and friendly, yet with that flasher in a long raincoat feel to them just under the surface.

The question I am continually asked is what it is like performing for gay men when I am straight. People assume that it must be a very difficult thing to do or that I am lying to them. That is to say that I am in fact gay myself. Neither assumption is correct and my feelings on the subject haven't changed in the slightest since that first performance. As a straight man, I take it as a great compliment that a large volume of gay men want to have their wicked way with me. To take it as an insult would be both simultaneously prejudicial and moronic. Instead, I am truly flattered by their interest. If people assume that I must be gay from watching my act then I am again flattered for a different reason. If my act is sufficiently 'gay' when performing in a gay venue, then I am doing my job correctly. If I am entertaining a largely male audience then I at least owe them the service of possibly fantasising that they might be able to 'pull' me. Many gay men have a fantasy about sleeping with straight men. However, a similar number are the complete opposite and border on being heterophobic. I therefore have to walk a fine line in the image I portray to the gay audience.

With regards to the actual performance itself, the more butch and macho members of the male populous struggle, particularly with the concept of a straight man performing to a gay audience. How possibly, for example, can a straight man allow a gay man to rub baby oil onto him? How can you let them touch you? These again are questions of a prejudicial birth. They often sprout forth from individuals with small minds and even smaller penises. I am not entering an arena whereby I am in any danger. I am perfectly comfortable with my sexuality and another man touching my dick does not threaten or endanger my sexuality. When I wander out onto the stage I am about to engage in an act. It is a performance that is devoid from reality. My alter ego, the stripper, is delivering the performance. He has a certain image and personality to portray. When I come off stage I revert to my real persona. The stripper and Nick are two different people. On stage the stripper is a sexual object who is available to all and sundry. When the stripper comes off stage, the body he inhibits is again controlled by Nick. It is Nick's sexual preferences and desires that then dictate to the body.

Most people have a real problem grasping the concept of being able to control your mind to the extent that you can portray a different sexuality. Again, I would refer people back to a sporting example.

People who are truly driven can put their mind to almost anything they want to achieve. Successful sportspeople are probably the most ambitious and driven people there are. Sports psychologists are now hired to help the genetically blessed but the mentally weak channel their mind more effectively in competitive situations.

A combination of factors have meant that I have developed into an extremely strong adult (on a mental level). Although my childhood was not traumatic in an abusive way, my parents and upbringing were certainly dysfunctional. I have developed many of the traits of adult children of alcoholics. There was a well known psychological study whereby children who had grown up under alcoholic parents developed certain traits and behaviours as adults as a direct result of their childhood upbringing. This study was eventually broadened out and the heading of 'adult children of dysfunctional parentage' was more accurately applied.

I undoubtedly exhibit many of the traits of an adult child of dysfunctional parentage. One of these is that the child tends to develop very strong coping strategies at an uncharacteristically early age. I learnt to deal with immense disappointment very early. It was very difficult at the time, but as it continued I developed my own way of dealing with it to the extent that very little of what anybody else ever did or said had a major effect on me. I found that mentally I was able to cope with virtually anything and the only person going to let me down, or affect me in a big way was myself. Also, in the sporting world I was not the most genetically gifted. I had to use everything else at my disposal to give me an edge. If I was genetically disadvantaged but psychologically advanced, the pendulum might just swing back in my direction. The result is that I am yet to meet anybody who is as mentally strong as I am. My coping mechanisms have meant that I can easily adjust to a variety of different situations. I am incredibly self-confident and assured compared to most. This is not to say that I am arrogant. I just don't concern myself too much with what others have to say or feel about me. If someone has constructive advice or help, I can't get enough of it. However, if they don't like me for personal reasons, that is their problem not mine.

In essence what I am saying is that although a straight man stripping for a gay audience may seem strange to many, it needn't be if you just expand your mind a little beyond its normal horizons. Sure, what I do is beyond the realm of most people. It requires a certain type of personality. Yet if someone is so closed minded that they are unable to grasp this concept then I would simply classify them as weak willed or even worse, possibly as inherently bigoted. I'm straight, but I love gay men. Many are now very close and dear friends. They don't bite, they haven't got contagious diseases and they are not dangerous. If you think otherwise you need a head doctor…

I wandered out of the club and along the road to the train station, looking a little conspicuous carrying all my gear in a huge rucksack that had toured with me throughout Nepal and Sumatra. One of the punters followed me back to the train station under the premise that it was time for his bed. It might have been, but you will have to call me a cynic. Given everything I had just experienced and witnessed, I am sure he was making a speculative attempt to get into my knickers. He babbled on about how he liked the performance and other strippers he had seen. As my train pulled in and I got onto it he was still babbling to me from the platform. I smiled and waved, thankful to at last be alone and free from his clutches. I sank into the comfy seat on a virtually empty train and drifted off with my slightly surreal thoughts.

*

I awoke the next day in the early afternoon to start what would eventually become a familiar pattern. I have always been a night owl so it wasn't exactly an earth shattering change, but the legacy would soon be cemented. I wandered into the bathroom to get a shower. When I had arrived back the night before I had been very tired and had crawled straight into bed. Zoe was already asleep and it didn't take me long to join her. The next day when Zoe arrived home she asked me how it went the night before. With typical understatement I said "fine". With her typical nonchalance she never mentioned it again.

I was all sticky and gooey from the baby oil the night before. As I arose and went to relieve myself it became apparent how sore my dick was from the previous night's activities. It was a little sensitive to touch, the skin was bruised around the base where the elastic band had been and it was actually uncomfortable if I pulled or stretched the skin on my cock. I washed my nether regions with unusual sensitivity and tenderness that morning.

I telephoned Michael to ask him what the feedback was from the night before. It was essentially positive. He began by saying that he is very protective of all the strippers that he introduces and people rarely critique them. This could have meant one of two things. Either Michael produced brilliant strippers all the time, or people were too afraid to offer their critiques to him. He went on to state that everybody had been astonished at how cool and composed I had been for the first time. The main critique had been about my hair and eyebrows. These were probably fair. My eyebrows met in the middle and my hair was how it grew. I had never put gel or any other hair product in it in my life! I did not know where you would even buy such products. Besides, such critiques were minor. Nobody had actually whinged about the show.

Michael had said that if I cracked the Bromptons' crowd the future would be bright. I appeared to have won their approval and this gave me a false sense of future optimism. As I was to soon realise there were many things wrong with my show, but I had to travel a long and lonely road to discover this.

Michael was my initial contact in stripping and he was widely respected by many people. He had started the careers of many strippers and they were mainly very grateful to him. The gay world is fairly small and he was widely known by a certain generation of people on the 'scene'. However, his time had largely come to an end a few years before. He was essentially out of it and on the fringes when I met him. He also has a somewhat formulaic view of stripping performances. It can and still does apply in many instances. However, it is also a bit old hat and things have moved on too. I was entering an alien world and he was my only advisor so I took much of what he said at face value. One of the 'problems' with Michael is that he is too nice. No matter how many times I would ask him what was wrong with the show or how it could be improved all he could say was "Darling, your show is just 'Marvelous'." It was a nice pun and well intended, but factually incorrect. As I performed more shows it became obvious that everything was not as good as it could be, but Michael persisted with his argument that it was.

Contrary to what Michael had said and what many people also subsequently assumed, Bromptons was quite an easy opener. The audience of regulars were very stripper friendly and supportive. They were certainly a collection of oddballs – but nice and well-meaning oddballs. They were understanding of one's first time and not too expectant. Furthermore, if you were to walk onto the stage naked and simply stand there for 15 minutes they would still appreciate it on one level.

As I performed more shows and elsewhere, that lenient expectancy of the first time performance was dissipating somewhat. I could see that some people were not satisfied with my performance or were expecting improvement. However, the position of mentor is a difficult one and one that few people seem to genuinely have a gift for. I certainly remember back to my childhood, when very few teachers at school were actually any good at it (teaching). Similarly, I have met very few people in other situations who were any good at it either. Those that can do are not necessarily good teachers, often fearing the imparting of any knowledge lest it come back to haunt or compete with them in the future.

I could see that people were becoming more critical of my performance (which hadn't changed) but they were unwilling or unable to enunciate why. I would ask constantly for constructive feedback or criticism from anybody who was willing to discuss it (especially those who I felt were detractors) and never received any. The great irony was that those people would still stand there and criticise even after being asked to share their critique. Yet were unwilling to do so. A touch of hypocrisy, I felt.

Also, how can anybody be expected to improve without some pointers in the right direction. If people were unwilling to share what was wrong then it would be fair to assume that I would think nothing was wrong! I have seen this phenomenon in virtually every area of performance on every level. Everybody is a critic but nobody is a coach. One of the things that stood me apart in my first job was that I was able to coach people through scenarios. Instead of just giving them targets and asking them to get on with it, I was able to actually show them how to get on with it and coach them through it step by step. That enabled me to clone my performance in others. This ability appears to be very rare. I was very lucky in that first job in that my friend, Chris, became my mentor and I was able to tap into his 15-year experience in that sort of role. He was also willing and able to share his knowledge. I didn't have this in stripping. Any attempt to garner any help or advice from a fellow stripper was a complete waste of time. They were terrified of imparting knowledge to the enemy.

The result was that I actually had to learn the slow and painful way by making errors. I began to analyse the reaction of the audience at various points in the act and glean as much as I could from talking to them afterwards.

I can look back with hindsight now and honestly say that my show wasn't very good when I started. In truth, most people probably aren't too hot when they first start. However, to counter that I would argue that if someone was given all the necessary advice and information there is no reason why they can't hit the ground running. Michael had given me a formula: five pieces of music, a couple of punters on stage, dick out towards the end, no choreographic assistance. He had assumed that my look would carry me through and to a certain extent it did, but only to that certain extent. Michael gave me as much help as he was able. His formula worked perfectly ten years before but times had changed. Poor Michael was getting on and he had recently been diagnosed as a diabetic. He had also had a couple of toes removed. Walking was difficult for him and he simply couldn't get out like he used to. He was seeing fewer and fewer strippers and lost touch with the scene. Still, if I never met him, there wouldn't have been a stripping career and you wouldn't be reading this. I'm eternally grateful to him.

I realise now that I was 'filling' far too much in my show. When I didn't know what to do next I would just shadow box. I felt comfortable with this, but clearly the audience eventually became bored with it. Also, the people I dragged on stage were also 'fillers'. I didn't actually do anything interesting with them because I wasn't sure what was expected. I was getting them to hold my ankles for doing sit ups or hold boxing pads. Essentially, I was getting them to enact the role of a trainer. It took up some time but probably left the audience slightly bemused. It was neither funny nor overtly sexual, which I learnt over time was the purpose of bringing someone on stage. Some strippers embarrass their 'victims' terribly when bringing them on stage. Nowadays I will only embarrass my victims slightly and some get a big thrill out of it. However, when I first started I was leaving them a little nonplussed.

Also, the whole cock flashing thing was the wrong strategy, I believe. People go to see strippers for very different reasons. Some go for the theatre of the performance, some go for a giggle, some are curious, but the common denominator in virtually all strip goers is cock. It dawned on me slowly that by flashing my cock at the end, for all of a few seconds, I was actually leaving people disappointed. A fair proportion of any given audience would actually want to play with it or suck it! Therefore, by denuding their eyes of the visual pleasure the whole strip performance suffered.

All in all, it took me about five months to realise where I was going wrong and then another year or so of reflection whilst working abroad. I believe that I have now got it right to a large degree, but improvements can always be made, as in anything. The day we stop learning we are no longer alive.

Chapter 6

Women Have Talons

The following Friday I was to perform my second show and my first hen show under the watchful eye and tutelage of Sissy Bells. It was to be held at a social club somewhere near Aylesbury in Buckinghamshire. An 80-mile drive ensued in the pleasant early evening sunshine, which was made less pleasant by the jams on the M25. I had allowed plenty of time and after struggling to find the place for about 15 minutes or so, I finally arrived and was greeted by Bells and his gruff Scotsman. They raised a few eyebrows when they saw what I was driving, but refrained from passing comment. Half my fee was being poured back into the Impreza just to arrive at the venues. Michael had mentioned that I would need an old, but reliable car, that didn't drink as much fuel. He was right, although I hadn't yet come to terms with the thought of trading in the Impreza.

I retrieved my bag from the boot and followed Bells through a side entrance into what looked like a boardroom (albeit a cheap nasty one). A wooden table sat in the middle of the room surrounded by chairs. Various amounts of costume regalia were strewn about everywhere.

I wandered outside into the hall and peeked beyond the curtain. There were a lot of women present; my best estimate was that they approached 250 in number. They varied massively in shape and size with a full age range spectrum. Tables dotted the room with between

10-15 women at each one. At the far end of the room was a slightly elevated stage. The din from the constant chattering was loud and seemed strangely intense.

I moved back to our changing area and sat down adopting my characteristic quiet observational stance on the world. Bells was in a state of near pandemonium and panic. The show was far from starting, yet he was pacing nervously up and down making the odd quip to his gruff other half about some item of regalia or another. Jason began wittering on about the number of assholes this business contained and how I would no doubt soon be meeting a few of them. "Stick with us, kid, and you'll be alright," he said reassuringly.

There was a little commotion at the door and a stocky gentleman accompanied by a leggy brunette entered the affray to a rapturous welcome from Bells. They kissed one another on the cheek and I was promptly introduced to 'The Bull'. The Bull was quite a big boy, although not down below as I was later to observe. He had an action man crew cut, spiked on top, was about 6 ft tall and probably weighed in somewhere around the 14 stone mark. He had the physique of a drugged-up bodybuilder and although not cut to the bone, was pretty lean considering his mass. He reminded me of Mike Tyson in a silly way. He had quite an intimidating physique but came with a girly high-pitched voice. Nonetheless, he seemed nice enough, although he was definitely a man of few words. His girlfriend was more chatty and acted as his mouthpiece.

I am very much the strong silent type. However, I can be very chatty when people talk back. If people aren't talking to me, I constantly have to make an effort to talk and thus not appear to be rude. The Bull wasn't one for idle chatter, he left that to his skirt.

I was to go on first, but not before Bells. Bells spent the half hour before he went out in a constant state of divadom, which for him is saying something. He was moaning about his dress, his make-up, the stage, how professionals like him had to tolerate amateurs and just about everything else around him. Meanwhile, Jason gave a knowing nod to all his concerns and acted as a counterbalancing calming force to his prime diva. After Bells had finally caked his face in make-up, adorned a frock and put on a ridiculous wig, he grabbed the microphone and strode onto stage. I was told that after he went out I had about 20 minutes in which to get ready and be on stage.

The circumstances to my getting ready were slightly different to Bromptons. I was sharing my dressing room with other artistes and the situation was slightly more public. I had already laid out my costume and began to play with my dick this time in front of an audience who politely pretended to do something else. The Bull and his skirt actually left the room, whilst Jason began to busy himself preening wigs. In the distance I could hear Bells twittering away, the words not quite decipherable through the walls. He had just finished 'singing'. This I knew because the decibels had been considerably heightened during the ordeal.

Wanking in the presence of a coy gay man was a slightly strange experience. Despite all my previous usage of sports psychology – the blocking out of all surroundings to purely focus on the job – I still found myself aware of Jason's presence as he was busying himself in the background, sneaking the odd glance. The result was that it took me a minute or two longer to get a full erection, but this was hardly a major problem. I made the same mistake I did the first time in tying off a little too soon and as experience would eventually show me, I was using the wrong size of elastic band.

As I was putting on my final garment, Bells began to chant loudly into his microphone:

"WE WANT DICK, WE WANT DICK, WE WANT DICK" in an attempt to whip the gathered throng up into an increasingly heightened frenzy. As the Eye of the Tiger began blaring from the speakers I began my short walk to the 'arena'. The doorman pulled back the curtain and I began bouncing up and down and broke into a slow jog as I had to make my way through the gathered mass of women to the stage. I was conscious of hands grabbing at my clothing as I made my way past and there was an inordinate and inaudible amount of yells and shrieks coming from the crowd.

It was a completely different experience to Bromptons in virtually every way. Unlike there, where the lights blinded me and I could hardly make out the faces in the crowd, this time the lighting was low and I could make out everybody on this bright, early summer's evening. Unlike the gay audience, which politely observed and showed quiet appreciation, the girls were rowdy, loud, drunken and unappreciative of any theatre. This was payback on men night. The strippers were not so much objects of adoration as they had been to the gay men, but multi-faceted symbols of both sexuality and rejection. The strippers were there for their express pleasure; to be laughed at, photographed and humiliated. Any fantasising over the strippers was to be kept low key. Peer pressure dictated that the stripper was an object of mass consumption, not a symbol of personal desire.

I made the mistake, but learnt the lesson, on this night of how a stripper must always control the audience. Having described the whim of the audience above, I must confess I fell victim to it. I have always had latent sexual fantasies about being controlled and dominated by women. Although this situation was not overtly sexual, I allowed myself to be physically stripped by the women in the audience. Whenever I walked out into the mass I literally had them tearing at my garments trying to remove them and the same can be said for the women I brought up onto stage. This obviously was not in the script (although as I have already mentioned my choreography wasn't up to much anyway at this time), but I allowed them to do it anyway. I thereby handed control to them and effectively lost the respect of the audience.

I completed the act and made my way back to the dressing room. The g-string I was wearing had gone. It had literally been pulled off and was no doubt now nestling in somebody's handbag as a souvenir. My dick was sore. A couple of them had grabbed hold of it and yanked on it pretty hard, not to mention the whole elastic band thing. The Bull's skirt pointed out that I now had several raised red marks on my skin – scratches – or war wounds to remind me of the experience.

I could see that Bells wasn't too happy that I had let the audience gain control, not the other way around. However, I can only see this with hindsight. His body language showed that he thought the performance was indifferent. I explained what he already knew.

Namely, that I was brand new to this and would welcome any constructive criticism that he could offer. I went on about how I could not possibly improve if people didn't point out my mistakes and as I had no industry experience I couldn't readily pick up the errors on my own. Despite requesting the feedback and explaining that my feelings would not be hurt by criticism, I could not get any. Bells merely stated with complete flippancy and insincerity that my performance was adequate for my first time on a ladies' night. The only advice he imparted was the suggestion that I pluck my eyebrows so that they did not meet in the middle. Although I think this advice was sound, it wasn't quite what I was looking for at that stage. He then suggested I go out and sell Polaroids.

I had purchased an instant camera for this very reason on the advice of both Bells and Michael. Apparently, there existed a phenomena whereby the women that attend ladies' nights are willing to pay £5 for the privilege of having an instant picture (such as a Polaroid) taken with the stripper. As the film averages out at around a pound per photo that is a profit of £4 per photo. Legend had it that a stripper could double his fee on a good night. As I was receiving £80, I would need about 20 pictures to do that. It seemed a tall order, but I was willing to try it under instruction.

"Sissy, how do you do this?" I asked, more than a little uncertain.

"Go topless, go and visit them at their tables and ask them if they want a photo," came back the reply.

"Don't you at least announce it over the microphone?" came back my logical reply.

"There is no need," said Bells, clearly not interested.

So it was that I wandered back out into the lion's den. I had previously been doing a sales role that involved constant cold calling and mass rejection. This sort of task wasn't exactly new to me. However, this felt different. Perhaps I didn't believe in the product. Everybody had been taking pictures during the show and here I was trying to sell them a grainy photo for a fiver. The unique selling point was that I was going to be in the photograph with them. Put simply, I didn't see myself as better than them, as a celebrity, or of any importance. Offering to sell the pictures felt like a phenomenal act of arrogance whereby I was proclaiming my betterment over the audience. I felt distinctly uncomfortable.

Wearing nothing more than a pair of tracksuit bottoms I began to circulate around the numerous tables with an instamatic camera. The fact that Bells had shown no interest and had failed to announce that I would do this did not help my cause. Half of the women were elsewhere (the loo, the bar, next door, etc). Some of them were openly rude and showed complete disdain to my suggestion of a photograph. Others gave polite refusals; some were put off by the price and a grand total of four bought a photo. At the end of this humiliating and degrading process, I returned somewhat sheepishly to the dressing room. Bells enquired how I had done. "That's alright," he said in attempt to make himself feel better.

Bells was now getting ready for the second half of the evening and it wasn't long before he again donned his wig and ventured back into the arena. My work for the evening was officially finished. I had been paid but I decided to stay, watch and learn. The Bull began to prepare himself for his show. A cowboy outfit had been neatly laid out on the table. A porn mag emerged from his bag with accompanying pieces of material. The Bull preferred to tie off using bias binding. This he soaked in water before wrapping it around his member. He then turned one of the chairs into the wall removed his underwear with his back to us and settled into a comfortable position – porn mag in one hand, his dick in the other. Everybody looked the other way while he did what he had to do.

Upon completing the necessary, The Bull donned his cowboy outfit, shy of horns, and strode out into his play area. I wandered out to see if I could get a look at his show, but the view was largely obscured, so I wandered back in again. The Bull returned about a quarter of an hour later devoid of his clothes and again turned his back to us all and grabbed a pair of scissors. He let out a large bellow as he cut the binding restricting the blood flow to his nether regions and he again began to breathe normally. Throughout the evening he had been very aware of preventing people gawping at his package, but being a stripper it was inevitable that people would have to see it at some point. The Bull definitely wasn't hung like one and he knew it. He seemed very aware of the fact and he kept it covered as much as possible. Using bias binding certainly allows one to tie off more effectively. It prevents more blood loss and therefore a greater percentage of the erect size remains. However, given the bellow the Bull let out in his release, I thought I'd stick to elastic bands for now – they didn't seem as painful.

Upon his release the Bull and his skirt were immediately galvanised into action. The Bull donned a g-string that rode high up his arse whilst his skirt waved around an instamatic camera. They went out into the foyer area where there was a fair amount of transitional movement and the skirt effectively acted as an agent and the chief photographer. Maybe it was my inexperience, maybe their tag-team system was a proven formula, maybe I'm just ugly; but The Bull sold far more photos than I did and he returned soon after with another 50 quid from his Polaroid sales. I won't pretend this didn't bother me – it did. I didn't resent his success, I just wanted to know how I could improve mine and they weren't exactly queuing up to tell me how.

I packed up my things and carried them out to the car. There were a couple of the girls standing outside having a cigarette. Their eyebrows rose when I opened up the Impreza. "Flash car for a stripper, innit. You must get paid well for this job?" she quipped.

"Not really," I retorted.

"Is it true that it was your first time tonight," she asked. I nodded. "It was good," she said, lacking sincerity.

It was early days and I needed to improve. Throughout my life I seem to have learnt most things the hard way. That is, by making mistakes with little outside guidance. It looked like stripping was going to be more of the same.

Chapter 7

A Learning Process

Over the coming weeks I began to market myself in the stripping world and learnt very quickly that there were no friends. Drag queens were bitchy and the strippers were even bitchier. To call some of them assholes would have been an upgrade. Prejudice was rife on virtually every level. In my naïvety I had expected a level of professional respect to come from the other performers. Instead, they were all carrying AK47s and they couldn't wait to gun you down at the earliest opportunity.

One example of this occurred whilst I was on a modelling job for a website. Several males had been hired along with a gymnasium for the afternoon. The idea was that we would go into the changing rooms, undress and go into the showers. Once showered, we would be required to get dressed again and leave the changing room. Shortly afterwards, we would again enter the changing area and repeat the process in a different set of clothes. The whole process was being filmed on camera and would be used on a website where supposedly there was a 'hidden' camera in the men's changing room. Sorry to shatter any illusions but yes, hidden camera websites are faked.

The whole day was quite enjoyable. In between filming I was able to train in the gym and the work was about as easy as they come. There were also 150 notes waiting for me at the end of the day. Scott, who ran the agency, introduced me to another one of the models. Scott knew I had just started stripping and said that Evander, the other model, was actually a longstanding member of the Bell Ends.

We shook hands at the introduction, but Evander did so reluctantly. He eyed me up and down with complete disdain and my conclusion was that he resented the prospect of further competition. Evander was a very large, muscular white South African. By the end of the day the old Spitting Image song 'I've never met a nice South African' had entered my head and didn't want to exit. Thankfully, I have met quite a few nice ones. Evander, on the other hand, could have been a prison guard under the old Apartheid regime.

He proceeded to tell me how the stripping business was "so tough and difficult, mate. It's not for the faint hearted". When I asked him to elaborate further, he was either unwilling or unable to do so. He continued to paint a very generalised picture in which the industry was "tough" and newcomers were not welcome. "If I were you I'd do something else," he said with sarcasm.

I returned the volley with an equal amount of sarcastic spin: "If it's so tough maybe you should quit and let others have a go."

Evander tried to stare me down. A more appropriate name for him would have been Tyson, for I was actually his Evander. Intimidatory tactics will only ever influence the weak. Evander and I didn't exchange contact details and were not going to invite one another to dinner.

On the way home from the fake peep show I gave a lift to one of the other models. Vinny, it turns out, had done a fair amount of gay porn. I should also point out that Evander and I were the only two models on the day that looked like they had ever been to a gym! The rest looked like they had only heard of the term. Anyway, Vinny explained that gay porn paid far more than straight porn and that shoots could pay around £300-£400 for a day. I enquired about whether the perceived rumour is true that large cocks need only apply. "Nonsense," he said. "If a shot is required of a big one they just bring in a 'Stunt Dick'." I tried hard not to swerve off the road with laughter (I managed, but only just). Thinking about it logically it made sense, but the thought of the stunt dick tickled me all the way home.

The very next show I did, the blind prejudice began in earnest. Michael called me and offered me the show. Apparently a stripper called Aimless had telephoned and asked him to help find a replacement for his absence. I filled the breach. I drove down to Brighton and found the somewhat small establishment, went inside and introduced myself as the stripper. I was met with a suspicious look by the manager who had very clearly already made up his mind that I couldn't possibly satisfy the expectations of an audience that wanted to see a male stripper.

I often make the mistake of taking people at face value (Asperger's) and automatically assume that people will show me the same courtesy. This they rarely seem to do, but it always takes me an excessive period to learn this. I look young and I often turn up to shows wearing baggy clothing hiding my athleticism. People often therefore assume that I don't look the part and wonder who this skinny youngster is trying to imitate the role of a male stripper. Probably because I have spent a lot of time around athletes and given my highly analytical nature, I don't make these mistakes. I can look at someone who may be dressed but certain clues will tell you what they look like underneath. (eg the tautness of their skin, the way they move, etc). People often get a surprise when I undress, but the first impression often sticks despite the fact that their eyes may now be betraying that first impression. Essentially, they are highly prejudicial.

I now go out to shows wearing a tight fitting top to combat this type of prejudice. However, if it is the middle of winter and freezing outside, I'll still enter the room wearing an arctic jacket and the prejudice often remains. I'm not particularly tall (at 5 ft 9) and athletic rather than stocky. The height should not be a problem; there are an unusual amount of short strippers. However, they all (to a man) wear platform shoes in a vain attempt to elevate their status. I wear trainers and the prejudiced don't seem to notice such an obvious irregularity. Furthermore, because I look so young in a distinctly adult industry I don't conform to the stereotype of what a stripper should look like. I even had a woman say to me once that being a stripper, I should be ugly. "Strippers are always ugly," she said. "That way us girls can go home without pining too much."

It wasn't long before the other stripper arrived and he joined me in a dingy office that doubled up as a store room. This was to be our changing area for the night. Wyatt Earp was a tall athletic type and as it transpired, he used to throw javelins. He was training to qualify as a masseuse or something similar. Stripping paid the bills, whilst he was completing his studies.

I explained that I was brand new and had been introduced to the business by the Rock of Ages (Michael). So too had Wyatt, who turned out to be very chatty and quite forthright in offering some sound and poignant advice (highly unusual as I was to discover).

He went on to explain that the business was nowhere near as glamorous or as demure as people are led to believe. By way of example, he pointed to our changing area for the night, but went on to say that compared to outside toilets in the middle of winter, this was at least warm and relatively (I stress the relatively) uncramped. He also opined that gay shows often go more smoothly that the hen nights. "It doesn't matter what you do on the hen nights. Every fourth show you will have a bad one. It's not you, it's not your performance, you just won't go down well. Do not let it get to you or affect you in any way and you'll be fine."

I thanked him for his contribution of information and began to get ready to go on. I tied off and donned my costume only for the manager to tell me that he now only wanted me to go down to a g-string and then the second stripper could do the full monty. He clearly had no confidence in me whatsoever. Furthermore, as I was now wearing my boxing gown, there was little on show to dispel the prejudice that was probably endemic in his head. I just nodded. As I saw it, I was getting paid and that was all that mattered.

There was no drag queen on that evening and I emerged into a fairly small cellar area with no stage. A small corner had been cleared for us to perform in. The audience of women were perhaps slightly more subdued than those the week before and the show went smoothly enough. I kept control of my audience this time and had to climb some stairs into the open air to escape the arena. Still wearing my g-string I walked back to the store room past the manager and his two door-staff. A raised eyebrow from the manager suggested that I had finally challenged his prejudices. but by that stage his position was so entrenched it wasn't going to be reversed completely.

As I changed the manager entered, gave me an envelope with my money and said I was free to go whenever I wanted. He seemed keen to be rid of me. I had barely spoken a word to him and I will no doubt forever wonder how a person can be so judgemental about somebody when they know nothing at all about them. If he had taken offence to something I had said it would be easier to swallow. However, his own little mind had created a reason(s) to dislike me. I abhor such small mindedness.

I actually stayed and tried to watch Wyatt's show but the view was obscured. We chatted briefly after he had finished. He had to dash off for another show, a late one in Birmingham (an 180-mile drive). We bade farewell. I was later to learn that Wyatt Earp is something of a stripping legend and strangely enough our paths have not crossed again to this day.

*

Things continued to progress slowly but steadily over the next few weeks. Sissy Bells telephoned and offered me a couple more ladies' nights which I readily accepted. To my dismay, however, he telephoned the day before on both instances to say that they had been cancelled. I was later to learn that this was a common problem with ladies' nights. When the venue doesn't sell enough tickets they just cancel the performer. Nowadays I make sure that everything is contractual and in the event of a cancellation a fee still has to be paid. Unfortunately, many drag queens and agents take in jobs on a wing and a prayer and there is no protection for the performer in the event that things go awry.

This is especially the case with Sissy Bells. We were never destined to have a long and fruitful relationship and I smelled a rat both times that he called the day before. The tone of his voice, his sentence structure and semantics; they weren't quite right. I subsequently found out that Bells got nearly all his jobs from an unscrupulous agent that was later to appear on BBC's *Watchdog* programme for sending out very poor quality strippergrams for nominal fees. (That said you do get what you pay for.) Bells was notorious for offering low paid work and wouldn't pay any of his strippers more than £80. I was later told that his budget for strippers was often considerably higher than what he paid them; he took a sizeable cut for himself (without any transparency). Also, if he could find a stripper who would travel to a job for less, he had a habit of cancelling the stripper already on the job so that he could accommodate the cheaper option and pocket more money for himself. I believe that is what happened on the two ladies' nights he offered.

I was still driving the Impreza and could not afford to travel too far for silly money. When Bells phoned and offered me a job in Great Yarmouth, I declined it on the basis that a 200-mile drive was fine but £80 was not. I wasn't going to do it just for the fun of it!

A week or so later Bells pulled a similar trick to get me to go to Barnstaple. This one I accepted for a couple of reasons. Firstly, I could do with the experience; secondly, Bells had offered £110 for this one (still not enough but I was learning) and I had also never explored Dartmoor/Exmoor and wanted to see if the rumours of Big Cats had any validity. Thus, I set off very early one Saturday afternoon.

I drove around the moors and had something to eat beforehand in an extremely picturesque Devon village. I distinctly remember eating my sandwich on a warm summer's evening admiring the small waterfall scene before finally setting off for the destination of the show.

The drag for the evening was called Jack Russell and I was to be the only stripper. No other stripper had been offered enough to entice them to travel so far. Only rookies, lunatics or sightseers would be so stupid.

Russell was a big fat bald bloke whose ego arrived at the venue some 20 minutes before he did. As with many drag queens he had a gimp in tow to carry most of his paraphernalia. The gimp is usually the other half and commonly the more masculine, hen pecked member of the partnership.

I explained to the terrier that I was new to the business and would welcome any tips or wisdom that he could impart (because, of course, he'd been in the business for 400+ years and had seen everything there was to see). He was about as charming, enlightening and generally welcoming as Bells so I didn't bother pushing too hard (why hurt your head on a hard wall?) He also tried to short change me on the cash at the end of the evening, but to be fair I think Bells had neglected to tell him that the extra was owed.

The show itself was another eye opener. I can now say without hesitation that performing as a stripper has given me a very dim view of the female species. I am privileged to get to see them at their most raw and exposed in situations where their bestial side emerges. They behave completely differently to men and this was the night that I first became aware of that.

The show itself was still in need of a lot of polishing, but I was a man (read victim) and that is what these country women had paid to see. I was stupid enough to drive over 200 miles to be the butt of their persecution and they certainly saw no reason to appreciate that (considering that three strippers had already dropped out on them they might have been a little bit more welcoming). The crowd wasn't vast, I would estimate that there was about thirty of them. Some of them were a little drunk, but definitely baying for blood.

I pulled up a late 30-something mum of three (probably) when I was down to my g-string. There were several cries of "get em off" and "rip them off him, Janice". She was a little lary and began clawing at the none-too-tight, cheap and nasty, early days of costumier g-string I had on. Initially, I prevented her advances, but the roars of approval from the rabble and therefore her efforts, grew greater. In the heat of the moment I bowed to the peer pressure, I let her remove my cock from my flimsy black g-string. She began to tug on it hard before promptly putting it in her mouth and performing a drunken act of fellatio on my tied-off member. The baying crowd had got what they were asking for. Several eyes nearly popped out of their heads and I thought one young girl was experiencing an aneurysm.

I retrieved my cock from her mouth, replaced it in the g-string and continued the act. By the time I finished, some jaws were still on the floor.

I emerged from the dressing room to try the Polaroid trick and was met with much the same problem I had first time. Also, there were far fewer girls at this one, compounding the problem. However, what was different about this show was the open hostility and nastiness that I was met with by an admittedly small faction of the audience. One woman openly said "you're not much of a man, are you?" whilst another offered the constructive criticism of "no, I don't want a photo, you were crap". I smiled politely and just mumbled something like "I can't please everybody". I now understood what Wyatt Earp had meant about ladies' nights and how no matter what you do, sometimes it just doesn't go your way.

I was still learning and my act could and would get better. However, comments regarding the size of my cock were clearly aimed to hurt. I have very thick skin; it would take a lot more than that to pierce my armour. Furthermore, it was irrational. To label a flaccid looking seven-inch cock tiny, is like calling Pamela Anderson flat chested! However, the eye opener was in the malicious intent. I was hired to perform a show, which I did. I had travelled many miles for not a lot of money. I had turned up where three strippers had let them down. The drag was less than welcoming and all in all I had a slight feeling of being in the lion's den. On the road back, I overtook the drag with an explosive burst as if to demonstrate in a childish way that I had a supercar and he did not. I glanced in the mirror wondering when I would see him next. It was late, the road was dark and I was playing a haunting Gary Numan album on the stereo (Human). I lamented on my thoughts all the way back on whether I was cut out for this stripping lark. Was it me or was this a business that just exuded a lot of unpleasantness? Either way, I needed to improve my game and I wasn't quite sure how to yet.

*

Over the coming weeks I performed at a series of new gay venues. Central Station was probably the most unnerving. It is hard to believe that the audience actually wanted to watch a stripper. Going into the venue I was accosted by a prostitute intent on selling her services (we were near Kings Cross and the red light district). She wasn't too amused when I suggested she couldn't afford me, even though I did sell the line with a smile.

The punters in Central Station didn't dare look at the performer directly, only out of the corner of their eye, lest they be construed as actually being interested. It was as if the drinkers were playing the stereotyped straight: big, burly and bearded. Why on earth would they look at that sort of thing?

It did throw me a little. I wasn't quite prepared for the total nonchalance of the audience. It didn't affect my performance in any way, but it was less enjoyable. If ever there was a feeling of 'I don't know why I bother' then that was it.

On a Sunday evening I performed my first 'double up'. I was invited back to the scene of my debut – Bromptons – for the first of the evening's performances. From there I was kindly given a lift to the next venue by a bloke who has since become a valued friend. Andy drove me to a place called Dukes near Vauxhall. It had perhaps the most salubrious dressing room I have ever encountered. A separate room upstairs that was well away from the action, it contained a full length mirror with small light bulbs ornately dispersed around the outside rim. I wouldn't say that I felt like a star getting changed, but it sure beat the hell out of getting changed in the broom cupboard.

It seemed slightly odd performing again only a couple of hours after the first time. Bonny, my stalker from Bromptons, had followed me across London to watch me again at Dukes. Michael told me that he had been blabbering something about wanting to wrap me up in cling film and mollycoddle me.

The performance at Dukes was novel because it produced my first ever tip. The British are not a nation of tippers, so it should come as no surprise that my tipper was actually German. At the time I didn't notice him slipping the tenner into my g-string, but he obviously attracted my good grace after the show.

I began to travel further and wider afield on the gay scene. The tiny stage at the Richmond Arms saw things pass uneventfully. My trip to Southampton saw me getting changed in an outbuilding. I remember getting soap in my eyes from the sponge and water routine. From then on I only used water as opposed to soapy water.

When I visited Cambridge the landlord was particularly enamoured with me and wouldn't leave me alone. As was to become a common enough practice, he felt the need to enter the room and ask a question at the time when I was wanking, only to offer a totally false apology. Not that I minded, I was becoming used to it. When I was leaving later in the evening he insisted on carrying my bag to the car only to tell me that there really was no need to leave as there was a spare room upstairs. His intentions were obvious and you have to give the bloke points for trying. However, I couldn't help feel that there was a cash for favours overtone to the whole scenario. If I was to go upstairs and 'oblige' to his whims I would no doubt receive several more bookings. Whether they would come without expected further obligations, one could only speculate.

My gig at Swindon was an interesting night and the first of many temptations to come my way. When I worked in recruitment I could never get anybody to go to Swindon. I began to think anyone that went there would catch the bubonic plague. People used to object on the grounds of a lack of nightlife. Maybe they don't have much to shout about and maybe male strippers constitute a highlight in Swindon. It certainly felt like it, because the show went extremely well and I felt like a true celebrity. When I arrived the female bouncer was chastising a female customer in a very provocative way (a clip round the ear). After announcing myself I was ushered in as a man of relative importance to the broom cupboard at the back of the club. An attractive woman with short dark hair and small build forced her way into my cramped changing area. Before I could utter a word, she introduced herself as a journalist for a local paper and asked if she could profile me for an article to appear shortly. I agreed to the intrusion on the basis that she would forward me a copy of the article when it was published (in true journalistic fashion she wasn't true to her word).

Several questions followed, none of them particularly memorable or unusual. The most eye catching response came when I said I had a girlfriend. I sensed a little disappointment in her, which also made me feel as though I had just given the wrong answer. As I began to tie off she pretended to avert her gaze elsewhere but was sneaking a look through the corner of her eye. The temptation to ask her to 'lend me a hand' was enormous and would have probably been well received. My little head wanted to tear off her flimsy clothes and aggressively fuck her against the wall. My big head was raising moral objections on the basis that I had a girlfriend whom I loved, who would not be best amused by any infidelity.

Because the journalist didn't do anything other than pout and be subtly suggestive, the little head remained under the control of the big head. The little head was revealed for the pleasure of the punters but nothing more. The crowd were great, probably the best I had performed to at that time and when I returned to the privacy of the broom cupboard, the journalist was hot on my heels. In pursuit of journalistic endeavour she had forgotten to ask a question of immense importance and needed to complete the set. The fact that she was eyeing my nether regions like a starved dog was purely coincidental. "Do you like girls," I asked.

"Fuck off, I'm straight," came back the reply.

"Would you like a lift home," I enquired.

"OK."

Little head was making a comeback.

We chatted rubbish as we drove in the Impreza through the dreary Swindon night. As we pulled up she mumbled something about needing a shower to get rid of the sweaty, smoky effects of the club. Kinky thoughts of what I might do with the shower head were running amok in my head, but somehow the moral argument was preventing me from enunciating them verbally. She wanted to be pinned to the wall by my cock. If I had stepped through her front door we would never have made it past the hall before we would have been naked and rutting like wild animals. Yet we were both reticent, for whatever reasons, to table the proposal. She thanked me for the lift and got out of the car, slamming the door in a kind of frustrated anger. I watched her go into her abode with a hard on that could have penetrated concrete. The big head had won the day, but for how much longer?

*

In an effort to promote myself I had launched a website which I could direct people to. It had a brief profile of me and a few pictures. I had put it together on a basic piece of software and as my computer skills were virtually non-existent it was nothing special. However, I received a call one day from a guy called Barry Wacko. He claimed to manage a group of strippers called the Bell Ends and he expressed an interest in me joining the group. He had seen my website, had heard about me on the grapevine and was sufficiently impressed to invite me to come and meet him.

It was a nice confidence booster and suggested that I must at least be doing something right. I agreed to the meeting and traipsed into London to meet him the following week at his flat. My intelligence had told me that Wacko was an ex-journalist who used his former contacts to spin a PR machine around his moderately well known stripping troupe.

He cut a colourful and flamboyant figure, reminding me of the media personality Laurence Llewellyn Bowen in the way he looked. With his long dark curling hair, a light grey suit and an open shirt he really only lacked a medallion. My first impression was of a man trying to defy the ageing process by applying new age metro-sexual principles.

We got down to talking business and Wacko began to drone on about how he had the foresight to create the Bell Ends, how successful they had been and how successful they still were. Newspaper clippings adorned the walls of his office with various mentions of the Bell Ends, all of them several years old. He then insisted on showing me a video recording of when his mighty boys had appeared on *Children in Need on* the BBC.

I steered the conversation away from his reminiscing to the present day and enquired as to how I fitted into the equation. He explained that he was constantly on the lookout for fresh talent and that I fitted his profile. He went on to say that I would have to attend rehearsals (led by a Bell End called Black Rod) and see how I got on with the choreography and the other guys. Wacko had painted a picture whereby the Bell Ends were the best and busiest set of strippers on the planet. As usual I was a little sceptical.

I had concluded at this stage that I would probably have to return to the rat race at some point soon. I had taken a huge hit on the motor racing project and the cash being produced from stripping wasn't preventing the haemorrhage. In fact, it was only slightly reducing the swelling. I was already in discussions with a company about a contract in Dubai. I began to treat this as I would any interview situation and started asking Wacko the questions I wanted to know. Basically, I was asking what he could do for me. He clearly wasn't used to this and didn't take too kindly to it.

Firstly, I began by enquiring whether it was possible to be a Bell End and have a day job. Wacko looked like he just swallowed a wasp. "In order to be a Bell End you must have total commitment. When I give you a date you must drop everything and move things in your diary to accommodate this, including other stripping bookings."

"Obviously," I countered, "the remuneration would reflect that?"

With astounding verisimilitude Wacko stated that Bell Ends were amongst the wealthiest strippers because they were so busy.

I pressed him on the detail. How many shows could I expect to receive from him and at what rates?

"The diary is full between now and Christmas with theatre shows," he said.

"How full is full?"

Finally, he crumbled and said that there were 12 shows booked between now and Christmas. As we were at the end of August, the ratio of bookings was well under one a week! Wacko had been at pains to add that the Bell Ends only perform theatre shows these days, did not do tacky hen night type performances and, heaven forbid, definitely no gay shows. It certainly seemed to limit his options. Furthermore, his theatre shows were hardly local and would involve meeting at midday to board a minibus to go to the other end of the country, typically returning at some horrific hour the next morning. All this for £120! It gets better. I wouldn't be paid until he got paid. If he didn't get paid, neither did I.

I pointed out the glaring inconsistency in his offer. How could I be committed solely to his cause, yet live off about £80 a week, which may or may not get paid to me? "I can't live off fresh air and sleeping rough may diminish my sex appeal," I said. Wacko blathered something about it was up to me and we parted company.

About a week later Wacko telephoned me at home and told me that one of his prime Bell Ends had made him aware that I had appeared as the centrefold in a gay magazine. This wasn't the sort of thing he wanted to be associated with. "I hope you got well paid for it," he sniped.

"The hourly rate was about ten times your offer," I replied. It was tempting to utter something about my conscience also being free of homophobia, but I thought better of it.

Wacko was to contact me again a couple of times over the coming years. On both occasions it was an e-mail he sent asking me to contact him stating something along the lines of how he liked my look. He had clearly not made the connection with my new websites and our previous meeting. I wrote a polite e-mail back stating that all contact details were on www.malestripper.org, including telephone numbers and he was welcome to contact me to discuss any potential proposals. As I suspected, prima donnas such as him would be offended at the suggestion that he should call me. He never called.

*

My next brush with the Bell Ends occurred at a place in Brixton called The Fridge. On a given Saturday about once a month, they held an event called Lovemuscle. I was booked to do it for the first time about the same time I met Wacco. Lovemuscle had become something of an institution over the previous decade. The format was simple. A drag queen who went under the name of Janice would parade onto stage and bring out 'her scantily-clad boys' one by one.

Once there they would 'dance' around for a couple of minutes whilst Janice would remove their garments and fling them into the crowd. The strippers were on stage for no more than about five minutes or so. The Fridge was a huge venue and probably held well over a thousand people.

When I arrived at The Fridge for the first time, I was 'lucky' enough to bump into Evander. He was also one of the evening's performers. He guided me through a labyrinth of passages and corridors to a room at the other end of the building. The strippers' changing area was basic and not especially large. Imagine somebody's bedroom with a few chairs. Evander and I were the first ones to arrive. There was apparently going to be six of us. Evander was a little less brash and slightly more subdued than at our first meeting.

Mr Multiface soon appeared in a blaze of theatre with a booming voice to match. He was like a headless chicken, constantly turning on his heels and strutting to the next person to utter a completely over-the-top greeting. Another soon arrived, a largish, good-looking guy, with a decent physique. I could instantly tell he was using mass steroids. His physique was developed but not especially 'cut'. His musculature was smoothed over by the water retention. Nevertheless, the masses would not be able to tell the difference.

Evander embraced the new entrant whom I recognised as Black Rod. I knew their connection as Bell Ends and knew his reputation for moodiness, no doubt not helped by the obvious steroid usage. I attempted to introduce myself to Black Rod, he was the only one so far who I hadn't met personally. My attempts at a handshake were met with a rebuffal (he just walked away). Looking over his shoulder he said, "You must be Marvelous, people have been asking me what I think about you." No doubt he was referring to Wacko, as they were apparently in league together. I couldn't be bothered to engage him much further. I have never been one for games unless they are on a level playing field such as a computer screen, chess board, etc.

We were two strippers short and the organiser was getting anxious. Multiface confided in Evander that Aimless (one of those missing) was not going to be here. He had been present in his company not more than two hours before and Aimless was drugged out of his head. The other one also failed to show for whatever reason.

I was finding it difficult to bond with my fellow performers. After the exchange of pleasantries with Multiface there was nothing more to be said. Evander and Black Rod were in a league of self obsession to the detriment of all others. I sat quietly, kept my own company and simply observed the organised chaos that unfolded before me. Soon it was time for the group wank. There was nowhere to hide in the small room. Multiface disappeared to the toilet, whereas Evander and Black Rod faced into separate corners. I stayed in the middle of the room.

Evander was most insistent that I didn't dance too much (if only I knew how). If I danced too much then the rest would have to follow and that would be creating extra and unnecessary work for everyone.

The show went smoothly enough. It was definitely easier than a regular gig. We weren't on stage half as long and that is easier on the dick. Lining up to go out there was a definite feeling of celebrity status. The crowd in The Fridge was huge and there was quite a din. The stage was large, high and elevated well above the audience. I felt like a rock star with the masses below reaching out to their heroes. The show was so short and we had to do so little that I actually felt like we were short changing the audience. Personally, I couldn't understand the appeal of Lovemuscle or the apparent installation of the drag queen as something of an institution.

I collected £80 for this feat of willy wiggling. I immediately handed the £12 commission to the agent who was present and thanked him for the job. Evander took a different approach. He bluntly told the agent that he couldn't have his commission yet as he needed it and that he would pay the arrears at some later date. Evander later confided that he never paid any agent's commission. Judging from the look on the agent's face he knew he would never receive the monies. Why then did he keep booking the guy, or alternatively why didn't he just deduct the money at source? This was a phenomenon I was to come across time and time again in stripping and to this day I still don't fully understand it. There is a definite element whereby certain bookers get a sexual kickback from the stripper, usually in the form of the booker performing a blow job on the said stripper. However, in this particular instance (with Evander), I don't think that was the case at all. Yet Evander was continually booked by this agent time and time again. The said agent and his ilk would continually whinge about the behaviour of the said stripper(s), but they continued to book them. If anybody can explain this gross act of obvious stupidity please get in contact – I'd love to know the answer.

I performed at The Fridge on a couple more occasions. The most notable was the night of Lovemuscle's 10th anniversary. Nine of the finest strippers on the circuit were to be wheeled out and little old me. As I remember there was only one omission, which as far as male strippers are concerned is a full house! Multiface arrived with a blond bimbo twice as tall as he was (some strippers were calling him the Hobbit because of his height). Evander was there, repeated meetings had softened his attitude. The rumour mill stated that he had fallen out with Black Rod, perhaps withdrawing some of his animosity.

Again I arrived very early and rumours were circulating that a rare appearance was to be put in by Smack Attack (a stripping legend who rarely frequented the gay scene). Paul Grunt, a short black guy with a Brummie accent was there. Paul seemed very nice, had an excellent physique and I wouldn't have believed he was in his early 40s. I assumed he was about 30. It wasn't until a couple of years later when I began touring the North of England that everybody in the know kept insisting he was actually in his mid 40s. Too many people were saying it and when I finally met him again in 2006 he confided that he was actually 46! He looks excellent and not just for his age. The grey hair is creeping in, but he keeps it short to hide it.

Private 96 was there. He was another legend on the gay scene and his name apparently represented the number of years he had been performing. He seemed really nice as well, but hadn't aged as well as Paul Grunt. I met the legendary Chips for the first and only time. Chips was another legend on the gay scene. He was famous for sticking a bottle of beer up his arse as a finale to his act (I won't tell you about the time he pulled it out covered in shit!) which made him strangely popular. Chips was very stocky and to be honest I would best describe his as barrel-shaped. Tragically he died in 2006 in the USA. His body was found in a shallow grave. It was widely known that he worked as an escort and was also into breath play as a sexual game. Speculation was rife over whether he was murdered or whether a sex game had simply gone wrong. Several friends that I subsequently made spoke very highly of him.

Finally, the legendary Smack Attack arrived. I was expecting some sort of bronzed Adonis with film star looks. My expectations were obviously a little outlandish. Smack was a fairly normal looking, probably in his late 30s, long dark curly hair (90s stripper stereotype). His body was OK, but lacked tone, shape and abs. I was guessing he probably looked really good ten years ago and age was simply taking its toll on him.

All in all, I was in legendary company and a few of them were looking like old men. They had undoubtedly seen better years, yet their reputations from yesteryear were elongating their careers.

Finally, Aimless arrived. I had spoken with Aimless on the phone. He was an arch enemy of Wacko as he ran a rival group of Bell Ends. There had been a dispute between them. Aimless used to be Wacko's Bell End, but split away and officially registered the Bell End name to himself. There existed this ridiculous scenario whereby Aimless called his group the Official Bell Ends and Wacko called his group the Original Bell Ends. Threats of lawsuits had been puffed about on either side, but nothing much occurred. I guess they settled on shared Bell End status.

I had been conversing with Aimless because he wanted more recruits. Perhaps he was interested because Wacko had been interested and he wanted to spite him. It sounded like the sort of thing he would do. In a close repeat of the Black Rod incident, I went and introduced myself to Aimless. With what I was beginning to perceive as typical stripper one-upmanship, he told me that he didn't consider me suitable at the moment. I was apparently too small. "It can all be changed with diet," he said smugly. For the record, Aimless was quite stocky, classically good looking, but lacked any sort of definition in his physique. He was carrying a little belly and I would be very confident that if we stepped onto a bodybuilding stage at that precise moment, I would easily have carried the judges.

Aimless wittered on a little more, stating 'facts' with unbelievable arrogance. As a consolation he offered me the chance to come and rehearse with him and his co-leader, Kent. I tried to take him up on the offer and phoned several times only to be fobbed off and messed about. I concluded that Aimless was a total bell end and not just on stage. He was full of contradictions and so self-obsessed that he would be a perfect candidate for today's reality TV programmes. I wasn't sure who was more obnoxious, Aimless or Wacko. They deserved each other.

The 10th anniversary Fridge show went fine. All the straight ones went to wank in their respective corners. The gay ones were less conscious. I noticed Chips staring at me intensely as I was wanking. Paul Grunt produced this huge penis pump out of his bag when the time came. He explained that it was quicker than wanking and it made it a little bigger as well (not that he needed that).

As I drove back home through Streatham I pondered over the evening's events. It had probably been the most enlightening single evening to date. There were certainly no friends in the business. Nobody was going to give me a leg-up. However, nearly all the legends were old relics waiting to die. From that point of view, there had to be a vacancy for some new, young blood. The bookings were building up slowly and I was starting to enjoy myself more and more.

*

I was approached by Smack Attack about performing at a regular event he was organising at a club in Streatham. I don't know whether our very brief meeting at Lovemuscle had anything to do with the approach or whether that was pure coincidence.

Smack explained that the whole concept was one of reverse lap dancing. There was no fee as such, but we would have to parade around in an effort to secure lap dances. We would receive tokens that we could cash in at the end of the evening. The fee would be

£5 for a dance to a g-string or £10 for a full strip. I was new and needed to learn. Also, I was free on the evening in question, so I had nothing to lose and accepted the offer. I played the lap dancing game twice before I learnt my lesson.

I arrived nice and early as always. A friendly black guy the size of K2 greeted me on the door and gave me directions as to where I needed to be. The reception from the other strippers was typically lukewarm as I should have expected by now. Only a guy called Glyn was friendly and talkative. I didn't know any of them and few of them actually played the regular circuit. Those that were busy and working wouldn't have entertained it, as I later discovered.

The lap dancing event was the first time that I met Chico, who later became famous because of the hit show *X Factor*. This was three years before his appearance on the ITV show and he was trying to distance himself from stripping and begin a career as a singer. He was compering the entire evening whilst throwing a few songs into the mix. He couldn't sing back then either, but he was extremely charismatic and did an excellent job on the microphone. Furthermore, I found him to be quite personable and affable and he did give me a few pointers as to what I could do in my show.

After all the strippers were gathered together, K2 emerged into the dressing room (the men's toilets) and began reading the riot act. Apparently, the week before, one of the strippers was caught shagging a girl in the toilets and was now banned. Also, this girl had cried rape bringing further disrepute on all those involved. Anyone caught shagging the clientele on the premises would be forcibly removed and quickly. A concerned look spread around all those present, which brought a smile to my face. I should have realised at that point that those present weren't there to earn the cash. By banning shagging in the toilets, K2 had just unleashed an almighty storm on their forest fire. K2 also mumbled something about adhering to the no touching rules.

One of the strippers went under the name Nathan. I am yet to this day to meet a more arrogant, but equally talented man. Nathan was so able that he could disappear up his own arse so as to be completely invisible! Amongst his various endeavours he could claim to have worked for every stripping troupe since the year dot (and have been the best member of the troupe in question), he traded oil for millions and was generally vastly superior in his very being to anybody on planet earth. I did enquire whether I might be able to tap into his vast experience of stripping. "Only if you're invited, mate," came back the reply. I have never heard of the guy before or since and can't verify or rubbish any of his claims. Needless to say, he had an average physique and an ageing look. Maybe he was good... back in the 1980s.

The lap dancing in Streatham was also the first time I met the legendary Canadian Shagpile. He did attempt to play the regular circuit and I knew of him because of such. He was another example of the ageing relic from the good old days. He had managed to keep a reasonable physique from using steroids but was showing all the symptoms of aromatised oestrogens. Indeed, he even injected himself in the changing room! Canadian Shagpile was so good he had to tell everybody about it. He used to be in the Californian Bell Ends, had travelled the world stripping, was known throughout the industry, etc, etc – you get the picture.

The next time I met Canadian Shagpile was a couple of years later on my return from Dubai. He turned up at a show I had in Southampton. He wasn't booked. I was doing the show with another stripper called Carpetburn. Canadian Shagpile was based on the South Coast so it was his local haunt. The first thing he did when he entered was to start verbally excreting all over Carpetburn about how he'd already done four shows that night for £125 apiece. He was so great he could command that sort of a fee and earn £500 on a regular basis!

To my absolute amazement he then suggested to the drag queen that he do another show, here and now. The drag told him there was no budget, but there was no stopping him. He gathered a pint glass and collected £9 as a whip round from the girls. After I had gone on and finished, Canadian Shagpile went on and did a show for £9! Far be it from me to suggest that his ego needed the affirmative boost from a female audience or to suggest that the four shows he had done earlier that evening were in fact fictional.

The same drag queen at that show once offered me a job in Plymouth which I couldn't attend because I was already booked. As it was so far, he was offering to drive and save me the petrol. He later told me that as I couldn't attend, he booked Canadian Shagpile. I enquired whether that was wise. The drag replied, "Bloody not. Not only did he twitter on about how great he was all the way there, I then couldn't get rid of him! I let him stay at my flat that night and all he did was burst into tears and go on about his girlfriend. Then he asked to borrow some money. Next day we literally had to throw him out. NEVER AGAIN!"

"I could have told you so," I replied sardonically.

"WELL WHY DIDN'T YOU?" he screamed as I fell off my chair laughing.

The next time I met Canadian Shagpile again was at a Christmas show in a Watford nightclub. What ensued was the stuff of pure comedy. The club asked us to play to their music rather than our own. It was a bit strange, but as a stripper we often have to ad lib. I was going on first and I told the compering drag queen that I would give him a wink when I'd finished as there was no musical cue. Before I'd even started wanking, Shagpile told me he was tied off. I told him he wouldn't be on for about 40 minutes yet! "I've been doing this a long time, I know what I'm doing," he replied. I can only assume that his dick no longer has any feeling left in it!

Anyway, I did my show and then Canadian Shagpile was introduced. The music was the sort that might be played at a rave. That is, very dance oriented. A series of railings across the stage separated the stripper from the crowd. When Shagpile got down to his underwear he climbed the railings like a WWF wrestler climbs the turnbuckle and began waving his arms in the air, gesticulating to the crowd. A couple of minutes later he was naked and the drag tried to bring him off, but he was having none of it. He kept climbing the railings and gesticulating like he had just won some major sports title (best stripper over 40 perhaps?).

I must admit it was quite an atmosphere. Shagpile had clearly got drunk on the fumes and was on a high that he clearly wasn't going to come down from in a hurry. After a couple more attempted interruptions from the drag, Canadian Shagpile was eventually led away from the stage. Somebody really should have covered his head with a blanket and put him in the back of a van. I was both open mouthed and giggly at what I had just watched.

Everywhere he goes, Canadian Shagpile's reputation is legendary. I write this whilst I am currently on a stripping assignment in Cyprus. The owners of the club where I am performing have also got personal experience of the legend. In a repeat of what happened with the drag queen, Nick and Bill had to eject him from their house and have vowed "never again".

Anyway, I digress. Back to lap dancing in Streatham. After K2 had read the riot act and the strippers had ceased injecting steroids, telling each other how great they were, had shaved off their body hair, strutted up and down like peacocks and pontificated some more, we were ready to begin. Nathan the Arrogant did a mini show to start the evening and then we all lined up like prostitutes in an attempt to procure a client. The girls would buy tokens which they would 'buy' us with and we could exchange these tokens for real money at the end of the evening. I was wearing my one and only boxing costume, which admittedly was perhaps not the best outfit in that sort of arena. Women undoubtedly go for uniforms and all the regular ones were worn by the other strippers (policeman, soldier, white naval and fireman).

Nevertheless, it wasn't long before an attractive young girl, wearing a white veil (presumably soon to be married) was thrust forward by her mates and I was handed some tokens. The deal was that I would then take her upstairs and perform a lap-dance for one or two tracks only. I would then thank her, escort her back downstairs, get dressed and return to my soliciting.

I must confess to being a little nervous and unsure at this point. Attempts at interrogating the other strippers as to what was expected had come to nought. They were too busy reassuring themselves of their own greatness. I was no dancer. In fact I can't dance to save my life. Performing a routine to music is very different to 'dancing'. I was therefore going to have to blag my way through it.

The first time I did it I was the epitome of professionalism. I stole a few things from my regular routine, did a fair bit of grinding up against her, didn't allow her to touch me (thereby sticking to the rules) and generally did as I was told. The 'private' area upstairs was nothing of the sort. It was a huge room with seating around all the walls. Strippers sat their clients down and performed in the nearest available space. Any client who paid their fiver or tenner could easily view all the other strippers performing for other clients as well as the stripper that they had personally bought. It certainly provided little incentive for the girls to repeat buy. Buy one stripper and you would certainly see more than one in action.

The first time I performed I was sneaking glances at what all the other guys were up to, just to make sure I was in the same ball park. It was pretty obvious that not everybody was adhering to the 'no touching' rule. They were cleverly hiding errant hands behind large flags.

After finishing the dance, I took my girl back downstairs, dressed hurriedly and hurried some more to get back downstairs so that I could continue my red light act. To my surprise most of the guys were entertaining for far longer than a couple of tracks. Business was slow, but it wasn't long before the same girl was approaching me again to be taken upstairs. She must fancy me, I concluded – most flattering.

As I started to entertain, I was again watching the other strippers with their non adherence to protocol. I was also aware that this girl had hired me again, presumably for a reason. Unfortunately, I didn't have a flag, or any other screening device for that matter. It was painfully obvious to me that the 'no touching' rule was not being enforced. A female bouncer was watching our every move and she was either very stupid or deliberately ignoring what was going on behind the flags. On that basis I decided to proceed by also ignoring the 'no touching' rule.

I started much as I did the first time, pulling bits from the routine and grinding. When fully naked, I increased the level of grinding and found this to be to her pleasure. As this was meeting with her approval, I let my grinding crotch rise up her body and when my dick reached her open neck top, I started lowering it into the space between her bra cleavage. This was met by an increasing broad smile and a little squeal, which I again concluded was a sign of approval. My dick was no longer pointing straight down.

I grabbed her hand, ran it over my chest and down towards my nether regions. She offered no resistance, hungrily grabbed by dick and began slowly tugging on it. She steadily increased the tempo in direct correlation to the stiffness so that when I was fully primed her hand was going like a motorised piston.

I'd be lying if I said that this was not a pleasurable experience and despite all the action going on around us I was in a completely different place. My tranquil dream state was shattered by a rather exasperated and concerned looking Chico, who came running over in a bit of a tizzy.

"It's no touching," he said.

Both I and the girl stared at him blankly, she carried on her pistonised action, obviously intent on me spunking in her face.

"No touching," he protested again.

"There's no touching going on over there behind that flag. Go and have a word with them and come back in a minute," was my response.

"No touching," he pleaded robotically.

"Go away, we're busy," I whispered.

At which point Chico leaned forward and slapped the wrist of the girl (gently) with another "no touching – naughty" thrown in for good measure. This had the effect of damaging the pistons and Chico began wittering on about regulations and getting him in trouble. I just groaned my displeasure whilst the girl looked on both sheepishly and cheekily.

I covered up my aching boner and escorted her downstairs. She skipped back into the crowd giving me a final naughty glance before she disappeared. In passing, one of the other strippers added, "It didn't take you long."

The rest of the night passed fairly uneventfully. After the initial rush of girls wanting to buy dances, it all died down and I spent most of my time in the red light area with little success. There were only another couple of dances in the entire evening. Two very young girls just giggled all the way through, but were very complimentary at the end. Although I wasn't their first choice for looks, I was the least sleazy and had offered the best routine.

Nathan, the ego-filled balloon, had been telling everybody how one punter had offered him £7000 to take him home, but he had turned her down. No doubt this was an everyday occurrence in his world. I had spent most of my time touting for business, whilst everybody else seemed to be securing business upstairs. I must confess to having been being a bit flummoxed and was searching for what I had done wrong. I concluded it must have been my choice of uniform. All the others had popular girly themes.

At the end of the night we went to cash up our tokens and I was standing there with Fireman Sam (aka Glyn). Glyn was the only other stripper I had taken to on the night and wasn't full to bursting with his own ego. He had been upstairs a lot compared to my constant soliciting without much success downstairs. I had put much of his success down to his fireman's uniform. Glyn, whilst being quite stocky, was balding and had the look of a bodybuilder in the off-season. That is to say, he looked a little bloated and chubby from steroid usage. He didn't have the best physique in the building, so I had concluded something else must have been adding to his allure.

As we were cashing up I was stunned to discover that I had actually earned more money than he had.

"Glyn…' I stuttered with amazement.

"What?"

"You were upstairs all night, where's all your cash," I said, scraping my jaw off the floor.

"Oh, we were doing them all for free, mate, it's a good laugh getting your knob played with all night."

I visited Caesar's in Streatham once more and attempted to earn money from lap dancing. I had even bought myself a white naval uniform to see if the uniform made any difference at all to earnings. It didn't, I was plus £10 compared to the boxer. A combination of strippers offering dick-sucks for dances and a non private playing area meant that it was never going to be a money earner.

My second night followed a similar format to the first. Chico was doing his best, attempting to sing; strippers were pontificating, giving away their wares for nothing and nobody was earning any money (except the venue). Chico was actually quite helpful in dispensing a few stripping tips and I distinctly remember him telling me to discard the jacket because it was 'making me look small' and hiding my physique. This was the first bit of useful constructive criticism anybody had really given me since I had started stripping. At the end of the night, he was upstairs attempting to get himself sucked with the rest of the boys.

If ever I have performed lap dancing again (it isn't often), it has always been after a show where I have already been paid a fee. Getting one's dick sucked by nubile young ladies is always nice, but, it isn't the reason why I do this. Not all strippers can honestly say that…

Chapter 8

Money's Too Tight to Mention

It was autumn 2002 and I had just got back from a brief climbing holiday in Ireland. Whilst going up Carrauntoohill (Ireland's highest mountain) I had been engrossed in conversation with a fellow climber/walker. We enjoyed each other's company for a couple of hours. He told me how he'd not had a proper job for nearly 20 years, was something of social outcast but had recently fallen for a girl and was having cold sweats about the prospect of returning to 'normal' life. In those 20 years he'd done a fair bit of travelling.

I explained my current predicament and how I was bit disillusioned with the way business operates in the UK, how I too had recently dropped out of society and started a fledgling career as a stripper. He suggested that two areas I should look at moving to were Dubai and Vancouver. Both, he reckoned, offered an interesting lifestyle with plenty of opportunity.

By coincidence, when I arrived back from Ireland, there was an e-mail waiting for me from somebody I used to work with. He was now the financial director for a leading recruitment company. They were looking for a dynamic go-getter to open up an operation for them in Dubai and they would like to talk to me. Although I have never been superstitious or believed in fate, it was one of those strange 'it's a sign' moments.

I decided to go and talk to them. After all, I had just lost a stack of cash on the failed motor racing venture. My asshole had been considerably enlarged by the experience of the last two years and I needed to get some money back. I was really starting to enjoy the stripping, but I was only averaging a little over a job a week at the time – £100 isn't the easiest income to live on. I still had some savings, but I was living on borrowed time if things continued at the current rate.

I had four interviews with BLT. It was clear that one of the four didn't like me, but the other three were positive, especially the chief executive. As is the way in the modern business world, he would tell the others what to decide and they would agree without an argument. Therefore it looked like an offer would be forthcoming. I decided to gamble somewhat. I told them that I had two other offers on the table, both offering six-figure packages. However, both were in the UK and I was keen to leave the UK. Therefore if they were prepared to offer something comparable on remuneration I would take their offer ahead of the other two. Yet I would be unable to hold off the other two offers indefinitely and would need to know their final decision soon.

Both of the other offers were pure fiction, but the take-away close is a powerful sales technique. In my experience if they were going to say no, they would prolong the agony. By forcing their hand, I was just speeding up their final decision. If they wanted me, they would come up with a written offer. If they wanted someone else, then I was only forcing them to say so ahead of their planned time. Some people may see what I did as a huge risk on my part. However, my tactics demonstrated that I am capable of negotiating difficult situations and people generally want what they can't have. By telling them that they couldn't have me if they dithered, they wanted me even more. My tactics worked. An offer arrived and after further minor negotiations, I had a one-year deal in Dubai worth nearly £8000 a month, tax free.

Whilst I was wearing a suit during the day to a high flying meeting, unbeknownst to my prospective employer I was working as a sleazy stripper by night (at least that's how they would see it). I would be lying if I said I felt comfortable in a suit back in a business environment. Suits are nothing more than a uniform worn to show conformity to a norm. Some suits work against their will towards a better good, others have had their brains totally washed away.

To me, the suit felt like a straitjacket. Furthermore, fraternising with the suits was incredibly difficult for me. The suit wearers are like ants acting out their part in a much larger colony. Some suits take to playing the game better than others. I always thought those that actually wear their suit with pride were weird in the extreme. Whoever invented suits should have been tortured... slowly. They are simultaneously both uncomfortable and dysfunctional.

By returning to the business game I was putting on an Oscar winning performance. There was no place I would rather not be more. Yet I needed the money. I had concluded that I needed to pay off my mortgage. I hate being in debt and owing things to people. When I had graduated I took out a loan for £3000. I hated it being there hanging over my head like a cloud and I paid it off as soon as possible. I paid off my credit cards every month. I never took credit except on the mortgage. Despite earning good money, I had concluded that the mortgage was too big to take on. Even if I saved £3500 per month, every month, it would still take well over two years to pay it off. It just seemed too daunting at the time. Besides which, there were everyday household items to buy.

Now, however, I had changed my mind. When running the motor racing project, the mortgage limited my ability to take risks, because I couldn't afford to risk losing the equity that had accumulated in the house. It needed to be paid every month and now I wanted to kill it – stone dead. The Dubai project would mean that I could kill it in a year. If I lived like a monk and saved everything at the end of the project I'd be mortgage free and with it I would have a lot more personal freedom.

In the meantime, the stripping continued...

*

I had managed to arrange myself a mini tour in Wales and the West. On Tuesday I would play a place in Bristol, on Wednesday a place in Cardiff and on Thursday a different place in Bristol. Money was tight and the succession of jobs on consecutive nights would save considerably on fuel.

Zoe and I were at the most strained point our relationship had ever seen. She was working full time but simultaneously studying for her Masters degree. I had seen a lot of hard earned cash go up in smoke whilst people seemed to be queuing up to screw me over. We were both stressed in our different ways and it showed.

We have always clashed over the issue of tidiness. I am tidy and organised. Zoe can be chaotic in the extreme. It had produced a few arguments over the years. Whilst I was trying to run a business from home, Zoe's chaos was starting to over-run my neat organisation. Previously, my complaints would be upheld, now chaos was running amok and my pleas were being ignored. My stress levels were rising.

I was enjoying the strip lifestyle and the thought of again renting out my ass as a suit was frightening in the extreme. I had sat down with Zoe and discussed the possibility of us paying off the mortgage within five years with me working full time as a stripper. Work was increasing and I had made some forecasts. I had historically been the one who had earned the money. It was my wage that had supported us both whilst she got qualified, it was my wage that bought the house, the car, the furniture, etc. Now the situation was reversed somewhat. She had a higher wage, but she was frittering her money away on items we didn't need. I discussed her spending habits and tried to implement a new plan of action given the reduced income. She wasn't very interested. It felt like in my hour of need I wasn't receiving the support I had hoped for.

Having arranged the mini Welsh tour, Zoe informed me that she would need the car for the Wednesday. I asked why and she said that she needed it for her Masters project. We established that it was a work expense. I explained that I had gone to considerable effort to arrange the tour and couldn't just change the date, so if work required her to have a car for that day she would have to hire one and bill them for the expense.

"But they'll just tell me to change the date."

"Well change the date then," I said, applying logic to the situation.

Zoe hired a car from our own pocket thereby wiping out the fee for one of my jobs on the Welsh/West tour. To say I was livid was an understatement. It may also have been a decision that changed the course of our relationship...

As I was driving along the M4 towards Cardiff I had to open the windows to allow the steam to dissipate that was continually emanating from my ears. It had been a considerable effort to line all the gigs up in succession and she had shown both contempt and disdain for my efforts. Besides her monumental nonchalance, I was affronted in the extreme by the fact that we did not have a huge pot of gold to waste. Money wasn't yet too tight to mention, but it could get there soon if this sort of behaviour continued.

I arrived in Cardiff lighter for loss of steam, with my self-protection mechanisms enabled and working on lowering my internal temperature. The gig the night before in Bristol had passed uneventfully. A small crowd of cautious gay men had produced nothing new to report.

The Cardiff venue was a large, modern, young person's club. It was a gay club, but the audience was very mixed with many straight women present. At first I made the incorrect assumption that many women in gay clubs were lesbians. On the contrary many straight girls often attend gay venues. They often claim the music is better. That may or may not be the case, but essentially they get left alone and don't have to continually escape from the hordes of desperate straight men who haven't got laid in the last quarter.

Many gay men have a 'fag-hag' in tow. Fag being derived from the derogatory term 'faggot' meaning a gay man and hag being derived from the derogatory term for an evil woman. Fag-hags are essentially straight women who like to hang around gay men. Their kind are on the increase. I'm particularly partial to them. They tend to have adopted certain values, norms and behaviours from their gay brethren. Notably, they tend to be more promiscuous and sexually adventurous with an overall enhanced liberalisation to their general attitude.

I was guided to a small personal dressing room, specifically set aside for artists and performers. It was essentially a large cupboard with a dressing room table in it, set back from the stage. Compared to much of what I had experienced so far, this was luxury.

The stage was large and the crowd equally so. The audience, although predominantly male, had a strong female content. One particularly caught my eye whilst I was performing. A young black girl who seemed as focused on me as I was trying not to be on her.

After I left the stage, the manager kindly returned my discarded costume and I performed my customary equipment check. I was a boxing glove down. I didn't really want the added cost of replacing them so I hurriedly dressed and returned to the stage. It was nowhere to be seen. I went to ask the manager if he had seen where it might have wandered off to. The bouncer was called and he suggested he might be able to track down the culprit. "Wait there," he said reassuringly, "I think I can find the girl who has it."

I spent the next ten minutes or so chatting to some lovely Welsh guys at the bar who were far more forward in their sexual advances than their London equivalents. Finally, the bouncer returned with the black girl, beaming sheepishly, my missing boxing glove in her hand.

After a couple of minutes of chatting rubbish I suggested she follow me whilst I dispose safely of the boxing glove. Upon returning to my dressing room, I found that an almost orderly queue had formed of Welsh women who seemed intent on fucking my brains out!

This was simultaneously both flattering and alluring in the extreme. I attempted to diffuse their intent somewhat by playfully suggesting that they were all lesbians. "I am normally," spouted one, "but not after watching you tonight," she continued.

I was somewhat taken aback by their bold front, but I wasn't sure whether to actually believe their intent. In essence, that girl was writing a cheque that her ass couldn't cash. All three of these newly emerged groupies were individual to each other; that is, none of them were friends. If they were serious, they were unwilling to share and as a result the competition for attention resulted in a frustrating stalemate for them. They cancelled each other out and drifted downstairs, leaving the black girl and I alone.

It wasn't long before we were kissing and shortly afterwards her head was bobbing up and down on my cock. Halfway through the act one of her gay friends walked in on us and promptly ran downstairs, screaming in disgust, "Stef and the stripper are doing it." A slight exaggeration, but still...

I gleaned very little information on 'Stef'. She was 19 years old and from Newport.

"I bet you get sucked off by all the girls after your shows, don't ya," she sniped.

"No," I said truthfully.

"Liar," she sniped.

"Although it may be hard to believe, I'm not getting on with my girlfriend and this is the first time this has ever happened," I added apologetically.

"I bet you say that to all the girls," she repeated.

In nine years I had never been unfaithful to Zoe. I had never really put myself in a position that would allow me to be so. Yet, here I was. It wasn't as if the sexy 19-year-old had fallen and accidentally landed on my cock. I took the bait when it was offered, in fact I swallowed it whole.

As I drove away that night a chorus of Welshman began shouting:

"LOOK, LOOK AT THE STRIPPER, LOOK WHAT HE'S DRIVING!"

The Impreza had flattered to deceive. A legion of Welshmen probably thought I was on £500 a show and my celebrity status for the evening was sealed. As I left the club, a leggy blonde told me I looked incredibly sexy and intimated strongly that she wanted my cock buried deep within her, preferably sometime within the next ten minutes. I thanked her for her flattery but declined to push it any further. I had just emptied my balls inside a woman other than the one I loved. It didn't seem right to do it again less than an hour later and I distinctly remember feeling strangely affronted by her interest.

I have never gone for blondes, but my reticence was more to do with a feeling of being a sex object. Although I would probably never feel it again, I felt like saying, "I have a brain too you know."

As I drove away I felt a strange sense of achievement and satisfaction. The guilt would hit me later in the week. I didn't even have Stef's number. I don't know if it was her real name.

The next night I was in Bristol. It was another gay venue and I arrived early. I was virtually the first one in the club. Two girls entered first. They were the only ones to enter the whole evening, but I ended up giving the pair of them a lift home and receiving a blowjob in the back of my car.

The evening had another memorable moment. The bloke that had booked it had seen my picture on a website and clearly wanted to get into my knickers. He was an employee of the club but had no jurisdiction to hire an act. The show wasn't marketed and had a poor attendance. I was only paid half the fee on the night on the promise that the rest would follow. It didn't and when I called the venue a couple of weeks later they denied all knowledge (conveniently). I learnt a valuable lesson that night. This industry is a bit fly by night, with its many cash in hand payments. However, in order to protect your livelihood, jobs are always best secured in writing. Strippers attract a lot of attention from unwanted pests. Many of them pretend to be bookers in the vain hope that they will secure a sexual favour on the evening. The minute you talk about contracts these stalker types tend to disappear.

On this particular evening, the booker was especially camp and slimy. The two girls had arrived especially to see the stripper, which was more than could be said for the rest of his meagre audience, most of whom seemed oblivious to my presence. The two girls shouted the loudest and had to be prevented from entering my dressing room (the toilets) afterwards by Captain Slime. Captain Slime was most put out when I went off with the pair of them after the show.

Normally, I would never rub somebody's nose in it like that, but Captain Slime had hired me for personal intentions and didn't really care whether I got paid or not. He didn't care if it cost me

£50 to get there and several hours in a car. All that mattered to him was the opportunity to lay me. I had no qualms about turning him down and going off with the objects he hated.

Both girls had annoying tractor accents, but still, my ambition was to play with the pair of them. For a while it looked good, however, the brunette cried off, leaving me to get sucked dry by the blonde. As I dropped her off she babbled something about how she was going to brag to all of her mates that she had sucked off a stripper.

As I drove back to London I had the windows open for a different reason. It seemed to stink of sex. I reflected on what I had done and this time I was repentant. I hadn't even fancied the blonde. I've always fancied girls with dark or red hair and blue/green eyes. The exception on the eyes is black/oriental women. Blondes automatically lose 20% for me and have to make it up elsewhere. This one didn't make it up, yet I still got a bit wild with her. I pondered why on the drive home. Was I getting back at Zoe? Had the well run dry? Was I just a typical man who couldn't resist it when it was put on a plate for him? What did this behaviour say about me? So many questions and at the time I had very few answers…

*

After arriving back in London little seemed to have changed in Zoe. She was still lost in her own private world, a world into which I had little impact. The next night after arriving back I was to perform a private show in a hotel room. I had already performed for this guy before. Some people may find it a bit strange that I perform private shows for men one to one. The first person to contact me and ask me if I would do that was an American guy called Steve. He asked me if I would come to his hotel room and perform my act as I would normally on stage. He was willing to pay my normal stage fee. His only request was that was he able to masturbate whilst he watched me perform. I explained that I was straight and he said that was fine. He didn't in any way want to compromise my sexuality, he just wanted to enjoy my performance in the privacy of a closed room rather than a club. All these seemed quite reasonable to me so I agreed to do it.

I told a couple of straight mates what I would be doing and they seemed to think I was mad. "What if there are ten of them in the room when you arrive, you could get raped." This appeared to be their consensual opinion. They might have thought I was mad in taking a risk. I thought they were mad with their prejudice.

Anyway, Steve was a real gent. It was a bit strange performing to one person only, but the money was the same and it was easy money as I saw it. In my first six months, my diary tells me that I performed four of these private shows. Two of them were so bland I can't even remember them. One of them was unforgettable. The bloke was very cagey from the outset, wanting to meet me at a train station in North London. This I did. He picked me up in a limousine, claiming to have his own company of limousines. We then went to a property he rented out where I performed the show for him. He clearly had plenty of cash and when he paid me he gave me £400, four times what I had charged him. The only anomaly was when he began asking whether I would be willing to incorporate some other things into my show – role play situations, dominating him, etc. I politely declined, stating that I didn't think I could meet his expectations of me. He duly hired me again within a week and again paid me £400. This time he was more explicit in what he really wanted. He offered me £1000 to take a shit and then let him lick out my arsehole. It didn't really rock my world so I pissed on his bonfire rather than shit in his toilet. He never hired me again, but I had to respect him for making the offer.

Steve, however, was more conventional and I again met him that evening. He sensed there was something wrong and before we began proceedings he enquired as to my well-being and I told him what had transpired over the last couple of days. I really did appreciate his concern and since then Steve and I have become friends. He might not hire me anymore (he says it would be wrong now we are friends), but we do see each other from time to time and keep in touch. We have a few things in common, most notably a dysfunctionality in our childhoods, and I enjoy our time together. The conversations have always been stimulating.

I collected my money from performing and went home. The next day I was performing at a private party. It was for gay men and when

I arrived, the host – who was Danish – enquired as to my sexuality. I told him I was straight and to my surprise he seemed pleased. "You might like my friend Natasha," he said laconically.

When I emerged into the living room, it felt like a packed roman amphitheatre. A man was tied to a chair in the centre of the room and everywhere else people seemed to be packed in layers, one on top of the other as high as the ceiling. I had little room to manoeuvre and when I turned around with a bottle of baby oil in my hand it was pretty obvious which one Natasha was. Apart from being one of only two women present, she was beaming at me with piercing blue eyes, cropped brown hair with her hand cupped ready to receive the oil to apply to my body.

I finished the act and disappeared to get changed. The host burst in, and encouraged me to hurry so I could be introduced to Natasha.

Natasha was just my type and we chatted somewhat cautiously under the auspices of our watchful party host who seemed intent on matchmaking. I was soon walking up the road with Natasha and a couple of burly gay Danes. They proposed going into a club, but my hatred of loud, smoky environments meant I politely declined their offer but wished them well for the evening. Natasha had clearly decided that I was more interesting than dancing and offered to keep me company as we shook off the gay Danes.

"Where shall we go?" she asked.

"How far is your place?" I replied.

"About a mile."

Natasha took me gently by the hand and began to guide me through the busy London streets.

"Is this one of the rewards of your job?" she asked after we had been walking for a few minutes.

"It shouldn't be – I have a girlfriend," I said sheepishly.

Unfazed by my honest reply, she just shrugged her shoulders and continued to lead me through the night. After about 20 minutes we arrived at an expensive apartment near Baker Street and I was ushered inside. After chatting nervously for a few minutes, she suggested I take a shower to remove the clammy baby oil. I rose at the suggestion and to the occasion. No sooner had I removed my underwear when Natasha let out a load moan and knelt at my feet beginning what would perhaps be described as phallus worship. Pulling my erect member back, it slapped into my stomach with a loud clap before she began to gorge heartily.

It wasn't the last time I saw Natasha socially. She stimulated my mind. She had a first from Oxford, worked as a high ranking civil servant and came from a well-to-do background. Her dad was in the House of Lords and clearly money was the least of her worries. I must admit she fascinated me. She had a very studious look to her, which I liked, and the intellect to match. She had a job which amused as well as annoyed me. She was well paid for doing very little and whilst she was a smart cookie she had limited experience outside of government. She was an excellent diplomat but often seemed oblivious to the practicality of real world solutions. Maybe she had been in the political arena too long.

She would often let me see what she had written about me in her diary. Most of it was complimentary and I'd be lying if I said it didn't make me feel good. I felt wanted in her company and that was something that I didn't seem to be getting at home and hadn't for some time.

Ultimately, however, Natasha had her issues and they were deep seated. Despite her outward self-confidence there was an insecure, frightened little girl inside. Her use of recreational drugs with all of her 'ra ra' friends was far from endearing to me. They made her moody and unpredictable and I didn't like the company of her numerous toff friends.

It became like a game to her. It was like she felt she had numerous assets with which she could lure me in. Money was one of those assets and she once talked about what was the use of having so much of it if she couldn't spend it with a man like me. She even then talked of throwing herself off an 11th-storey balcony. She was prone to depression and her drug use can't have helped. Although she was too selfish, I felt, to ever seriously contemplate actually jumping, it was representative of her state of mind. She was used to getting her own way and she hated it when she didn't get it.

I soon became an object which she wasn't getting her own way with. In her eyes I was malfunctioning. She had an intellectual arrogance about her that was not very attractive and she despised it when I proved her wrong. She even wrote in her diary of how I kept 'logic chopping' her into submission. By contrast, I welcomed her intellectual challenge. She, however, wanted to control my thoughts, not run with them.

I liked Natasha but she had a nasty side to her. Like too many women I've met as a stripper, she was incredibly selfish and ultimately that turned me off.

*

The minute I had put my mind to it I had emptied my balls into the mouths of three different women, from three different shows in four days. All of the women had been bona fide fag hags and there was a certain addictive quality to what I had undergone in the last few days. Things were not going well at home. I was convinced I had lost Zoe's love because she didn't respond to me anymore.

These new women had watched me perform and wanted to have me. Their motives were different in each circumstance, but it probably is fair to say that it boosted my ego and made me feel wanted at a time when I was a little low.

Also, it was starting to unleash elements of my true sexual character. I've always had this 'darker' side. Zoe had kept it in check. She preferred 'normal' sex. I was more kinky, exploratory and adventurous. I was always straining at the leash whilst Zoe would pull me to heel. In a wild three days the leash had lost more than just its tension. It appeared to have snapped in two.

Whilst my inner demons sought to overrun my inner goodly heroes, I had the added complication of dealing with my depleted finances. There was no way that I could continue to strip and not have another source of income. The company that had headhunted me for the job in Dubai had weighed in with a firm offer. After some bluff calling on my part we settled on a 12-month contract at just under £8000 per month tax free. The way stripping was going

I would do well to clear that in a year. There seemed little option but to take the job.

I really didn't want the Dubai position all that much. I welcomed the finance it offered, providing a genuine opportunity to clear the mortgage quickly. Also, I was disillusioned with the British culture somewhat and this presented an opportunity to test the old adage that a change is as good as a rest. However, the thought of once again joining the rat race terrified me and gave me nightmares.

Also, I was really starting to enjoy and embrace my fledgling strip career. What started out as an act of rebellion, mixed with a peculiar curiosity for me, had become a form of chemotherapy attacking the cancerous cells all too prevalent in the corporate slave nation our society is rapidly becoming.

I had discussed with Zoe at length about the possibility of a five-year plan to kill the mortgage with me as a stripper. Given the then current growth rate of bookings, this was not an overly ambitious plan assuming her salary was managed properly. However, her reaction was lukewarm at the time of discussion and her actions were downright contrary to my suggestion. My head hurt from banging it on a wall and our relationship was going downhill fast. We were approaching terminal velocity and the brake pads appeared to be worn to the bone.

It seemed like I had no choice. The only person that could have helped me fight off the cancerous corporate lifestyle was Zoe and she offered no lifeline. It stands to reason that on some subconscious level I had to resent her for doing this. Reluctantly I agreed to take the Dubai assignment and almost simultaneously I came to the conclusion that the rock in my life was no longer hard. She had melted away and only ashen remnants remained.

She took with total amazement and utter shock my suggestion that I should move into the other room. I felt I was being forced to start afresh and I told her that I was going to pay off my mortgage. In the meantime, she was welcome to keep wasting her money away, but no longer mine. I was truly expecting complete nonchalance in her reaction to my bombshell, but the opposite was the case. It hit her like a combination from a peak Mike Tyson, but I was hurting too. My pleas had fallen on deaf ears too many times. I simply didn't believe she was going to change now. We had just been put on probation.

I felt like a man on death row. On December 9th 2002, my life would end as I knew it. I would be enslaved again into a sort of corporate living death and my rock of the last nine years was no longer there to lean on in support. I was feeling the strain. For a condemned man, every breath tastes sweeter than the last and with the stripping in those final weeks that's exactly how it felt.

I returned to play a gay venue in Portsmouth. The first time there my reception had been OK to lukewarm. This time there was a visible improvement in their reaction and the personnel had changed little. Even the compering drag queen offered words to that effect as I left the stage.

I did another gay club in Kent where prior to going on I also did a photo shoot with a photographer in the cellar. The pictures probably appeared in some gay magazine stateside but I never heard from the photographer again. It's a shame as we actually got on quite well that night and when I returned from my Arabian prison over a year later he had changed his number.

The night was made most memorable because of the behaviour of the resident fag hag – a big girl with dyed red hair and a foreign accent. I tried to talk to her, but didn't get very far. Several lesbians were present in the club that night and one particularly pretty one kept sneaking me glances. However, she was with her girlfriend so I continued to probe with the fag hag. What little I did glean from her was that she possessed a high degree of insecurity coupled with a fear of rejection. She only seemed comfortable around gay men and ostracised me the moment she realised I preferred women. I gave several of them a lift home at the end of the evening. Matt (the photographer) called me the next day in a state of anguish. The large fag hag had tried to jump into bed with him and a couple of the other gay men where he stayed the night. Talk about wanting what you can't have!

I performed at a club in Brighton where they wanted me to play only to their rave music, rather than my usual music. It was a slightly unnerving concept at first but I soon got into it. Dare I say it, but I actually danced (sort of). The performance was on a very high raised stage and it certainly seemed to go well. It was a very surreal setting where everybody seemed high rather than drunk. Arms of both sexes were raised towards the stage reaching out in a vain attempt to grab me as I performed my act. It reminded me a lot of the archive footage you see from rock concerts on the TV. If someone had handed me a guitar I could have smashed it up and dived into the audience to complete the scene.

My penultimate show was a gay pub in Watford that had seemed reticent to book me at first. However, the show again went very well and one of the publicans reverted from hostile to pleasant within 20 minutes. That is, from going on stage to coming off. With that said, one could hardly call it a stage. It was more like a couple of beer crates with some wood over the top. There wasn't room to swing a spider let alone a cat. I was starting to get a feel of how to interact with an audience and what was expected from a performance. I had made a few little adjustments as I was going along but nothing major. My choreography was still lacking, but I had learnt what was expected and had started to adjust to it. It was starting to show because my reception was improving everywhere I went and it wasn't just because people wanted to get into my knickers.

I also acquired a few more hen shows in those final few weeks as Marvelous. Most of the work as Marvelous had been on the gay scene and the hen scene had proved more difficult to access. On the gay scene they were keen to view new, young blood. Many of the strippers playing the circuit had been doing so for three decades. Few had more than one or two acts, a few were saggy where they were once toned and generally audiences were tired of the repetition. New pretenders were welcome to come and challenge the established elite. The gay scene also likes its 'chickens'. The term chicken is an extension of the abbreviation 'chick' as in newly hatched. Gay men, by and large, like their quarry young. If one demonstrates an ability to pull a chicken half one's age, I guess it does wonders for one's self-esteem. Because I look a lot younger than my real age, I fall into the chicken category. Although there is a demand for older performers, the mass market demands youth and this is on my side compared to a lot of the competition. As a result, gay venues were willing to give me a try with little or even no recommendation other than an accompanying picture.

The hen night circuit on the other hand was much more of a clique with a certain air of Mafiosi about it. Although Michael had provided me with a list of drag queens to contact who regularly partook in hen shows, they were far too diva-ish to return my phone calls. If they picked up the phone the reception was mild to lukewarm. In essence, hen shows were declining and there were not all that many about anymore and those that were available went to the established clique. Certain agents used certain drag queens, who, in turn, booked the strippers. Why the said agents left the booking of the strippers to the drag queens is beyond me. Agents should book the entire show – that's why they are an agent after all! There is also this assumption that drag queens are the centre of professionalism, whereas strippers are a modicum of unpredictability. By and large I would agree with the accusation levelled at the strippers, but in my experience drag queens fall into exactly the same category. Too many of them fall ill at the right time, have their cars explode on them at a convenient moment or have their fourth mother die on the night of the show. Their excuses for not turning up are as dire and as prevalent as those of the strippers.

Furthermore, given that the drag queens are often handed the reins when it comes to recruiting the strippers, many of them have also turned into miniature Don Kings. They will recruit the cheapest strippers they can find because then they pocket the rest! Win-win is not a concept many of them believe in.

Strangely, the drag queens have little difficulty in recruiting cheap strippers in this way. The majority of the strippers are straight. Hen night audiences tend to scream loudest and often give the biggest ego boost. Thus, you will find many of the leading strippers willing to take bargain basement money just to appear on a hen show. The drag is often paid double or even treble what the stripper is paid, yet still beats the stripper down that extra tenner so he can keep it for himself. Some drags are notorious for booking strippers that will allow themselves to be 'given a hand' prior to tying off. Those that allow this are asked first. The whole stripper-drag thing is an unholy alliance, far from harmonious, steeped in tradition and ultimately unnecessary. Drag comperes are not essential for hen shows but they are traditional. Britain is nothing if not a traditional country.

As a result the whole hen night thing was a bit more difficult to crack and even today I wouldn't pretend I have it sussed. Back then the offers were few and far between. Sissy Bells offered me a few shows but over 50% of what he offered fell out of bed before it happened. The cynic in me suspects that he found a stripper to perform at a cheaper rate and therefore cancelled me by telling me that the venue burnt down (or some other lame excuse).

One show I turned up at looked like a complete disaster. The drag queen was calling the audience names and stormed out of the venue. When it came to my turn to perform, the DJ played the wrong music and then accused me of messing it up because I didn't come out! With what had happened earlier in the evening with the drag queen, I think they were looking for a fight with everybody and anybody. I don't know exactly what had happened, but as far as I could gather the drag got heckled and didn't take it too well. If heckling is a problem to a performer, he or she really ought to look at something a little quieter – maybe a librarian's role might suit him better.

At the end of the evening they gave me only half the agreed fee citing the whole show as going wrong from start to finish. Short of taking the till, there was little I could do. The girls seemed happy enough. I could hardly forget the one that told me she had just split up with her boyfriend and asked me to sleep with her so she could get back at him! I figured I would sort it out later as they just seemed upset at the drag queen swearing at them and storming off.

However, discussions with Sissy Bells on the matter the next day didn't prove very fruitful. He clearly had no contractual arrangement with them at all and was a middleman for another cowboy agent. Everybody had skimmed their bit off the top and the performers went out for rock bottom. I said I would just have to sue the club for the excess unless he could provide the precise details of the booker.

"If you do that I'll never book you again," came the reply.

I weighed up the options. Bells was hardly booking me much

anyway so that didn't make any difference to me. Now I had said it, whether I did sue or didn't sue, he wasn't going to be in contact again anyway. We were only talking about £40, but more important to me was the principle of the matter. I typically push principle a long way, but on this occasion I let it slide. I was scheduled to go to Dubai in a matter of weeks and could hardly justify returning to England for a court case over £40. Reluctantly I let the matter drop.

My final hen show before departure was a more pleasant affair. I had responded to a posting on a website called the muppetboard from a drag queen called Lady Jayne Van Campen who was looking for a couple of southern based strippers. He accepted my offer of work and we met one night in Corby.

At that point, my experience of both strippers and drag queens was highly negative. This was the first occasion where negativity became at least neutral. Lady Jayne was professional, likeable and a good performer. The girls loved him and his Northern accent completely belied his Dutch heritage. His partner was also totally delightful and a pleasure to be around.

The other stripper was a fellow called Heartburn. At first he came across as a little 'Tim Nice but Dim'. He seemed totally in awe of the discovery that we both had the same underwear. He clearly had a history of steroid use, possessing the size but also that watery, flabby look that also often presents itself with usage of testosterone-based steroids. However, Heartburn was the first stripper I had met that had the potential to be likeable. The ego was in check.

I performed first, often a disadvantage on hen nights. Commonly the girls are a little unsure at first and the first stripper often releases their inhibitions and 'warms them up' a little. By the time the second stripper arrives, they are typically more rowdy and raucous. The decibels have risen in direct correlation to the amount of alcohol consumed. The second stripper is therefore typically better received. By way of contrast, the second stripper may also receive more abuse as a result of the afore mentioned alcohol.

Perhaps it was a measure of my progress, but for the first time on a hen show, I felt I actually went down better than the other guy. I was standing at the back watching Heartburn perform his act whilst two or three girls were constantly vying for my attention, paying little attention to Heartburn. Towards the end of his act, one of them even threw in the comment, "You've got a bigger dick than him."

There are some big boys that play the circuit and some average ones too. Heartburn was one of the latter.

A good night was had by all. I had not performed on many hen shows, but my final one before flying away had left me with a warm glow.

My final show before departure was where it had all started back at Bromptons. I was on stage at 10 pm and due to start work the following morning at 9 am Natasha had come to watch my final performance. It struck me as ironic, but also reflective, that Zoe had never seen me perform. She had never shown the interest or inclination to view my new form of earning a living.

It was quite an emotive occasion for me. I actually debuted a new act, where I started out in a white naval officer's uniform. It was a remnant from the lap dancing club. Halfway through the act I peeled off all the naval clothes to reveal a boxer underneath where I picked up from the old act. Although it may have seemed a waste of time, I wanted to do it for a couple of reasons. Firstly, I wanted to prove to myself that I could add to my stripping repertoire. That is to say, that I wasn't just a one-trick pony. Also, the good folk of Bromptons had seen my boxer routine a few times now and I wanted to offer them something different.

The change certainly seemed to pleasantly surprise a few regulars. I went out with a bit of a bang and a bit of cheek. I kept winking at Natasha and people picked up on it. An unwritten golden rule in a gay venue is that you never bring a girl on stage, unless specifically requested to. Neither do you play to the girls that much either. They are paying customers too, but the gay clientele has a tendency to complain if the stripper even so much as looks at a girl in the audience. My playfulness that night was tongue in cheek and everybody knew it was my last show. I'm glad to say everybody took it in the spirit it was intended. All the regulars muscled in on Natasha and interrogated her, asking if she was my girlfriend. There was a strange air about them that night. I don't know whether it was my complete nonchalance and apparent disregard for the gays, or whether the presence of a woman to whom I had an affiliation intimidated them somewhat. Certainly, her presence had an effect on them and some of the dirty old men types, including Bonny, my stalker, had been consigned to the shadows.

We left the club together and as I got outside the realisation that it was over hit me. In about ten hours' time I was about to return to the life of a drone. The last few weeks had been great, in fact the previous six months had been great. It had become climatic in the last few weeks. Just like sex, I was about to experience that post orgasmic come-down.

I spent the next few hours with Natasha and her friends. We went for something to eat and I remember her showing me what she had written about the night in her diary – how she had loved the attention I had lavished on her in the club. Of all the people in the room I could have selected, it was her that the most important man in the room at that moment, the man who all eyes were fixed upon, chose to single her out as being special. It made her feel good, wanted and important. It was nice of her to let me know that I had made her feel like that. It added to my warm glow about stripping. I got home late and finally nodded off to sleep at about 4 am, only for my alarm to sound three hours later. My torture had started.

www.malestripper.org

Training in my spit and sawdust gymnasium. The image attached to the cracked gym mirror is of Marvelous Marvin Hagler. He inspired my first stripping name and as you can see by the pictures below my first stripping persona was a boxer.

Front squats produce a seX-ecute sign with the arms. This time Bernard 'The Execution-er' Hopkins adorns the gym mirror. He largely inspired the name Sexecute and as you can see from the pictures below I stole his mask and even some of his moves !

Other stripper guises. As Clark Kent I was able to recycle my corporate uniforms

Yet more stripper guises.

Only the very best athletes can earn a living from sprinting and I wasn't good enough. Here I am with a few mates warm weather training in Spain. Professional athlete would have been my dream job. Professional athleticism as a stripper is a good substitute.

Giving the seXecute sign on the summit of Africa (Kilimanjaro)

Sometimes I love to get away fom it all. It took over a week to walk there, but here I am on top of the Thorung La in Nepal just shy of 18,000 feet.

 I saw someone do this on TV once. Any explosive athlete should be able to do it reasonably comfortably.

'Just a thought.......'

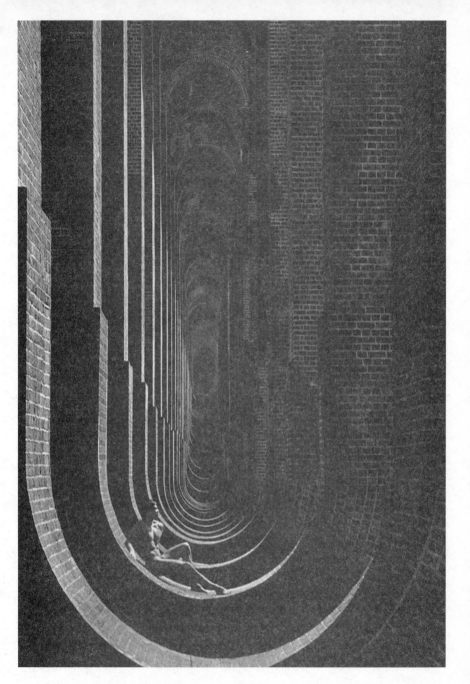

My favourite photo of Sexecute. Although, I barely feature, the naked male adds something to the amazing setting.

Chapter 9

Reflection in an Arabian Prison

I hurriedly ate breakfast, pulled on my uniform (a suit) and frogmarched myself to the station. Upon arrival at my station I reported to my new owners. I knew it was going to be bad, but even I hadn't anticipated how bad. My owners hadn't quite delivered on what they said they would. The arrangement meant that I should be in Dubai within a month, but preparations had not been made.

The owners were quite strict about etiquette. On the first day it was mentioned that we drones were not allowed to answer mobile phones whilst in the premises of the owner. I could see this was going to be difficult. It was as clear as day that I wouldn't last long in this set-up. I had to get to Dubai, away from the owners, before I murdered some of the upper hierarchy of the owners.

At the end of that first day, I went home and immediately phoned Chris (my ex boss from Passive).

"I've just had the worst day of my life," I said in utter exasperation as he picked up the phone.

"Why, what's happened?" came back the worried reply.

"I returned to work," I sobbed.

He began laughing, but I couldn't. I simply could not see the funny side of it and although his advice of "think of the money" was correct, it appeared much easier said than done.

I set myself the goal of clearing a mortgage and even wrote down in my diary each day how I was approximately £225 closer (accounting for non-working days and all living expenses) every day.

The new owners were very hard work. They had not kept their part of the bargain and I anticipated problems ahead. I was meant to have complete autonomy with regard to the operation, yet when I asked questions about my budget and the facility to hire staff, it was as if I spoke Arabic. The director who had objected to my hiring was determined to make things difficult for me. He wanted to keep me in London for a few months before going to Dubai. I objected to this on a couple of grounds. Firstly, it would ruin my tax-free status and secondly, I knew I would never manage to survive that long in the London office without killing somebody. Something had to be done.

My solution as usual was that of a maverick. I let it be known to one of the girls in the office that I used to be a male stripper. Although I told her not to tell anyone, I knew full well she would tell everybody. I even gave her the website address. Telling her this actually filled me with a sense of pride. If the truth be known I was proud of the fact that I used to be a stripper. Only a select few can say that they have done it for any length of time and for that brief period I felt like a professional athlete. It was time that vindicated me for all those hours I had put in honing my body over the years. What I was doing now was something that just paid the bills. I chose to be a stripper. Needs demanded that I was now back in recruitment.

Sure enough, the leaking of information had the desired effect. I was soon called into the office by the person who had recommended me for the role. As was his manner he stuttered and stammered his way through things, blabbering something about his favourite football team before bringing up the disturbing rumours he had heard about my past life as a stripper. Staring him straight in the eyes I asked, "What's the problem?"

"I don't have a problem, Nick, but others do. The CEO of the parent group now knows about this and he's wondering if it is a good idea to have somebody who used to work as a stripper heading the operation in Dubai."

"What I did in the past has no bearing on the job I have now been hired for. I don't see what all the fuss is about."

"Nick, I'm only trying to help, I suggest you pull the website."

In fairness to him, I think he was trying to help... himself. He had recommended me for the role and probably saw me as a potential embarrassment to himself. I did take the website down but only after the director who had the grudge against me had made the cardinal error of putting the stripping issue in writing. He sent me an e-mail stating that we had to be clear about my 'out of work' activities otherwise they would not be sending me to Dubai. I promptly paid him a visit showing my distaste for his written statement. If they did not want to send me to Dubai they were free to pay up the contract that had been agreed (one year's money). Otherwise, I suggested they hurry up and arrange my transfer to Dubai as was agreed when I was hired. Short of these two alternatives we were going to end up in an industrial dispute.

I had made my position pretty clear and with his statement now in writing I felt I had a clear case based on discrimination if they failed to follow through on their promised agreement. I was able to call their bluff.

My tactic worked and it was agreed that I would be dispatched to Dubai within a few weeks. I knew that I wouldn't survive very long in their offices with their regimentation, so I made up my excuses that I would need to prepare properly to relocate. They were paying me a daily pro rata rate whilst I was based in the UK, but I forfeited the money for a few weeks in a bid to successfully escape to Dubai where hopefully I would be left to run things the way I wanted. They had, after all, hired me because of my previous track record in setting up and winning new business from scratch.

I spent the last few weeks before departure in a very dangerous limbo state. My relationship with Zoe was hanging by a thread. She was begging me to give it another go, but I was hurting from so much needless head banging that I was reticent to give it a try. I thought she just didn't care for me anymore. In turn my reticence really hurt her, in a way that she had never been hurt before. In fact it was a pain from which she never truly recovered.

157

My transition back into a corporate life was far from smooth. To say I hated my new job was far too mild a statement. I loathed it and everything it stood for. I was now working in central London and would regularly meet Natasha for lunch, who was just up the road in Whitehall. I must have really brought her down with my depressive state

There wasn't a single maverick at the London office so I constantly met friends for lunch who could offer some sympathy to my plight. I once met a photographer friend of mine after work and remember arguing with him. I got quite angry and frustrated with him because he couldn't understand my situation. He said that in the few weeks since I had stopped stripping I had "changed" and that I wasn't the same person. He reasoned that I shouldn't go to Dubai because the job was making me unhappy.

"But, can't you see, Mark? I have to go through this pain now because in a year's time things will be much better and I won't have to worry about money too much?"

He simply couldn't see my point. Mark isn't materialistic and has never worried about money. He lives day to day, but his Highbury abode is heavily subsidised by the council. I had no such luck and try as I might, I just got frustrated in trying to make him see my position. I guess it's a lot easier when the state pays the majority of your bills.

I flew out to Dubai to start a new life, not knowing if and when I would return to the UK. It didn't take too long to establish that Dubai was not my new long-term home. I was feeling disillusioned about the UK, but Dubai was not the solution. My best friend out there was a Greek guy called Dimitri. He was a professor at the local American university. He summed it up perfectly when he said shortly after I met him that he considered anyone who actually liked Dubai to be "weird".

The Dubai authorities operate a propaganda campaign of which Joseph Goebbles would have been proud. If I had a pound for every person that had told me that Dubai is great (even when they have never been) I'd be a rich man. Even when I tell them that I lived there for nearly a year and that they have been misinformed they insist I am wrong.

Contrary to what may be believe over here, Dubai is not a middle eastern city with progressive western values. It is very much an Arabic, Islamic state. It might not be quite as culturally repressed as Saudi Arabia, but it hardly has the liberal values of London or New York. Decency police still wander the streets assessing whether people are wearing clothing that is too short. It is illegal to be gay, pornography is banned, magazines such as FHM have blacked-out images throughout their pages, the films at the cinema are censored, as is the internet! You have to register with the state for internet access via their server, so the state actually censors what you can see online.

The first thing I tried to do when I arrived was to join a sports club. I tried the track team, a couple of football teams, the national boxing team and a power lifting competition. In all cases I was rejected because "they were only for Arab men".

Dubai openly has a system that I liken to apartheid. People are categorised according to their nationality, colour and creed. They are then paid accordingly. Emiratis head the system, followed by Americans, followed by Brits. Then came the rest of Europe, followed by Australasians and South Africans. The 'lesser Arabs' (such as Palestinians and Egyptians) were actually quite low down the pecking order but then followed the true 'slaves' of the economy. Those from the Indian sub-continent and the Philippines were treated appallingly. These guys used to work 13 days out of 14, for 12 hours+ every day. A bus would pick them up from their 'township' every morning and deliver them to their place of work. For their slavery they were usually awarded about $100 per month.

Dubai was a terribly superficial, contradictory place. I was effectively ostracised and prevented from penetrating the foreign communities. Everybody stuck to their own and I didn't want to mix with the British. Dubai seemed to have attracted the worst of the worst of the ex-patriots. The average British ex-pat was about 20 years older than me. He seemed to have embraced the culture with no qualms and often referred to the 'slaves' as "jinglies" or "coolies". I thought these terms had disappeared about 60 years ago with the British empire! Ex-pat man thought it was great that he could have a live-in slave for next to nothing. In answer to my objections that Dubai offered no women to a young, red-blooded male, they suggested I visit the whore houses (yes Dubai has several of these, but obviously the authorities deny it).

Dimitri was on a two-year contract at the university and he said he nearly went insane in the first year. For the second year he had arranged for his fiancé to come and live with him. He warned me I was going to have a tough year ahead and he was right.

Incidentally, Dimitri was a professor of marketing during his stay in Dubai. He later confided in me that he actually knew nothing about the subject at the time he applied for the job and simply read a couple of books on the subject. He is a very smart guy, blagged the interview and landed the position. He concurred with me that it was a mickey-mouse subject that didn't belong in a university.

Living in Dubai might not have been so torturous had it not been for the fact that I was working for a company that didn't seem to know its arse from its elbow. I thought once I landed in Dubai I would be allowed to get on with it, but I was very wrong. I had made one cursory visit, a week in length, prior to my permanent move. During that week I wrote a report recommending that they change their planned office location. The director who had it in for me stole the credit on the recommendation, but when I arrived nothing had been put in motion. I had told them that I would sleep in the office for the first few days until I found a place to live. Except there was no office! I ended up spending the first two weeks on somebody's floor that I met in the gym.

During those couple of weeks I was unable to do anything. I had no phone, no office, nothing. Still, I was being paid to do nothing and it led to a lot of introspection on my part. I had never felt so alone and so in need of Zoe.

The ensuing months were torturous. I was working for complete amateurs, nay idiots. My location was about as welcoming as a concentration camp. Even the weather was terrible. About seven to eight months of the year in Dubai the weather is oppressive. With 50-degree heat and humidity off the scale people go from their air-conditioned buildings into their air-conditioned cars back into an air-conditioned building. Nobody dares venture outside. The remainder of the year is pleasant.

I quickly figured out that I just needed to do the bare minimum and keep my mouth shut as much as I could. That is, take the money. I would work one month and post some good results and then take the next month off (I would blame it on Ramadan or some other Islamic festival). My employer had lied to me on numerous levels so I hardly felt bad lying back to them. Also, they never listened to a word I said to them. They clearly thought I was living in a third world country (Dubai is actually technologically ahead of the UK), as they once sent by courier from the UK – wait for it – photocopying paper. It was as if I couldn't have bought it from the shop in the building I worked.

The idiots also never gave me the budget I asked for on day one, so I never hired the team that was required for growth. It didn't help my state of mind that I arrived in an empty office in the morning and went home to an empty flat at night. I told them after only a few months that I wouldn't be staying with them for any length of time. They had conducted no research into what was required in a candidate for the position. Instead they made some lofty crystal towers assumptions from their base in the UK. They were particularly keen that they hired an unmarried man. Yet, Dubai was a sexual desert. The position would have suited a married man, who could bring his wife with him and therefore help him settle (sorry if this sounds politically incorrect but they would have been foolish to hire a woman for the role – they are virtually second class citizens in Dubai and would never receive the sufficient credence from the locals).

I spelt out to them in plain English why I thought they were idiots and how bad I thought they were. To my amazement, this caused them to offer me a contract extension rather than a rebuttal. Having spelt it out again for them I agreed to stay only for the initial term that I had agreed, whilst they find my replacement. In essence they didn't replace me, they just bussed out a few people from their London office on a lot less money. They also never listened to my recommendation that they hire an Arabic speaker.

All the time I was in this role I missed stripping terribly. It was as if a part of me had been taken away and I was operating with only one arm and one leg. If ever I needed confirmation that I didn't really fit in as a suit then my Dubai experience was it. I was also conscious that I wasn't getting any younger and stripping should be a young man's game. The more I flitted away my life as a rat playing corporate games the less time I would have to live the life of a professional athlete – the life I had always desired. I could always return to being a rat when I was older if I needed to. However, I could hardly start stripping when I was old, grey and fat. I couldn't resist telling virtually everybody I got to know in Dubai that recruitment was just a time filler for me.

"I will probably return to my former profession soon," I used to say.

This in turn led them to ask what I used to do and when I told them it was always a great topic of conversation. Think of it another way:

"What do you do for a living?"

"I'm in recruitment."

This is followed by a long silence generally followed by snoring.

"What do you do for a living?"

"I'm a male stripper."

We could follow this up with a further dozen pages of discussion.

I was actually offered two jobs as a stripper whilst I was in Dubai. They both came through a Philipino friend of mine, Leon (whose floor I slept on when I arrived). Leon worked in the hotel game and knew a lot of people. He was also gay (and therefore underground in Dubai) and proud of his association with a stripper. A couple of clients of his had enquired after my services, but in both instances they had got scared of the authorities finding out and possible repercussions.

My sanity was only held together in Dubai by my training in the gym with Dimitri, my frequent visits by friends from the UK and the thought of escape at the end of my term. Zoe also came out for two months (she quit her job). She looked at working in a Dubai hospital, but being a woman (and thereby a second-class citizen) the pay didn't justify it. My employer also specialised in recruitment for the health sector. Despite my requests, they offered me no help whatsoever at placing my girlfriend in a job in Dubai. I'd swear they didn't want me to settle there.

I resigned from the idiot company slightly prematurely, but only slightly. It would have been nice to take the money for another six months or so, but I couldn't bear them any longer. The director who had long had it in for me said something out of turn one day, so I told them to stuff it where the sun didn't shine and served them notice. I had earned enough to fulfil the objective. I sold the Ford Mustang I'd acquired on arrival and readied myself to leave.

When I boarded the plane to leave Dubai it was a fantastic feeling. I can only liken it to how a prisoner must feel on being released. Upon my return to Britain, my dad met me at the airport with the Impreza (I'd given it to him as a gift but he felt unable to accept it). I drove back to Wales but soon set off for London to visit friends. I needed about two weeks of friend visiting and unloading my Dubai torment onto sympathetic ears before I felt fully purged. Several of my visitations were to people I had met through stripping. All the while that I had been in exile I had been planning my comeback and now that I was back in the heartland I could smell and taste it! Yet before I could do anything concrete, I had to disappear again to satisfy the tax people.

Zoe and I embarked on a truly fantastic four months. I can say without any exaggeration that it was four of the best months of my life. We started off by hiring a 4x4 in New Zealand and driving nearly 5000 miles in the six weeks we were there, exploring most of what it had to offer (a lot). Two weeks were then spent in Bali followed by two weeks in the jungles of Sumatra looking for Orang-Pendek (the alleged Western Sumatran apeman). This really did turn into an adventure, one we nearly didn't come back from. Our guide managed to get us lost for four days without food in the world's second biggest jungle (only the Amazon is larger). I've never been more scared in my life but that story is for another time. It could fill an entire book in itself! Needless to say, when you have been lost in the jungle for two days without food and the guide bursts into tears stating that he doesn't believe he will ever see his wife and daughter again – you know you are in trouble. Anyway, we escaped in the end courtesy of some jungle natives who had never seen white people before. Finally, the highlight for me was the six weeks in Nepal, trekking in the Himalayas, reaching a pinnacle on the Thorung La at 17,820 ft.

Nearly 18 months had passed since I had retired from the stage. In essence, that first six months had been a learning curve, a toe dipped in some murky naked waters. What I was now planning went beyond a comeback – I envisaged a career.

Zoe and I had reached an uneasy truce. We were both still hurting in a strange sort of way and we were both transformed somewhat from our experiences. But we had a plan and a goal and in that we were very much united.

When we returned from Nepal, Zoe found work within a week as a locum. In the meantime I would dedicate myself full time to finding a place to live. Our new home was to be purely functional. It had to be within easy commuting distance of London (for Zoe, who envisaged herself working in a London hospital) and near all the motorways (for stripping).

I looked at several areas to the west and north of London, eventually settling on Hemel Hempstead. Finally, I found a two bedroom flat. It cost less to buy than I had money in the bank and satisfied all the requirements. It was within walking distance of the station, was within a few miles of the motorway, had off-road parking, space for me to build a gym and a loft that had been partially converted (no junk allowed in the main rooms).

The bid was accepted and due to my belief that all lawyers are evil I decided to conduct my own conveyancing. This led to some snooty letters from the lawyer representing the other side (as per usual they seem unable to talk unless it is down their nose at you). I cut the lawyer out and went straight to the seller telling him that unless his lawyer started acting professionally and courteously I would pull out of the deal and buy somewhere else. It seemed to do the trick.

Conveyancing needn't be a difficult process. Done properly it should only take a few weeks at most, but most people don't feel confident enough to do it alone, so they hire a lawyer. This causes inevitable delays. Lawyers string out every process in an attempt to justify their ridiculous fees. If people could actually see what they pay these goons for, they would never make the same mistake again.

Anyway, I had to sit and wait whilst the other side pontificated. This meant lots of preparation time for my new career...

Chapter 10

Total Rebuild

First things first – I had to get back in shape. My last couple of months in Dubai had been devoid of training. There was no reason to train. I wasn't allowed to compete because I wasn't an Arab and both Dimitri and I grew slack towards the end. I then had nearly three months in the UK where I spent the time visiting friends (no training and then four months' travelling (no training). In all I had gone nine months without doing anything, the longest break I had had from training for about ten years.

When I had moved to Dubai, my old track mate James had taken in my gym equipment. His dad was worth a few quid and had an outhouse in which it could live. So when I arrived back I based myself partly at Zoe's (who had a room at the hospital where she was locuming) and James' where I could train.

The first training session was quite a shock. I could never imagine that I would lose so much strength. I had managed to get a couple of gym sessions in before I left Kathmandu. The signs were worrying, but I blamed the poor equipment (wishful thinking). I also flattered to deceive, because the Nepalese are small people and they all thought I was still strong!

My best bench press ever is 140kg weighing 70kg (touch and go, no pause). When I tried a max bench I was horrified to note that it was down to 95kg and my weight was about 67kg. I was struggling to deadlift 160kg (my best is up at 210kg) and a full squat felt heavy at 120kg (best of 186kg). My abs had disappeared and compared to old photos I was a sorry state. My chest measurement was down and my waist measurement up! James obviously found all of this most amusing.

Cue the *Rocky* music and the pictures of enemy strippers attached to the mirror in the gym. The first few sessions back are always the hardest. You have to start very light otherwise your muscles will be stiff for up to a week afterwards, preventing you from training again effectively anytime soon. However, my body began to respond very quickly to the training. I incorporated some sprint training into the regime to get that toned look back into my body and within a couple of months the poundages were again at a level that was acceptable to me.

In the meantime, I had begun the other preparations. Whilst in Dubai, Zoe had taken a set of photos which I sold to a magazine (nude photos in Dubai – if only the authorities knew!) I used one of these, blew up the print and had 1000 run off as my new publicity photo.

I had parted with my Impreza and bought an old diesel workhorse for the many miles ahead. I christened it 'the chug'.

My old name of 'Marvelous' simply had not worked. Nobody got the connection with the boxer and indeed, people kept telling me I had spelt it wrong. I got fed up with telling people that it was the American spelling after a world famous boxer. Unbeknownst to me at the time and to quote a now dear gay friend, "gays don't do sport". The same can be said of women. In truth, 'Marvelous' was my fantasy. I wanted to be a boxer and there I was, sort of, being one with the name and the gown to boot. However, in terms of stripping practicality, it could have been better. It could have been worse, some of the names doing the circuit have clearly been plucked out of a hat, but at best it was a C+.

I had decided my new name over a year ago in Dubai. Whilst stuck in my desert prison, my thoughts were never far away from the life I had left behind. I had decided on the new name of 'Sexecute' (pronounced Sexy-cute). The choice behind the name was threefold. Firstly, I thought the name was an apt description. My athletic physique would hopefully depict the sexy part and my baby face the cute part. Secondly, I had been planning my comeback act to be that of a medieval style executioner. Sexecute was therefore a play on the word execute. Thirdly, in keeping with tradition and most importantly in my book, I was naming myself after another boxing hero. Bernard 'The Executioner' Hopkins was another great blue collar middleweight champion and a worthy successor to Marvelous Marvin Hagler. Thus, Sexecute was a derivative of The Executioner. Also, Sexecute was a much more appropriate stripping name than Marvelous. Anyone could believe and identify with a stripper called Sexecute. Only I would call a stripper Marvelous. In death, Marvelous gave birth to Sexecute.

In Dubai, I purchased a real Arthurian type sword in one of the souks (Arabian markets). It was unsharpened, but even so I had to dull its edges a little more to make it safe. This was to be my executioner's weapon.

I visited Michael who is an artistic genius. I described to him my vision of the new outfit and he drew it before my very eyes in a matter of minutes. He also sent me to see a friend of his who he said would be able to make it for me. This turned into another wild goose chase. His friend was the strangest chap imaginable. I just so happened to turn up with a black, butch, athlete friend of mine and this seemed to frighten him to death. I think he thought I would turn up on my own and then he would be able to measure me up for a g-string. Because that wasn't the case he threw a camp hissy fit and refused to help. It was probably just as well, because Lynn, who I initially found through the local wedding dress shop, did a fantastic job and very reasonably priced too!

Michael also sent me to meet a stripper called Arson that had enjoyed some success whilst I had been away in Dubai. Arson was in touch with Michael regularly updating him on his alleged successes. He had supposedly spent £3000(!) on his first costume, but had apparently recovered the money in a matter of weeks because it produced so many bookings. Thus it was that I began to get my first whiff of bullshit. Nonetheless, I called the man called Arson to seek his advice and contacts. Michael was less than complimentary about Arson's appearance but stated that he was reasonably popular. Either Arson had stumbled on some magic formula, or perhaps he was exaggerating his claims of his own stripping prowess.

Arson agreed to meet, albeit with hesitance, so I made my way to a pokey flat near Peckham. Arson opened the door and I immediately understood what Michael had meant. Someone (a punter) was later to describe Arson as having a "face like a bag of spanners". Another stripper perhaps summed it up better by describing him as "old rubber face – he reminds me of Deputy Dawg with such pliable jowels". I wouldn't like to compare myself with Brad Pitt, but Arson had definitely been hit a few more times with the ugly stick than most. Physically, he was hardly imposing. I am certainly not large, but Arson was smaller than I. He had worked hard on his physique, but it looked like he needed to work harder. Apparently, his saving grace was his large cock.

Perhaps, I thought, Arson woos the audience and bookers with his overwhelming charm and smooth talk, rather than his stunning good looks. I was soon to be disabused of that notion. At the time, I was yet to meet a stripper I liked and I was clearly going to have to wait a bit longer. Arson was loud, obnoxious and full of shit. Nothing new there then. He was also insecure, paranoid and had a voracious ego. In addition to all the normal stripper ailments he also liked to name drop a list of famous people he supposedly had as friends.

Initially, he clearly perceived me as threatening and probably thought I was planting listening devices around his flat. But, as Michael had recommended me, he said he would be prepared to hand over a few of his illustrious contacts (I'm still waiting to this day). I made my excuses and left. Arson clearly wasn't going to be much help to me and I categorised and filed him with the rest of the strippers I had met so far. I was going to have to do this all alone.

With regards to the music, this time I didn't mess about trying to get favours off other strippers. I just went straight to a music producer (a blue collar one, of course) who cut the music for me, blended each track into the next, added sound effects and even put a voice over onto the introduction for me.

I worked out my act, acquired myself a skull for a dark grand entrance and was ready for the re-launch. In truth, my executioner act was really aimed at the gay scene. Although it may sound silly, I didn't really realise it at the time. I had learnt a lot in my first incarnation but I was and still am learning, albeit at a diminished rate. In my first six months I hadn't done an awful lot of shows and the majority of those I had done had been on the gay scene. This perhaps explains why I designed the executioner act in the way I did and why I thought it would work.

I began to phone around in exactly the way I had before. I started with the gay venues and then tried the drag queens. The results were similar to before, but seemed slightly more positive. The gay venues were willing to book me; one even turned around and said they would have me within a few days. This caught me a little unawares, but I accepted. The drag queens prompted little or no response. I also re-contacted some of the agents I had used previously. One of them, Andy at Xanadu, had been far and away the most professional I had dealt with previously. So he proved to be again and he came up with a booking for me immediately that weekend. I had anticipated getting bookings within a few weeks, but now I had them within a couple of days and had to get 'in the zone' earlier than I expected to.

*

I performed my first strip on the comeback as an executioner at a house party for a gang of female teachers. The show went fine, although they perhaps found my entrance a little strange. It was only after the event that I found out that they were a group of secondary school teachers. The chemistry teacher was soon to be married, but it was the French teacher who enquired as to whether all girls behave in the way that their group had. It was with a wry smile that I tried to imagine the teachers from my school days behaving in the same fashion. Try as I might, the image proved very difficult to conjure. The show had reached its climax with the chemistry teacher wanking my cock to raucous encouragement from all the other educators.

In all honesty, the executioner act did not really work that great for the girls. The teachers were fine, they took it for what it was – a man taking his clothes off in a different way. However, as I was to discover pretty quickly, certain female audiences were not quite as understanding. They found the whole masked entrance with a huge sword (designed to be a phallic symbol) intimidating and as stupid as it may sound, some were actually frightened by it! Only on a couple of occasions did girls approach me and say they found the whole entrance incredibly sexy. Both of those girls had a certain gothic look about them and they were both in gay clubs at the time!

I performed a large hen night with Arson and a stripper called Lucifer's Offspring only a few weeks later. After the show I had quite a few girls come up to me saying that I was the best looking of the three, but they preferred Lucifer's Offspring's act. As for Arson, no comments were offered. I performed the act only a couple more times for girls, with some modifications, only for the same thing to happen. I quickly discontinued it from the ladies night scene.

On the night in question Arson spent the entire evening parading around like he was a demi-god of strip, boosting his own ego to all and sundry whilst reducing his own insecurity. This was the first time I had seen Lucifer's Offspring since our encounter in Bromptons before I left for Dubai. He had transformed into a completely different person. Whereas before there had been a real person and a stage character, there was now only his stage character left. He had taken a leaf straight out of the Arson manual (they were good mates at the time). He arrived in a blaze of arrogance, proclaiming his own greatness as he went. He seemed to look down his nose at all around him and spoke with a contempt for everything bar himself and his routine. He arrived in an old BMW chariot with the personalised number plate 'Kit Off'. When the relationship between Arson and Lucifer's Offspring cooled, the devil child lost some of his prickly heat and we got along much better. Anyway, on that particular night, no allies were going to be made, so I exited promptly at the end of proceedings.

By contrast to the ladies' night circuit, the executioner act seemed to go down a storm on the gay scene. My first strip back at a gay club immediately followed the teachers and was received very well. I was approached by a man in the audience that night who introduced himself as Diamond White (a drag queen). His name had been on the original list provided by Michael and I had called him several times previously and left messages. He had never returned any of my calls. I talked to him for a good while that night, or rather I attempted to talk to him whilst he talked at me. He was full of bluster, bold claims and mighty statements. He critiqued many drag queens, professed his greatness and told me he was about to have his own chat show on a mainstream television network (to my knowledge it has never appeared). He became very cagey when I pressed him over details and enquired as to how he secured the alleged deal. I was to come into contact with Diamond White again on a couple of occasions. I'm afraid he was yet another example of a delusional, bitter and twisted drag queen. It transpired that whilst he was telling all and sundry that he earned a six-figure income from dressing as a woman at night times, he lived off the state during the day. I don't know what is worse – his hypocrisy or the fact that he gets away with it.

Incidentally, whilst I was talking to Diamond White the drag queen performing on stage was trying to get volunteers to perform in the amateur strip after I had been on. He wasn't getting any takers and came out with the line "come on – nobody is going to be as bad as Arson".

Everywhere I performed the executioner on the gay scene it seemed to go down very well. On more than one occasion after performing it, I was approached by men who said "that's the most interesting/innovative/original show I've seen since Uniboy".

Uniboy was clearly a new stripper who had appeared during my stay abroad. Everywhere I went on the gay scene, I kept hearing about how great he was and I kept getting compared to him. Finally we met one night at a hen show. Uniboy was tall, over 6 ft, but lacked a traditional stripper's build. In fact he was quite slim, normal even. He was young (early 20s) and handsome. As I was to see later he also possessed a very large stripper's weapon – the one between his legs. Uniboy was openly gay and had a much older boyfriend (now husband). Before you start thinking it, let me say it – NO, he isn't with him for the money, they are very much in love with each other. That night I had my first contact with another stripper that wasn't about bravado, ego, machismo or one-upmanship. Soon Uniboy and his husband invited me around for dinner one night (they can cook, I can't) and my first stripper friendship was born.

Uniboy also has that rare stripper quality – a full brain rather than just a collection of cells. In fact, he was a straight A student at school. He has his issues like most performers, is sometimes more than a little insecure, but has his feet planted where most have floated away into the clouds. His long-held ambition is to make it as an actor and stripping has always been a sort of theatrical performance stepping stone for him.

To this day, apart from Uniboy, I have only made two other friends who are strippers. I was booked on a hen show one night in Birmingham with a guy called Stimulation X. He too lacked all of the unpleasant stripper qualities. We had a good laugh that night about the over-the-top antics of all of the other strippers we had worked with along the way.

Again, Stimulation X doesn't fit the stereotype. In fact he is now a granddad! He is in his mid-40s, trains hard in the gym and fully enjoys the stripping lifestyle. He once lamented to me about how he used to work in a factory for 40 hours every week, for not a lot of money. He now accurately points out that he can earn the same for a lot less hours and a whole load more fun. Stimulation X has very thick skin and cares little for what other people say about him. That is, he lacks the insecurity of a typical stripper. In fact, he even appeared on *The Trisha Show* with his niece. They were paid to act out a scene whereby his niece had a go at him for being too old to be a stripper (for those who haven't yet realised – yes many of those shows are fake).

Petrol is another one. He's actually the same age as me, but has been stripping for 17 years (since he was 17). He started when the business was at its height and has watched the steady decline from within. Petrol is a real non-conformist and has a tendency to ignite occasionally. He doesn't suffer fools, has no ego problems and is well grounded.

Along the way I have met a couple of other strippers who I have got along with OK, but a friendship hasn't formed; but I wouldn't categorise them with the rest. However, the number is very small. In nearly six years since I started, I have only made three stripper friends.

It wasn't too long before I began to broaden out my array of costumes and acts. Some strippers have only one act, one costume and have performed the same show for over 20 years. At the other extreme, Uniboy (who enjoys dressing up in various outfits) has about a dozen different shows with accompanying outfits. I have taken a middle ground. The executioner, whilst popular on the gay scene, didn't cut it on the hen nights so I needed back-up. I resurrected the boxer from the canvas, giving the act a complete overhaul. Some further tweaks along the way meant that it was getting complimented in a similar way to the executioner, but crucially this time, the act was unisex. I could perform it for either audience.

Clark Kent/Superman was next, originally devised for the hen scene, but it proved to be more popular with the guys! A lot of the subtleties and nuances just seemed to go over the heads of the girls. Whereas the guys got it and had a higher level of appreciation for the comedic 'theatre' I was trying to engender.

Most strippers have one of the three 'girly' routines and I was determined to avoid them like the plague for that very reason. However, I kept getting queries from the website where I would be asked specifically to supply either a policeman, a fireman or *The Officer and a Gentleman* (white naval uniform). It therefore made good economic sense to acquire the outfits. The naval uniform was easily acquired on Camden market, the others proved more difficult. My sister is a police officer, but refused point blank to help me acquire any old uniforms that were being thrown out. Apparently, I could be arrested for impersonating a police officer and rightly so in her view. She pumped up her face considerably when I told her I would just pay someone to 'acquire' the uniform for me. As it was, I was talking to a gay policeman one night after a show and he directed me to a shop in the East End where they sell police issue uniforms under the counter. As for the fireman, I paid another policeman to 'acquire' the uniform for me.

The fireman thing still mystifies me to this day. It has to be the unsexiest outfit anyone could ever wear. Yet the girls go crazy for it. My friend Russell is a real fireman and he can't understand it either. We met one chilly morning at 7 am at Heathrow Airport. Russell also drives a fire engine limousine (Hothire). That is, a fire engine that has been especially converted to carry passengers. Some bloke with more money than sense had hired the fire engine to pick up his girlfriend from Heathrow and I had been hired to pose as one of the fireman drivers. Actually, I was hired as the stripper, and had to surprise her on the right cue. I was serving champagne one minute and then taking my clothes off the next, all in the back of a moving fire engine. The guy that had hired us all found it hilarious and I think he could justify paying all the money given the amount of laughter it produced for him.

Russell still talks about it today as one of the most outrageous things he has ever seen. Every time I see him, he is usually telling somebody else about how we met. About how there was "shock and horror on the firemen's faces as some bloke got naked in the back of the engine and waved his cock around… We dropped him off at the station with nothing on. The commuters queuing in suits looked terrified."

I have worked with Russell again a couple of times since as he regularly picks up hen parties and transports them to their chosen destination. Firemen probably have as many sex tales to tell as a typical stripper! The girls all want to bed a fireman. Both Russell and I don't get it at all! However, having interrogated several girls on this matter, the fantasy would appear to be that the fireman rescues the damsel in distress from the burning building, throws her over his shoulder, kicks his way through the burning beams, bursts through a second storey window (she is still over the shoulder), has a perfect landing onto the concrete, throws down the said damsel and shags her senseless on the grass outside. She then bears his children, he protects her forevermore and supports her on his fireman's wage. At this point Russell was choking most alarmingly on his own innards and nearly crashed the fire engine!

Russell told me that the question he nearly always gets asked is, "Do you still rescue cats from trees?" Obviously, he tells them what they want to hear, but the reality is that in this ridiculously politically correct jobsworth-led society we now live in, health and safety regulations usually prevent them from doing it. Once the owner is quietly led away, they turn the hose on it! He also tells me that girls often perk up in casual conversation when they hear what he does for a living. Another fireman friend was even talking to a girl in a call centre who wanted to meet him when she found out that he was a fireman. They exchanged e-mailed pictures of one another. The one he sent was me in a fireman's outfit! Needless to say, nobody got that girl in the end because he didn't want me posing as him and he didn't look like me! It is a disturbing number of girls that buy into the fireman fantasy. In fact, it borders on delusional.

Chapter 11

Why Do We Do It?

One of the things I am regularly accused of since I became a stripper is of wasting myself and my life. Apparently, I could be so much more. Whilst I reject this out of hand, I simply don't meet the expectations of most people.

There is a stereotype that all male strippers are dumb blondes who take lots of steroids. Because I don't fit this profile, I in some way often astound and disappoint the accuser.

Furthermore, their version of 'being so much more' in reality usually means 'be more like them'. This is the very thing I don't want to be. I still occasionally sit up at night with a sudden jerk, cold sweat pouring from me, awakened as I have from a nightmare where I am back in a regular job wearing a suit. We now live in a big-brother-watching, slave-nation society. Everybody has a number and people are forgetting their names. The toxins of rebellion have been denuded from people by the ever rigidifying conformity imposed on them by society's rulers. Few people dare speak out of turn. The teeth in your mouth have long since become more important than the words that come out of them. Implement, not question, is the order of the day

The whole children-and-mortgage-trap is openly encouraged by our rulers. Get a mortgage and have a child. Buy a car. Have another child, buy a bigger car and a bigger house to accommodate the new arrival. Get a bigger mortgage, increase your debt. This is all underpinned by the rule of 'do as you are told at work'. Most people are only a few mortgage payments away from disaster. How could they possibly rebel? They are trapped on a treadmill that can only get faster and more demanding in the shorter term. It takes a rat to win the rat race and I decided long ago that I wasn't a rat. Why, therefore, would I want to run like one in a wheel?

Perhaps, understandably, when I point this out to my accusers, it is not always best received. I guess the truth often hurts. In essence, my accusers usually envy my position. Occupying the role of male stripper produces more jealousy than you can possibly imagine. If looks could kill, I'd be dead a thousand times. When I am introduced to people in a non-stripping setting and they inevitably ask what I do for a living the response is generally one of two. The first is one of genuine interest and curiosity which leads to a dozen further questions. The second response is one of malice because those people would actually like to be me. The latter group often make the error of assuming that they can talk down to me like I am in fact the dumb steroidal blond stereotype. These people don't like it when they get my sermon about breaking out from being a drone and they can do it too if only they have the will to do so (usually said with smile). The more they attack my position, the more they usually reveal about the sadness and desperation of their own personal situation. Depending on how condescending their initial attack is, depends on how much of this I point out.

My family detest my choice of profession. They are far from alone in being unable to reconcile why I would choose to give up a six-figure salary for a job where I constantly 'humiliate' myself for a fraction of the earnings. This isn't even to mention the shame I have no doubt brought upon the family name.

They too are thinking strictly within the box that society has prescribed them. Many people ask themselves what is the meaning of life? However, most people ask this question far too late. They begin to seriously probe in their 60s after they have wasted away their life, working all the hours in the week for an employer they hate, for just enough remuneration to pay their mortgage, bills and buy enough food to prevent them from starving. This is no life, but because most other people we know are experiencing the same pain, it somehow makes it more bearable.

Some seek solace in religion. The pain then becomes bearable because they believe we will all go to a better place after we die. This in my view is a false reality that enables those people to live out their daily lives (and if it works, good luck to them). Their belief system, or faith, is like an aspirin that takes away the pain of their daily existence. I am convinced that when I die there is nothing. Therefore, the purpose of life is to maximise my happiness. If I don't do this within my finite lifetime, then I have wasted an opportunity.

Economists theorise that happiness can be measured by something called utils. The individual with the most utils gained is the happiest person. I subscribe to this theory. Life isn't quite as simple as a mathematical formula because the utils we seek are not tangible. However, it is very important to pinpoint exactly what gives us utils. Money is definitely a key factor. If I had sufficient money to live out the rest of my life in relative comfort I would never work again. I'd probably be off adventuring in various parts of the world in between keeping the company of people I like.

In the same way that the guy who said "it's the taking part that counts" (not the winning) was a loser, the guy who said "money can't buy happiness" was severely misguided. It may not be able to buy complete and total utility but it does buy an enormous amount of utils. Essentially I am a stripper because the lifestyle brings about a high degree of utility. However, I couldn't afford that lifestyle if it didn't pay at all. I may have been earning a six-figure income at the age of 24, but the penalty associated with that reward was a very util-low lifestyle. My financial reward for stripping is low, but my lifestyle is very util rich. I was fortunate enough to pay off my mortgage before I was 30. This was the by product of a util-low existence. However, the sacrifice was definitely worth it. I now need very little finance to live out a high-util existence.

Money should not necessarily buy material goods. Its key facilitator should be the purchase of TIME (read utility). Most people seem to have failed in their understanding of this basic principle. Too many are working all hours to generate finance to buy bigger and better material goods, which in turn inflate their egos and self-esteem in a pointless competition with their peers. I too have previously been a rat in this pointless race, but thankfully have long since jumped from the train.

Too often I seem to meet millionaires who have acquired vast funds (either from inheritance or hard work) but don't know how to convert this into utility. I never know whether to feel contempt or pity for them. If I had to go and do something I hated just so I could eat I would feel very frustrated and angry. I feel envious at those that don't have to do this because they get a leg-up in life, usually from friends or family. If I no longer had to work to eat/live you wouldn't see me for dust! I would be off gallivanting around the world visiting and exploring lots of places of interest amidst performing a range of other util-high activities. I certainly wouldn't be at home moping around whinging or getting bored. Anybody who has sufficient money to see out the rest of their days and not work – yet is still unsure how to live out a fulfilled existence – needs help of some sort (psychotherapy?)

Stripping is my admittedly temporary answer to this conundrum. Whilst my financial situation may be comfortable and more affable than many, it is hardly complete. I still need an income in order to eat and live. This generally means working for a living and this is therefore a drain on my utility score. I have pondered this long and hard and I have scoured various sources. It appears there are very few 'jobs' out there that I would actually want to do for any length of time without the thought of slitting my wrists coming to the fore on a regular basis. I have worked for myself before and that was just as hard as being employed, so that was no great solution. There are lots of jobs I'm sure that I would enjoy or could do for a short time and then retire. However, these are not readily accessible. Jobs working in investment banking or venture capital are not readily accessible by doing an internet search. Furthermore, if my experience is anything to go by, wearing the correct school tie goes a long way in those sectors.

Jobs that offer utility rather than finance are virtually non-existent. If you are going to be paid badly you don't want stress and how many jobs can offer you that?

My ideal job from as far back as I can remember was to be a professional athlete. I use the word athlete in a broad generic sense here. At first I wanted to be a professional footballer and when that dream evaporated, a professional boxer. With that opportunity denied, I turned to track and field and eventually power lifting. At each turn I was denied for different reasons. My parents moved me away from my home and I never played football again. My mum wouldn't let me box. On the track I lacked the genetics to be the very best. Despite winning a national title in power lifting there was no money to be made.

Thus, when stripping stumbled along and fell into my lap, for the first time I felt like a professional athlete. I now get paid (in part) to train my body and look after my physique. This is what I call professional athleticism. I have considered myself a professional athlete for years. My attitude to sport, the implementation of training and diet and the resultant performance would put many a professional team player to shame. However, diligence doesn't necessarily make a professional athlete. A whole concoction of factors go into the mix to make a professional sportsman. As well as diligence and attitude, an athlete must have genetics and, crucially, opportunity.

I almost certainly had the genetics for certain sports but lacked the opportunity. I had the opportunity in others but lacked the genetics. Stripping finally blurred the boundaries. I was given an opportunity where my genetics were sufficient. I obviously wasn't going to be let down by a lack of professional attitude and diligence. I haven't looked back and can safely say that being a professional stripper actually rates as one of the proudest things I have ever done. All I ever wanted to be was a professional athlete and in a very round-about sort of way, I have made it.

However, I would not be so arrogant or naïve to say that is the only reason why I strip. There are an assortment of reasons. I have already alluded to another of the key ones. Stripping brings in a high degree of utils to my existence. I am my own boss. Nobody tells me what to do. My obligation is to the client and nobody else. If I want to turn a job down I can. The feeling of well-being that comes from such a high degree of freedom is substantial and not to be sneered at.

I actually quite like the road warrior existence. I am a bit of a wandering nomad averaging about 40,000 miles per year in my car. I traverse the country in many ways, not to mention some limited foreign travel. I sometimes find the long night time drives (no traffic) therapeutic. I get to see plenty of different places and I am sometimes able to coincide stripping and pleasure. For example, every time I venture on a tour of northern England I usually find time to go climbing in the Lake District. The job has yet to become boring. Every assignment is an adventure – put simply you don't know what will await you when you get there. Sometimes the experience is fantastic, others I'd rather forget. Dull, it most certainly is not.

The job certainly has 'minge' benefits, which are discussed in more detail elsewhere. Male strippers are able to pull girls with considerable alacrity when compared to Mr Joe Public. The male stripper has a sort of minor celebrity status when he emerges after performing. This means he receives attention from women. Some are 'bedpost notchers', some are drunk and others just start competing with a room full of women vying for the attention of the only man in the room. This tells us much about their fragile egos. Some (although these are very rare) simply just want to sleep with you (no strings). Either way, the average male stripper gets his end away more than most.

There are also the psychological reasons as to why I strip and this brings us into the more general area of the psyche of strippers as a breed. It appears to this author at least that strippers as a whole are very damaged individuals. I would of course like to think that I do not fit the stereotype, but there are aspects of it which I almost certainly fall into.

For example, all strippers I have met are exhibitionists. I have met some who are not but I wouldn't call them strippers (for example members of the Bell Ends who don't go fully nude and don't play the circuit). All genuine professional strippers can be categorised as such and many psychologists would classify this as a condition/illness in itself.

Although I would disagree that exhibitionism is an illness, there is a by-product of it that is perhaps a little more sinister and this relates to attention seeking. A psychologist would probably analyse much of what I have said and conclude that I felt unloved or unwanted as a child. My reaction to that could manifest itself in my current behaviour as a male stripper. Because I felt unloved/unwanted I could now be seeking the love and attention from a different group of people outside my immediate family. That is, I seek the love, attention and affirmation of my audience. At face value you would probably expect me to refute the charge. However, why should I be massively different?

I would certainly point the finger accusingly at the rest of the stripping community. It has long been an enigma to me why it has attracted the individuals it has. They certainly seem to come with truck loads of excess baggage with very few exceptions. The stereotype of the dumb steroidal blond is not far wrong but I would go further. They are not all blonde. There are many brunettes as well. Most of them are low on the IQ scale. Many take steroids, which doesn't help their cognitive reasoning. However, a vast number are also completely unprofessional and unreliable. They have a tendency to show up when they feel like it and only if they feel like it. In the real world this sort of behaviour would not be tolerated. Any real business that hired them to supply a service would terminate their contracts upon non-delivery. A reputation would be garnered and soon they would go out of business. In stripping, however, the laws of the real world do not apply and these individuals continue to find work.

As yet, the definitive reason to this eludes me. Many theories abound. Certainly many no-shows occur because the strippers are high on drugs and are no longer in control of their faculties. I have witnessed this firsthand. Many strippers have never had a 'real' job. Several are the terminally unemployed, claiming benefits on the side. They have a tendency to agree to take the first job that comes in and then when offered something for £10 extra they attend that one and call the other job at the last minute to announce that "the car won't start". Such short-sightedness, one would think, borders on stupidity but they continually get away with this unprofessional behaviour.

It is certainly frustrating from a professional viewpoint that this sort of conduct is tolerated. Part of the explanation for this, maybe, is that the market is very small. If someone wishes to book strippers for the first time they typically won't know the good from the bad, or the diligent from the unprofessional. They will get probably get stung and won't book anyone ever again. Yet their misfortune remains a local tale and allows the cowboys to continue plying their trade in another region.

There is also the slightly more disturbing explanation that is perpetuated and facilitated by the bookers and agents. Many a drag queen books a stripper and the choice of stripper isn't always wholly based on their performance or professionalism. All too often their choice depends on whether the stripper allows a certain amount of 'extras' or whether he will allow the drag to 'give him a hand' when tying off. Far be it for me to cast aspersions on certain individuals, but I can confirm it does go on.

I have been asked enough times personally whether I would oblige. One drag called Camp Pixie assured me if I got my cock out for him personally (in private) he could guarantee another booking at a said venue. I haven't played at the said venue again. Other drag queens have alluded heavily to the benefits of sexual compliance. I haven't been booked by them again. Other strippers have told me of the benefits of sexual compliance. Essentially, certain drag queens know that they will receive a sexual kickback by booking certain strippers. They run a gauntlet as to whether the stripper will turn up, but they benefit personally if they do. If the said stripper doesn't turn up, the drags whine constantly about unprofessionalism, yet they will offer the offender the next available booking in the hope that they will show up next time.

Some agents behave in a similar fashion. I find their behaviour even more stupefying as very few of them even attend the shows.

It should simply not be in their interest to book strippers who don't turn up or do so in a (ste)'roid rage. Yet, they do book them and don't immediately blacklist the person concerned. Answers on a postcard please...

One particularly well known agency, are famous for cancelling shows at the last minute and replacing the stripper with their preferred strippers. Their modus operandi is to call the venue concerned and explain that the booked stripper is ill or has broken down, but their stripper will be attending as a replacement. Although I can't prove it, my theory is that the agent gets a good seeing to from the stripper at a designated time. I know the alleged actions of the agent to be true because I caught her trying to pull the stunt. She cancelled me on the morning of the show with some ludicrous excuse about the venue manager being ill. Before she had hung up I had the venue on the other line stating that they didn't know what she was talking about. Everything was going ahead as normal. Needless to say I haven't had another offer from that agent.

Strippers are a very fragile breed as a whole. Contrary to what might be one's initial perception they fundamentally lack confidence and have major self-esteem issues. For example, I have met very few that will actually go on stage without applying their make-up for fear of people seeing their real face. Personally, I wouldn't know where to buy it let alone how to apply it. Some border on paranoid. In order to counteract their low self-esteem many of them have egos the size of a planet. Indeed, a stripper's ego will typically arrive at a venue before his physical being. When strippers gather to form a pride there is much strutting around amongst the pride members in an attempt to ascertain the alpha male. This is usually measured in terms of the amount of shows performed in the last week. Stripper A will typically offer Stripper B a totally false greeting followed by the line "So, are you busy?" (whilst puffing out his chest so far you would think his nipples were attached to a stampeding elephant). Stripper B will return the false niceties and proceed to explain how he has been incredibly busy having performed 87 shows in the last week alone. Stripper A will retort with, "That's good, but I've performed 91." In all seriousness, Carpet Burn once assured me that he would perform ten shows every Saturday. The most I have ever done in a night is five and that was because logistically they all slotted into place. I have been offered 10 shows on a given night, but typically would have to turn seven of those down because it is simply impossible to go from gig to gig given the time parameters they demand and the inability of my transport to teleport.

If Arson is in the room he will typically inform all and sundry of how he has just returned from the last leg of his world tour via Moscow. The Adrenal Gland actually introduces himself as follows: "Hi, I'm the Adrenal Gland; I am the best stripper in the country." For the record, the Adrenal Gland is short, old, fat and bald. He has a cock which is about 4 inches when erect. Make your own conclusions.

The pride will also typically feel the need to mock the gay audience so as to protect and enhance their own masculinity. They may do gay shows, but they hate doing them. The lady doth protest far too much, me thinks. Some strippers do struggle with gay shows. The audience can be far more difficult to please and won't scream at a chimpanzee in a sailor's uniform as the girls often do. However, some strippers need, yes *need*, this level of attention and adoration. I recently worked with a new guy called Timberland (again old and bald – maybe it's the steroids) who at the end of his show (it was a hen night) literally sprinted for the door. He stated that he didn't like the audience because the girls weren't screaming loud enough for him. He isn't alone. Him and his ilk typically steer well away from the gay scene.

Other strippers feel the need to constantly seek attention in many different forms. Some like to appear on television. We are all offered some appearances on gutter television from time to time. *The Trisha Show* are regularly on the phone. I have declined to appear because they refuse to pay for my time. However, they know if they phone enough strippers, sooner or later they will get one. It's always the same ones. They take time out of their schedule to make somebody else money whilst they can claim to have been on television. Other strippers still, have to spend all their time posting on internet message boards, proclaiming to the world how great they are. I can't help but compare this behaviour to that of another internet forum. Marunde Muscle is a forum where fans discuss activities within the world of Strongman competition. Some of the world's greatest competitors, including former World's Strongest Man titlists, post on that forum. They come across as humble and likeable. This is in stark contrast to the strippers who have won nothing, haven't proved anything, yet shoot their mouths off as if they were gods. I refer you back to much earlier comments where talking fills in the gaps when the performance doesn't deliver.

I have watched some strippers on ladies' nights deliberately try to deflect the attention from the stripper on stage back over to them by playing up in some visible part of the room. One stripper is particularly bad for this. His character is that of a Benny Hill style cheeky chappy and to my ire people fall for it. Everybody tells me what a wonderful man he is despite his obvious falsities. A recent homophobic rant of his caught on tape has altered about all of two opinions.

A couple of strippers have started off as pleasant and soon transformed in a swampy mire of egoism once they have received an injection of audience love. The first time I met the Looney Warlord he was just beginning and was quite polite. Six months later he walked into the room with an arrogant swagger that was deserving of a good right hand. The shit that came out of his mouth did little to alter my opinion. To be honest, I wasn't sure which hole was his arse and which one was his mouth.

What is it that attracts individuals of this fragility to the business? I have deliberated over this often and have concluded that by and large the industry doesn't actually attract them, instead the industry recruits them. I think there is much in the psychological argument that strippers receive affirmation from their audience. Some of them cry when they don't get it. However, strippers don't usually apply for their positions on Jobserve or via newspaper classifieds. The only such advertised positions I have seen are for troupes who aren't really looking for people to strip. Most strippers I have met have stumbled into the profession by accident, or alternatively, have been lured into the profession by those with an agenda.

Those strippers, agents or drag queens that put on their own shows have recruited strippers into the business to meet their own requirements. In all examples, they have recruited vulnerable individuals who can be easily controlled, moulded and manipulated. Black Rod has recruited many a stripper. Every one is as stupid as the rest and follows him around like a lapdog telling him how wonderful he is. This has the dual benefit of meeting his troupe requirements whilst massaging his own ego.

Many agents and drags have trialled new strippers just so that they could see a young attractive man with his clothes off. They all, of course, have to be shown how to tie off. The most compliant of these individuals usually get offered the shows. More than one agent and one drag queen have admitted their motives to me in this area.

The downside with recruiting new strippers in this way is that they tend to be stupid, unreliable and unpredictable. They are often damaged individuals with unstable backgrounds. They are easily influenced from all quarters and soon start to believe their own hype. When they see their face on a poster they really do believe they are a superstar, as opposed to the lowest form of entertainment on a cabaret ladder where people typically laugh at them rather than along with them. Once the ego has landed they become difficult to contain and the bookers move on to recruiting the next gullible wannabee. If strippers were recruited from other areas, they would be more liable to have their own ideas and rebel against their instigators earlier. This obviously doesn't apply to everybody, but within any given population a high percentage will conform to the norm. Strippers are no different and many are best avoided!!!!

Chapter 12

Shattering the Myths

When I meet people and they find out what I do for a living they often come out with typical pre-conceived notions of what being a stripper must be like. Very few of them are true. Allow me to try and straighten the record a little here.

The first myth has to be that male strippers actually earn really good money. I have lost count of the number of times on hen nights where an aspirant gold-digger makes her initial approach with the line "I bet you earn a few quid". Despite refuting her statement she will typically follow up her initial query with "what do you drive". Typically, they dismiss my answer of "I drive a battered old diesel" as modesty. It has been known for a look of horror to spread across their face when they actually see that I wasn't joking. The look of horror directly correlates with a tightening of the vagina.

This is the where myth and rumour seem to go into overdrive. If I had a pound for everyone that tells me I must be rich from stripping, I would be rich. Also, there appears to be a trend that when I tell women that I am a male stripper, an unusually high proportion of them have a friend who is a male stripper who has allegedly become rich from the experience. When I assure them this couldn't be true, an argument ensues. Maybe this arises because we have different definitions of rich. However, these stripping 'millionaires' usually turn out to be gay. If there was any truth to these rumours of stripping millionaires, I can assure the reader that their wealth was not brought about from stripping, but maybe the performance of 'extras'. Generally, women – even wealthy, predatory ones – have yet to embrace the empowerment of paying for sex. For gay men it often comes as second nature. Male strippers can supplement their income if they are so inclined.

Some of the strippers will spin out their yarns where they work as £1000/night escorts for wealthy women. I am yet to see one scrap of evidence of this. 'Escort' agencies may be cropping up everywhere, but the term 'male escort' is effectively the same as 'gay prostitute'. Men have few qualms about paying for a sexual service (be they gay or straight). Women have a tendency to feel dirty or inadequate about doing so. In this liberal era of equality, women still don't feel empowered about paying a man for sex. Escort agencies spin a different yarn, where they will of course ask all aspiring male escorts for a fee to join their books and then never find them any work. I could list well over a dozen straight mates who have made this mistake. They struggle to find a girl in normal circumstances to have sex with (before you ask – no they aren't ugly) never mind the luxury of getting paid to have sex.

I have been asked several times by women how much I would charge, for "a night of passion". They invariably don't mean it. In fact, they expect that since they have shown an interest, I will follow through and offer it for free. Some have been visibly offended by my response of "make me an offer". For the record, I have been paid to fuck a woman once in the last three years. I could have probably received well over 100 similar fees if I was willing to oblige the male of the species and some of the offers have been from very wealthy men. One could certainly exploit this situation if one was so inclined. It is hardly a well kept secret that certain strippers have 'sugar daddies'. One, the Purple Maverick, has allegedly earned very well from this lifestyle.

Stripping itself, however, will categorically not make a man rich. On average, in today's market, a busy male stripper can expect to work 200-300 times a year. Sometimes he can expect to perform ten shows in a week, on others the diary will be empty, like his pockets. The typical show pays approximately £100. Minus his expenses, this hardly makes a pot of gold at the end of the rainbow.

However, it is not only women that make this inflated earnings assumption. Most men also assume that strippers do pretty well for themselves. The logic is understandable. Few people have the necessary gumption and confidence to undress themselves completely whilst a room full of strangers gawp at their actions, scrutinising all their flaws with no remorse or sympathy. One would think that because the supply of people willing to do this is low and the demand to witness sex and nakedness is pretty high, strippers could command a decent price. If the law of supply and demand was the only factor here, the price would probably be considerably higher than it is. However, several outside factors impinge on this.

For the record, the average male strip show pays around £100-£110. Some pay as low as £80. When the location is remote and there is a lot of travel involved, it may pay £200. However, these instances are rare. Many people have had the wool pulled over their proverbial eyes when booking strippers for the first time. Stripper man senses their vulnerability and will fleece them for as much money as possible. The punter invariably finds out that they have been had and never books again. This also happens a lot with troupe shows where the booker will often pay £1000 for what is essentially a traditional ladies' night when £500 would have sufficed. The booker loses money and also doesn't book again. The greed and short-sightedness of many within the industry is stunting any potential growth.

Furthermore, there is the problem of the 'wannabees'. Whilst I think this is one of the best 'jobs' in the world, I wouldn't do it for nothing. I may be an exhibitionist, but my sexual kicks still involve vaginas. This is not the case however, with all strippers. In order to secure a 'job' strippers will undercut one another, sometimes to a ridiculous amount. If a show on a ladies' night is available, certain well known strippers will half their fee to secure their position on the show. There is, after all, a heightened chance of minge benefits and the adulation from the female audience, in terms of decibels, far outweighs that of the gay audience. This feeds the monstrous ego and dampens the self-esteem demons. Bookers know this and exploit the weaknesses. The reduction in fee is never passed on to the client. It's simply redistributed into the pockets of the booker.

There is also the problem of the '20-quid weekend granddads'. Although they would never be booked on a proper show, these guys go out and perform strippergrams for petrol money whilst the booker takes a further £40. Their reward is no doubt based on attention and the potential for a blow job. All of this does little for the genuine strippers. Their work has been stolen by impostors and the clients don't book again because they were unimpressed by the balding, middle-aged flabby bloke that turned up (despite the promises of a bronzed Adonis).

The frustration mounts from the stripper's point of view when many a booker will start an auction. Funnily enough, this is nearly always instigated by women. When male bookers phone they usually ask only whether you are available on the date in question at the appropriate time. If you are, they invariably book you. When women contact me, however, a circus act often begins. They telephone every stripper, booker and agent on the internet searching for the best price. They spend a grand on phone calls and manage to save themselves £40 by booking the granddad. I have had them call up after the event sometimes saying they will book me next time. Conversely, I have turned up for others where I have been booked via an agent and the customer had actually called me directly for a quote. Despite my quote being £25-30 cheaper they actually went for the sanctity of the agent. Then, of course, they tried to avoid paying the extra by using the argument that they had contacted me direct. My sympathy in these situations is always slim to none and slim has usually left town.

I am often confronted by those that band around the claim that stripping is "well paid for 15 minutes' work". I must confess to finding this statement slightly galling. If one were to pro-rata the rate upwards to £400/hour, that would be very good – especially if we actually earned that. However, we don't earn anywhere near that. The actually hourly rate is nearer that of manual labourer but with no guarantee of stable work. Everybody seems to conveniently forget that the stripper may have just driven 150 miles for four hours in appalling traffic to arrive at the show. He will have the same amount of miles to get home (albeit in slightly better conditions). The stripper's car does not run on air and he will have to put petrol in the car in order to make it go. Also, given that he is a road warrior, his metal chariot takes considerably more strain than the average commuter's. Therefore, his chariot maintenance bill is higher than most. Furthermore, I for one did not get my body by sitting around watching TV whilst eating packets of crisps continually. My 'day' job is based in the gym or on the track. Many hours each week go into this. Moreover, my appetite is that of a professional athlete. That is, high. I eat plenty due to my higher than average level of calorific expenditure. My other 'day' job is spent on the telephone and the computer actively chasing bookings and fielding queries. These hours add up.

In total, given both my day and night-time working activities, my hourly rate would be closer to £10/hour before the deduction of expenses. From his pot of gold the stripper must also deduct other costs: the costume purchases, professional music production, baby oil, replacement of stolen costume items, publicity photos, gym membership, agent fees and maybe bed and breakfast. If you still think it's well paid I'll be seeing you on the circuit sometime soon.

There is some debate about the decline of male stripping on the straight scene. The general consensus is that the first real wave arrived with the advent of the Chippendales in the late 80s (although they weren't really strippers as they kept their knickers on) and received another boost in the mid 90s with the film *The Full Monty*. This heralded the arrival of many new strippers and a surge in the demand for ladies' nights. Ironically, the film led to a decline in the amount of work available for the then established strippers due to the influx of newcomers outweighing the increase in demand.

Today, many of the relics from 20 years ago are still plying their trade. When I perform in the gay clubs, a frequent jibe is often directed at certain strippers in their 40s and how they have let themselves go. All of the strippers from that 'golden era' tell me that it just isn't as good as it was back in the day. Fees are down and demand is less.

Even the gay scene is in decline. Many venues that used to have strippers have ceased to do so and have now changed their entertainment formats. About 15 years ago there were apparently 28 gay venues inside the M25 that had a regular stripper; now that figure is just three. The venues argue that strippers were just attracting a band of hard-core regulars who never bought enough drinks. Some have griped about a lack of new faces. Others simply say that stripping is old hat and that it is not in fashion anymore. If that is the case, it will no doubt see a revival some day in the form of a retro movement. Some gay venues will always have strippers thanks to the whim of the owner/manager. Typically, these venues will also only receive visits from strippers that please the booker.

Personally, I have often found it easier to play the gay scene, simply because you tend to be looked after better. Because the gay venues are used to receiving strippers, they have somewhere for you to get changed, they offer you a drink and although a gay crowd are frequently very expectant, they are usually very appreciative and rarely malicious. This applies also to the majority of the female audience, but there is usually a far from silent minority who find it amusing to heckle. Such behaviour has to be expected by any performer; where it becomes more annoying is when people try and invade your dressing room while you are changing or steal your costume as a memento of the evening. This rarely happens at the gay venues, but frequently does so on ladies nights. I have lost count, for example, of the numbers of pairs of underwear and sailor's hats that I have had stolen.

The internet can probably account for a large proportion of the decline of stripping. When strippers first became popular over 20 years ago there was no internet. Hard-core porn wasn't available in this country and had to be illegally imported. Nudity was rare and a privilege. Men in swimming trunks were risqué. Naked men swinging their bits around on stage was outrageous. The viewing of such copious amounts of penile tissue was unusual and desirable. Times have changed. Now hard-core porn is available from every sex shop. Hard-core images are available instantaneously on your computer at the behest of a search engine. Male strippers are no longer risqué, trendy, different or even sexy/sexual.

One of the stripping relics once relayed to me the story of how things used to be. He would arrive at the venue and park up in the reserved parking space. The doorman would greet him with a smile and a handshake. The doorman would invariably offer to carry his bag for him. He would then be led through the parting throngs with people pointing, staring or slapping him on the back. He would invariably have a pleasant area to change in, often with a special room set aside for performers or in the personal headquarters of the landlord. How the times have changed.

Although I considered the source of the story a little dubious, it is a tale that has been repeated too many times by others not to have validity. Strippers were in big demand and could work almost every night if they wanted to at that time. As a result of the increased demand they were given much more of the star treatment. Their groupies were higher in number and more intense in attitude. I list some of these former 'groupies' as friends now. They talk of a time when strippers were revered and looked upon with genuine respect. They lament frequently on their demise.

Nowadays a stripper arrives at a venue and will first have to scout around for a safe parking space. Spare change may be necessary to pay for the parking bay. The doorman will often meet you with a 'where do you think you're going with that box' look. After eyeing you up and down suspiciously (with smatterings of additional jealousy), you will be allowed entry. If you are lucky somebody may come out to meet you and guide you to the changing area. If not, you will have to stumble around asking for directions. Jealousy override seems to have kicked in with the majority of people as they deliberately shun you and shrug their shoulders at your request for assistance. Finally, somebody from the venue will realise that you aren't going to find the secret changing area without assistance and will come out and guide you to the disabled toilets.

Local government is also contributing to the decline. Some gay venues have been denied licenses to allow strippers to perform. This is despite numerous female lap dancing clubs being under the jurisdiction of the same local authorities. No doubt some over-officious prat with a small penis working for the local council vetoed such occasions. Unfortunately, few people have my maverick qualities. Whenever a show has been cancelled due to over-zealous local authority anal retentiveness, I have offered to take the said local authority to court on the grounds of discrimination. Most people don't fight the system, even when it is wrong. As yet, nobody has taken me up on the offer.

Girls have always viewed male strippers in a slightly comedic light, whereas gay men have viewed them through a more sexual lens. For girls, that comedy has become slightly 'old hat' and gay men can now find that sexual outlet elsewhere. There exists a hardcore audience that appreciate the cabaret of the stripping art. Even they are disappearing.

As traditional big strip shows have declined, there has been a slight upturn in the hiring of strippers for private parties. Strippers do provide an excellent opportunity to embarrass the birthday girl or hen before her marriage. Nearly all these private events seem to be booked for women. Very few are booked for gay men.

It is well known on the gay scene about the practice of tying off. This is the trick that strippers use to give the illusion of being extremely well endowed, thereby impressing a naïve audience. Of course, the illusion is further enhanced if the stripper is already well endowed (and some most definitely are). A number of times I have been approached by punters (mainly women or gay venue virgins) asking if I exceed ten inches when fully erect. Alternatively, cries of "look, it's Mr Big Dick" will reverberate around the room. All I can say is, if only. Some strippers are obscenely large but the art of tying off certainly allows Mr Average to join the party. In fact, the majority of strippers fall into the average category. I haven't seen too many that are below average (one or two).

When I tell people that I am male stripper, one thing men often say is that they couldn't do that because they are not large enough downstairs. They obviously don't know about tying off, but it is a fallacy to assume that the only thing a stripper needs is a big dick. Various things go into the mix: a good costume, decent music, an athletic physique, props, youth, dance moves, an innovative routine, a big dick; all are factors that contribute to a popular stripper. Obviously, the more of those qualities a stripper possesses, the better the act. Height is another factor; many strippers wear platform shoes on stage. For white strippers, their skin tone is another. Once one punter complained that I was "too white". As a result white strippers tend to either invest in sunbeds or fake tans to darken their skin.

In essence, the main four qualities that makes a male stripper are probably: big cock, a good physique, handsome face and a good act. Each probably accounts for roughly a quarter of the total package. The best strippers will score highly in all four areas. Some don't score at all and shouldn't be allowed. Others score well in one category and this carries him through poor scores in the others. I have known some strippers trade purely on their looks, which excuses their non-existent routine and average equipment. Others are nothing to look at until they drop their trousers. Others still are pure cabaret. On the gay scene a big cock and a 'dirty' act will always usurp a good looker. On hen nights a good looker will usually make up for a lack of inches.

The term 'road warrior' often springs to mind with male strippers. It is not uncommon to make a round trip in excess of 300 miles to reach a venue and get home again. If travelling further than that, it has to be worthwhile. Either a premium is charged or there needs to be more than one show in the evening or succession of evenings. For example, I frequently travel to the north of England and spend a week in the region, performing each night, before returning to North London at the end of the week. I do something similar in Wales/South West England. I average about 40,000 miles per year travelling with the job (not including air miles). Of course, other strippers may have a different spin on the story. Black Rod recently told me he is so busy he never travels out of London. Arson, apparently never travels more than five miles from his house anymore. Such is his popularity he can apparently buck the national trend of decline and have the punters come to him. At the other extreme, one stripper told me that he was so busy he covered 104,000 stripping miles one year. Eat your heart out professional truckers (and call me a cynic again)!

Contrary to what is sometimes assumed by a large proportion of women, all strippers are not gay or bisexual. Where this myth gets its origins from I do not know. There definitely exists an arrogance on the gay scene that there is no such thing as a straight man. The running joke is: "What is the difference between a gay man and a straight man?" Answer: "Ten pints of lager." This is just representative of an unbelievable arrogance that borders on the obscene running throughout a disappointingly large proportion of the gay community. I often wonder why an oppressed minority can sometimes be so grossly prejudicial.

However, few women suspect that the strippers performing before them will also ply their trade in gay clubs. Why then the accusations that we must all be gay?

Perhaps it is borne out of their own insecurity. If the stripper is gay he is unattainable. This may boost their own self-esteem because there is no danger of rejection. Gay men do tend to preen themselves more than straight men and spend more hours in the gymnasium. Strippers do the same for their profession. Whatever the reasons for this bizarre assumption, let me dispel them here. Yes, there are a lot of gay strippers. The percentage figure is quite high – I would guess perhaps as high as a quarter of performers. However, that still leaves a lot of straight strippers.

Paradoxically, whilst it is assumed by some that all male strippers must be gay, this lifestyle is often held in conjunction with having slept with at least 3000 women! If I am to believe what people tell me, then I must have a queue of gorgeous women waiting to sleep with me at every show I attend. Whilst this is discussed in more detail in a chapter of its own, to summarise – the claims are wildly exaggerated. Whilst I will concede that being a male stripper does present more 'minge' benefits than are available to the mere 'mortal' man, they do not represent the kinds of figures that are supposedly generated by rock stars. Firstly, I suspect that the 'minge' figures that are often accredited to rock stars are also wildly exaggerated. However, with that said, the stripper/rock star is often perceived as a 'celebrity' and there definitely exists women who are celebrity bedpost accumulators. The rock star has far more celebrity than the male stripper and with that comes a perception of wealth. As mentioned earlier, women often assume male strippers are a good monetary catch and many a vaginal opening has closed up when they have realised the truth. Personally, I have always been deeply saddened that women attempt to woo men based on what they perceive their wallet contains. Prostitution is fine, but at least be honest about it! A regular user of whores once said that "the modern woman is a whore who doesn't deliver the goods. Teasers are not pleasers... they greedily accept gifts to seal a contract on which they renege." In his opinion, buying sex in a straightforward transaction actually costs less in the long run.

Fifteen years ago strippers had a higher celebrity rating and it is possible that strippers were scoring with more regularity then. However, I doubt it. Amongst the tall-tales told by the stripping elite, the truth must be carefully extracted from the bullshit. The adage of 'any hole's a goal' has always rung true. I have heard many a story of, and seen with my own eyes, strippers shagging women in the toilets post show. To put it mildly, the sort of woman who indulges in such instantaneous sexual predatory of the male performer would rarely befit the cover of a glossy magazine. Also, their conduct usually arrives in hand with having drunk copious amounts of alcohol. I wish I could tell you that Angelina Jolie-alikes were waiting for me at the end of every show to fuck my brains out. I regret to report that post show my brain rarely ever leaves my head.

Also, as I mention in more detail later, it must be noted that the stripper is often perceived as unattainable. As a species, women fundamentally lack confidence and sprinkle large doses of insecurity on their breakfast cereal every morning. Given that, why then would the bronzed Adonis on stage with his pick of the 100 or so women in the room possibly pick them? Of course he would pick them, but frequently they won't believe it, even when the stripper makes his intentions clear. After all, he has slept with at least 3000 women in the last month alone. He is so sexually experienced and perfect that he leaves her feeling woefully sexually inadequate. Why then should she embarrass herself by even considering that he might like her? It is best, therefore, not to even go there… It takes a very confident (sober, not drunk) woman to consider going with a stripper. As I don't drink or do drunks, my field is somewhat narrower. In fact, a few friends of mine have benefited from the 'roadie effect'. That is, I take a friend with me to shows as my assistant or 'roadie'. The truth is that he is there to freeload off my 'minge' benefits. With the stripper seen as unattainable, his roadie is seen as a more ordinary and less intimidating sort of chap. A few mates have reaped the benefits of this scenario. Whilst they have been boring her a larger hole in her bedroom, I've been asleep on her couch. Worse still, I could have her gay friend trying to seduce me in her living room. It has happened…

Chapter 13

An Unholy Alliance –
Drag Queens Versus Strippers

Although the average man in the street probably won't realise it, strippers and drag queens go hand in hand. I certainly didn't know it before becoming a stripper and I see little reason for them to continue to do so. However, that is the history of the business and traditional methods have a habit of lingering.

Drag queens are often working the same gay venues as the strippers. Sometimes they act as the compere prior to the stripper appearing on stage. Strippers might see them as the warm-up act; drag queens probably view strippers as an unnecessary inconvenience in the middle of their routine. Drag queens nearly always act as the compere on a ladies' night. Done properly, they do a very good job of psyching the women up prior to the appearance of the stripper. On ladies' nights it is clear who the majority of the women turn up for. Ask 100 women after a show and 80 of them will say they came to see the strippers, first and foremost. The drag queen was a nice accessory.

Despite taking apparent top billing on such events, the strippers still typically come out second. Drag queens usually command twice the fee of the stripper. Strippers perhaps understandably resent this and although they go together like chips and salt there is an underlying tension between the two camps.

Drag queens often book strippers on their shows and vice versa. Both camps tend to favour themselves monetarily when this occurs. However, I have noticed a lot of resentment often displayed by certain drag queens booked on shows by strippers. By contrast, some drag queens sell their strip shows to the lowest bidder and as a result frequently bring a wheelchair ramp for granddad to get to the stage. The nurse required to undress him is not usually included in the budget.

Drag queens will argue, with some justification, that they often bring a PA system with them as part of their fee. This is true... sometimes. If strippers were going to double their fee, then I'm sure they would bring a PA system too.

Drag queens always state they have more expensive costumes (ie frocks and dresses). This is not always the case. Strippers can spend a considerable sum on outfits and some drag queens wear dresses from a charity shop. One drag queen very honestly opined to me that in the same way that strippers are exhibitionists, drag queens are transvestites. They simply like dressing up in women's clothes.

Whilst I don't think this applies to them all, it does apply to a fair proportion of them. Certainly those drags that spend considerable sums on frocks have more of a penchant for dressing up. I have yet to meet a drag queen who is straight. If we are to accept the argument that drag queenery is nothing more than performance cabaret (as the drag queens would insist), then it would seem odd that the industry is completely gay dominated. Another book would be required to explore the world of the drag queen in depth. However, my observations would indicate that the drag queens, as a breed, are every bit as damaged as the strippers they sneer at from afar in their crystallised towers laced with sequins.

Don't misunderstand me here. I know some drag queens who are very dear friends. Eighty percent of those are based in the North of England. There is a very different culture between the Northern and Southern drag queens. The northern drag arrives as David, transforms into Penny Change and departs as David. The Southern equivalent is more likely to arrive and leave as Diamond White because the drag persona has blurred the boundary between creation and reality. How's that for disturbed?

Drag queens have a tendency to view strippers as the brawn to their brain. In some circumstances this is justified. As a stripper with a whole brain, rather than just a collection of cells, I have a tendency to threaten many in the insecure drag world by simply breathing. This particularly applied to one drag duo known as Dumb and Dumber. Their malicious rumour spreading keeps reaching me from other sources. I only met them once and hardly said anything to them all night!

Strippers do attract more than their fair share of jealousy and more than a few drag queens fan the flames of the green-eyed monster. On ladies' nights, the drag queen is essentially a well paid warm-up act. If the strippers and the drag queen work together on an equal footing, the night works so much better. Frequently though, there is a fractious division between the camps as they strive for the betterment of recognition. The 'warm up man' tag has produced many a bitter argument from drag queens justifying their place in the hierarchy. In fact, many a bitter drag has claimed that women don't come out to see strippers, they come out to see the drag queen. When they start putting on drag queen ladies' nights I'll start to believe it. Until then (yet again), call me a cynic.

There did exist an internet forum called hunkymuppets. It was set up initially by a computer geek on behalf of his partner as a sort of fan forum. It was inspired by watching the performance of a Midlands-based stripper who had no internet presence. At first the forum was quite entertaining. People made reference to shows they had seen and strippers posted comments on stripping related issues. Soon, however, it was filled with lascivious drooling drag queens pontificating about sequins. It had barely anything left to do with strippers at all. The site was eventually revamped as a stripper and 'female impersonator' forum. The name remained despite the fact that all but a couple of the most egotistical strippers remained. PP O'Rourke needed people to reassure him that he was so wonderful. He began getting his friends to post on there saying how wonderful his shows were. A stripper called the Purple Maverick was famous on there as being the best stripper ever to walk the earth. Yet, few people have ever worked with him and those that have speak of his overwhelming ordinariness (belying the reputation). It turned out that he had a few fake internet profiles from where he built his own brand value by extolling his own virtues.

The last time I saw the site it was infested with vile drags and bitchy queens. A few sensible drags had made a public exit from the vile, inane sycophantic drudgery. My point is that the site was set up to discuss stripping and strippers. Yet, many an insecure drag queen latched onto the perceived fame and attraction that the strippers brought to the table. The site grew on the back of strippers. To my knowledge there is no drag equivalent by its name.

Today, gay venues have a tendency to promote drag heavily, whilst the stripper barely gets a mention. If you ask the audience – as I have – what brings them in, they usually say the stripper. Often a rush of people arrive just before the stripper goes on, but unfortunately they have a tendency to leave again almost immediately at the end.

I arrived at a gay venue in Hastings one night. There was a huge poster of a well known drag queen above the door. They hadn't even advertised that there was going to be a stripper. The drag queen nose-dived and left the venue in a blur of divadom. The stripper went down a storm. The drag probably got paid two if not three times what the stripper got paid. The manager seemed to resent the fact that the advertised act was a failure and the 'surprise' was a success. I have never been back to the said venue and as I left I noticed another big poster for next week's drag queen. Jealousy of strippers comes in many forms and on many levels. Although strippers pull in the punters, even some of the venue managers clearly resent us.

It is true on a ladies' night that the drag queen is on stage much longer than the stripper. They typically do two spots on stage of around half an hour each time. The stripper will do 20 minutes once. However, strippers put in far more work behind the scenes. Both parties rehearse their acts equal amounts, but strippers have to train every week and watch their diets constantly. They live their profession whereas drag queens simply rehearse theirs. Also, strippers mutilate their genitals before every performance. No danger money is paid to them for this.

I don't begrudge drag queens the money they earn, but I do resent those that say strippers are overpaid given the work they put in. Dumb and Dumber have been particularly vocal and vociferous about this. In their mind, strippers just turn up, go on stage for 15 minutes and then go home. Dumb and Dumber have a reputation for booking strippers so that they can bow down and worship on their knees before them. They wonder why the strippers they choose don't show up on a regular basis. Their name says it all...

Chapter 14

Expectations and Nastiness

Before embarking on his journey into the unknown, the male stripper should ideally have surgery to thicken his skin. A thin-skinned stripper won't last very long. Admittedly this may seem something of an irony, bordering on an oxymoron after what I said earlier about male strippers being a generally very insecure breed. Most of the time strippers do receive a joyous reception. I have never seen anyone booed off stage or had rotten vegetables thrown at them. However, I have seen strippers storm out of buildings because the girls hadn't screamed loud enough to inflate their ego. Also, once off the stage, members of the audience make personal approaches. Many of these offer complimentary appraisals, some offer constructive critique, most have a list of Frequently Asked Questions (for example, "How did you start off in this?"). However, some go out of their way just to be plain nasty. Others just have unreal expectations. This borders on a fine line with pure nastiness.

Sorry girls, but the unreality/nastiness factor almost exclusively arrives from the female audience. An example of unreal expectations comes when a booker proclaims that the show is too short. PP O'Rourke is well known within the industry for having a short show (about 8-9 minutes). Many a venue has complained about this as the average is nearly double that. However, some girls have expected an hour-long show!! My riposte to this is always simple – you try taking your clothes off for an hour whilst maintaining somebody's interest! Alternatively, pay me three fees and I'll do you four shows – buy three get one free.

Typically, someone who whines about the length of the act before they have even seen it is attempting a very poor method of fee negotiation. Someone who whines about the length of the act after the event is attempting the same with an added dose of malice. After all, they did know exactly what they were getting.

Private parties invariably run pretty smoothly, although occasionally there can be a malicious individual who tries to ruin things. One tends to feel slightly more exposed and vulnerable if you are coming under attack when you are naked. On the rare occasions where this has happened, the host usually gives a heartfelt apology for the behaviour of the perpetrator and then goes on to comment that her boyfriend dumped the perpetrator only yesterday! Physical attacks are very rare. Snide and nasty comments are more likely.

However, on the big ladies' nights I have come to expect a disgruntled faction. When women roam in tribes, men are often the target for their vitriol. Because the strippers are the only men in the room (drag queens are viewed as honorary women) they can become the target of illogical ire. On a base level, this nastiness may manifest itself by the waving of a little finger to indicate that you have a small dick. This has happened to every stripper I know. Frequently, this occurs before they have even seen the evidence! The irony, of course, is that most strippers can hold their own in that department and when they are tied off, they look huge.

This finger-waving unpleasantness often occurs after the offending female has decided the stripper has rejected her. Stimulation X recently told me the tale whereby he was talking to a girl before the start of the show. It all looked good for a steamy meeting post show. During his show, the said female began finger-waving and shouting obscenities. Somewhat perplexed by the change in behaviour, he sought an explanation afterwards. In a fit of rage-filled expletives, he was told in no uncertain terms that he was a liar, a cad and a cheat. She had watched him look at, walk over to and allow other women to touch him in the process of his act.

Although poor Stimulation X was the victim of an extreme loon in that example, similar stories abound. Whilst standing at the bar I am regularly approached by utter fruitloops with lines such as:

"Well… that wasn't very good, was it!" she says condescendingly.

"What was wrong," I ask.

"You went over to those other women and didn't come over to me."

I try not to roll my eyes but I can't help it anymore. In a room full of 100+ women you can't get around everyone. Also, I will approach those first that give me some eye contact. If somebody is looking at the floor (as is the case with a lot of fruitloops), I will naturally assume they are unwilling and will be difficult to involve in the show. As much as I'd like to be psychic, I'm still working on gaining my Uri Gellar-approved qualification. I can't read minds yet.

There have also been a couple of incidents of memorable note which exemplifies the nasty lengths that some women will go to if they don't get their own way. I was asked to perform a ladies' night in Birmingham. I was the only stripper with a drag queen (a vile Brummy queen who fortunately, to date, I have never had the displeasure to meet again).

There were many women crammed into a large hall. I have had better receptions and I've had worse. Mediocre is a fitting description. Yet the women were on heat that night. I had many approach me afterwards, fishing with a sexual net. I stood at the bar as they approached, one after the other. Eventually, I sat down with a Julie and we chatted for ten minutes or so. During this time, I was approached by two other parties attempting to get me to come and sit with them instead. I took Julie's number and said I'd call her later as I attempted to be a good celebrity and do my public relations bit.

"Why are you talking to her, you should be over here with us," scowled a blonde Brummie angrily as I approached. The rest of her group were similar in their greeting.

"We don't want to talk to you any more, fuck off," added another.

The second party were only slightly more lukewarm in their welcome. I have pretty thick skin, so I re-established my acquaintance with the hottest woman in the room and we soon departed so that we could get to know each other better. She certainly made my next few visits to Birmingham well worth looking forward to.

A couple of weeks later I telephoned the venue to see if they wanted to book another event for later in the year. They declined. There had been some complaints. As I have very thick skin, I always welcome constructive critique. How else can one possibly improve? Naturally, therefore, I probed as to the nature of the complaint. At first he was unwilling to divulge the nature of the complaint. This instantly makes me suspicious. If you buy a washing machine and it doesn't work, you take it back to the store and explain why you are returning the goods. If you brought it back and were unwilling to divulge what was wrong with the machine, the store would be unlikely to replace the machine or refund your money. They would be rightly suspicious of your motives (statutory rights aside).

I noticed a very similar phenomenon in my years in recruitment. It was in that environment that I learnt to read people very well. Unconscious body language signals often divulge a lot face-to-face, but even on the telephone people unwittingly give themselves away unintentionally, particularly under clever questioning. The semantics of their sentence structure, their tone of voice or the manner in which they respond to a question all reveal whether somebody is likely to be telling the truth. It used to drive me insane when in recruitment a prospective employer was unable to be honest with prospective employees. They used to tell me the real reason why they didn't want to hire Candidate A, whereas Candidate A usually came on the phone full of optimism imbued by client feedback at the interview. If the client is unwilling to give honest feedback to this person, how can he/she hope to improve their approach next time? They will keep running into the same brick wall. You shouldn't dent egos by constructively critiquing some of their failings – you give them a better chance next time! Failure is the greatest teacher, but if someone doesn't know they have failed, they can't learn from it!

Typically, however, in the recruitment situation, the prospective employee didn't fail. The decision of an employer was rarely based on sound logic and instead came from an emotional standpoint of a given manager. Usually they would hire the wrong person for the job. The wrong face seemed to fit better than the right face.

When I was in recruitment, I was successful. I was told much later, however, discussions were had amongst management about the fact that I didn't drink. Because I didn't go down the pub with the other lager louts, I didn't fit in. As a result, I was considered a bit of a liability due to non-conformity. In that instance, my results made up for my lack of alcohol consumption, but another guy who didn't drink wasn't so lucky. His results were not as good. He didn't go down the pub, management didn't like him and he didn't last long.

I have a habit of exposing such irrational and bigoted thinking head-on. This has never made me popular with management bigots. It is easy to see such bigotry as it attempts to mask itself and logical questioning soon exposes it. On the gay scene critiques have come my way from certain individuals because I have rejected their advances. They don't criticise my act.

I was confronted with a similar situation here. People had made a formal complaint. On the gay scene nobody has ever gone to this extent as far as I am aware. Instead, they just bitch into their beer about me not being gay. Making formal complaints is a step further. I knew why this had happened and I half expected it. I had spurned the advances of a few women. The old adage about a woman scorned rung true and the claws were out.

I may have thick skin, but lies still hurt. I therefore probed the manager as to the nature of the lies. He was cagey but apparently people had complained that I looked nothing like my photograph! Further probing revealed that what he meant by that was that apparently I was far less muscled than in my photograph.

This was complete nonsense and an outright lie. I have training diaries going back to 1999. I can tell you what I weighed on a certain day, how much I was lifting, how fast I was running, bodily measurements, etc. I do have a deceptive look. I don't dress to advertise my physique. I'm not vain or egotistical in that way. I typically wear a baggy tracksuit because it is comfortable as opposed to a skin-tight top that might show off my physique. As a result people are often surprised when I strip off and comments of "where did that come from" are not uncommon.

At the time of that show I was a little lighter than normal. I had been training for boxing. I would have liked to have had a few fights, but the black eyes from sparring weren't helping stripping. Furthermore, finding a trainer willing to help out was like searching for the holy grail. Boxing is my favourite sport, but its training methods are in the dark ages and getting involved is like joining the Masons (see a book by Dave Matthews entitled *Looking for a Fight*). Anyway, I was down to about 145lbs. However, the publicity photo they were using at the venue was taken the very same afternoon as I had competed in a powerlifting competition. For that competition, I had to boil down to 148lbs. My body composition had changed little. I hadn't gone bald or grey, I hadn't grown any lines or a gut. I looked very similar to my photo.

I offered the venue manager a challenge. I would drive back to Birmingham that instant. If he could successfully demonstrate by way of photograph that I looked different to my publicity photo, I would give him the fee back. If not, he should double the fee. Needless to say he didn't take me up on the challenge. I think he knew and accepted the complaints were false. Why else would I make such a challenge? However, in that particular venue I had made some detractors for life. I won't be going back.

There was an even more bizarre complaint one night at a private party. It was a busy Friday night and the birthday party in a private flat was the third assignment of the evening. I had discussed things with the host beforehand and everything had seemed perfectly normal.

On arrival, however, things began to get a little bizarre. Although I found the correct road, it was a new development made of hundreds of blocks of flats. I couldn't find any numbers to locate the flat. A phone call through to the host didn't help much either as her directions were rubbish. Only after she emerged onto the street at about the fourth time of asking could I find them.

On the way up to the flat, she asked me if I could get changed in the hallway. I explained that as I would be wanking, I didn't think that would be a good idea. She seemed somewhat shocked by this revelation and instead led me into the bedroom and promptly asked me if I "needed a hand" with anything. Given what I had just told her and her tone, I took her comment to be highly suggestive.

"If you are asking whether I *need* anything else to get ready, I'm fine. If you want to stay and help, it would be gladly accepted," I replied diplomatically.

This wouldn't be the first time an obliging host had helped get my dick hard. It is just another one of those 'minge' benefits that sometimes comes along with the job. Don't get the wrong impression, 99% of assignments are strictly professionally conducted. I am not in this for the 'perks'. If, however, a lady makes a formal offer, it would be rude to say no.

In this instance I must have been too diplomatic. The Irish host was far from drunk (unlike the hen) and I think her question was far from innocent. If I had torn off her clothes and shagged her senseless there and then it might have been more agreeable to her. The fact I responded with such diplomacy seemed to raise her ire.

Having spurned my offer to help increase my total cubic volume, she went into the other room and left me alone to apply my own elastic bands. The act was completed with a strange air. The hen was far too drunk to remember much of what occurred. She seemed to sober up pretty quick when my cock appeared in her line of sight (she was on her knees at the time). Women react differently. At one extreme they react with delight and try and suck it dry. At the other extreme they react like they have just seen Freddy Kruger. This was more Freddy Kruger. So as not to offend I covered up, gave her a kiss on the cheek and closed the show. Half of the admittedly small audience seemed to have daggers in their eyes whilst the stench of hatred hung in the air.

I emerged fully clothed to collect the remnants of my discarded attire. Two or three of the girls said they hoped I wasn't in a hurry as they wanted to ask me some questions. This is normal (how did you get into this, how often do you do it, do you have another job, etc). The questions began normally enough but the tide soon turned. On a couple of previous occasions I have seen women turn quickly in their attitude. This occurs rapidly if I happen to mention that I have had a vasectomy. I don't want children, I don't like them and don't want to be responsible for them. Call me selfish, but I want to be able to climb mountains, take risks and not have dependents who need me to live. The world is already heavily overpopulated and I shouldn't needlessly add to that. Therefore, my behaviour is as much responsible as it is selfish. Anyway, I have watched on more than one occasion as I have turned with the utterance of one sentence, from potential father of their child to murderer of their unborn baby. Apart from causing some unnecessary illogical unpleasantness, it also ruined the chance of a shag with some delectable nubile young ladies. Therefore, I have stopped mentioning it in discussions.

This time, however, there was no mention of vasectomies. I merely answered the questions as asked. I used to have a well paid job but I elect to do this as an alternative. Suddenly and unexpectedly, one of the women went on the attack. Whilst commending me on my professionalism and a job well done, she said it had gone too far. Obviously I requested a more detailed explanation. Apparently, taking all my clothes off had offended some sensibilities. Amazingly the whole room rallied to her cause.

I explained that the role of a male stripper is just that – to remove his clothes. Also, if they wanted me to keep my knickers on, why had they requested me specifically to take them off? Despite logic chopping all of their arguments away, the claws were out and logic simply enraged them further. They had one detractor in their midst (an Australian psychologist) who quite rightly asked what they were expecting when they hired a male stripper.

"You haven't hired him to do the washing up," she quipped.

As the argument became more heated, I asked the two main detractors what they did for a living. I hazarded a guess at either PR or HR. Both the Irish host and her main ally refused to confirm or deny whether I was close (arising suspicions that I may have hit the jackpot). They had certain mannerisms exhibited by protagonists of those two professions that I had encountered in my former life. Eventually, they asked me to leave. Of course, I did so without fuss. I had only stayed on at their request in the first instance.

The Australian psychologist followed me out of the door only a minute later and we ran into each other as I was loading the car. Thankfully, she confirmed that I wasn't mad, but they were. She hadn't been in the country long and didn't think she would be invited to any more parties within that group! She also confirmed that one of my detractors was in HR and the other in PR!

I have often described ladies' nights as a 'Get Your Own Back on Men Night'. That is, the men are objects of hatred and humiliation for a room full of women. Part of that humiliation is the removal of all his clothes thereby making him more vulnerable. In these instances psychological domineering and taunting, free of any retribution, heighten the experience. This was one of those nights with bells on. It was a shame for them that the object of humiliation had a higher IQ and was therefore able to speak back!

Chapter 15

The Role of Agents

I really shouldn't dislike agents. After all, I used to be one. However, I hated being in recruitment and I hate recruitment consultants. Most are complete pricks who can't spell 'professional' let alone understand the meaning of it. Too many fit the stereotype of a fast talker in a sharp suit with a mobile phone stuck to their ear. If only they realised that repeat business is the key and they don't get much of that by shafting everybody but themselves.

Unfortunately it's not just recruitment agents whose actions are questionable. All agents, in every line of work I have come across, have lacked professionalism and stripping is no different. Most agents have an agenda and couldn't give a flying fuck what anybody else thinks or whether the customer gets what they sold them. There are a few exceptions to this, who have been the epitome of professionalism. It's a shame these guys are members of an elite tribe.

Mostly, agents just enhance the bad name of the industry. It is to my perpetual dismay that despite their poor performance, bookers of events continue to use their services. It is one of the great enigmas of this industry that poor performance is often met with continued delivery and acceptance. Personally, I'm a consumer champion. I challenge poor service or delivery and tackle it head on. A judge recently said in summing up against a retailer, "Unfortunately for you, Mr Molloy is that one in 10,000 consumer who knows his rights and is willing to enforce them to the letter." Whilst that may be true, I have long lamented that the British would rather lie down than complain. Alternatively, they will complain until their throat hurts in private, but never action anything to retribute against the offender. The stripping game seems to accentuate these points even further.

There is a well known agent on the circuit who is famed for supplying strippers from £50 upwards. The granddad from Eastern Europe who turns up (if he turns up), gets a tenner and a blow job if he is lucky. The agent takes the remaining deposit, usually by credit card. Consumers complain but never take any action. A few complained to the BBC who put him on their *Watchdog* programme. All that did was boost his sales. I have even had women contact me and ask for his number!!!

I have turned up for jobs booked by some agents where the client has been given completely unrealistic expectations. I distinctly remember one strippergram in a Chicago Rock Café. The venue refused to play my music and forbade any nudity. I had to perform with very little space at their table. I made the best of a bad situation. The booking woman asked for a discount afterwards because the show wasn't 30 minutes long as she had been promised! I obviously explained that she had been spun a line and that she had to take it up with the agent. I also asked her if she could show me the contract that the agent had obviously supplied her with detailing what she could expect. Needless to say she didn't have one. I tried to ask her what factors led her to book through the said agent, but I was met with an embittered response. I tried to explain that next time (highly unlikely) she should only book from someone supplying a contract. It no doubt fell on deaf ears. People have a moronic tendency to book with someone who gives the big talk but writes down nothing of their talk.

So much of the industry is cash only. Many regular venues prefer this. It avoids any sort of employment legislation, National Insurance contributions, etc. Strippers are happy because they avoid income tax and it doesn't affect their benefit claims. However, bookings that are arranged in such a fly-by-night fashion also have a tendency to fall out of bed at a moment's notice. No contract – no comeback. I prefer to book direct in most circumstances. If the venue cancels at short notice I will charge them a cancellation fee as per the terms of my contract. If they don't pay, I take them to court. If an agent cancels at short notice they will usually attempt to wriggle out of all responsibility. Legally, it becomes a lot more complicated when a third party is involved and everybody denies responsibility blaming the other party. This makes it far more difficult to obtain the money.

I take a very dim view of such short-notice cancellations and I like the terms to be clear at the outset. Once I commit to a booking I begin to turn work away for that particular time and day. As a result, a short-notice cancellation means I have lost other potential bookings. In essence, the food has been taken out of my mouth. It grates me even more when flippant comments such as "this isn't your real job anyway" are offered as an excuse.

The great irony of this is that the very same venues will often pay exorbitant fees for other artistes without question. One night there were four of us performing at a gay venue in Watford. They seemed reluctant to pay us the agreed fee in cash and instead wanted to pay us by cheque. The venue was owned by a large parent company so they were probably good for their cheque. However, the stripper known as Petrol had told them in no uncertain terms that he was going to take the till (by force if necessary) if they didn't produce cash. Rather than risk Petrol igniting whilst still in the club, an underling was dispatched immediately to a cash machine. In the interim the manager told me the story of how they had recently had a *Big Brother* winner come and perform at their venue. She sung her one song (badly, allegedly) and left immediately, refusing to mingle or pose with punters. Alleviated of £7000 for the privilege, I put it to them that there was no way they could possibly justify that fee economically for a personal appearance. They didn't generate anywhere near that amount from ticket sales on the door and would have been lucky to scrape it back on drink.

Their argument ran that the ensuing publicity for the club brought punters back in on a regular basis. A quick straw poll of four punters in the club that night confirmed what I suspected. None of them knew about the event let alone remembered it.

A similar story came my way when I was performing in a club in Stoke. They hired the singer Blu Cantrell for a more acceptable £2000. She apparently demanded they order her a pizza and when it arrived it was the wrong sort. She refused to perform until the right pizza arrived. Only then did she sing and she again ran for the door and refused to meet her adoring public. In both cases, I asked what the club had contractually agreed with the agent and why they didn't demand a discount for such poor service. If I hired somebody for my club for a few grand I would at least expect them to fraternise with the customers! Surely that isn't too much to ask for a few grand?

It gets right up my nose when somebody tries to short change a stripper by a tenner. This is heightened further given that strippers often pack a place out when they are advertised in advance. This stripper hangs around afterwards talking to people and giving out posters. I also offer to help promote the venue in any way I can. The reward for this is sometimes to be treated like a right pussy. Remember what happens to pussies – they get fucked. Yet the very same people will book acts from agents for several thousand and get very little in return. After being fucked silly they still say thank you. WHERE IS THE LOGIC?

Other bookers work on a more perverted logic. One particularly ugly female agent is rumoured to hand all her work to a small handful of strippers whose penance is to go around and be dutiful to her. I have long suspected this of occurring with many other agents, but other than circumstantial behavioural traits I can't prove a thing.

One night I turned up at a show with five strippers. The show was booked by an agent I have no respect for whatsoever. Two of the strippers present were a disgrace. One could have drawn a pension and another could have entered a Sumo wrestling contest. I had not heard of either man and to call them a professional stripper was/*is* a joke. The girls present voiced their disapproval or more accurately sat in stunned silence. The agent concerned has all the strippers on the circuit on their website. I know several of them were available to work that evening but hadn't been called. Why they booked the two blokes from the bus stop I have no idea. Even more perplexing is that the lap dancing club concerned continued to use their services as an agent!

This sort of behaviour is bizarre in the extreme! I have listened to agents complain about certain strippers letting them down and yet they offer their very next show to the same guy! When I moved to Hertfordshire, one well known agent was actually located within walking distance of my abode. He refused to meet face-to-face. Locked in a time warp he told me he used a stripper who I knew had retired. Yet his praises are sung by many a drag queen. I have sat there as drag queens have slagged off a certain stripper to an astonishing level, in one case even threatening to slit his throat should their paths meet again. Yet the very next show the aforementioned queen booked himself and secured the services of the stripper with the razor blade emerging from his windpipe. No reconciliation had been made to my knowledge. The stripper concerned has a reputation for drugs, unprofessionalism and unreliability. If this isn't circumstantial evidence for sexual favours, then I don't know what is! The stripping industry is far from meritocratic and can't really be called a business. Any genuine business run in such a way would go bust.

Chapter 16

Propositions

It is often assumed that male strippers receive sexual propositions on an almost daily basis. For the most part this is true, but not quite in the form that most of you may imagine. A whole chapter is dedicated to the topic of female propositions later. Suffice to say they are rare and far less common than one might imagine. It may be true that I once had sex with five different women in a day thanks to my profession. I have had women pay me for sex and I have literally had the clothes torn from my body on hen nights. However, these incidents are rare as a percentage. Women have offered me money for sex on a regular basis, but there is a veiled implication that by asking they should get it for free – if that doesn't occur, the claws come out!

Mostly, the propositions come from the much more confident gay sector. Rejection is handled well by most parties and rarely accepted until about the tenth brush-off. Whilst flattering, the attention can become a little tiresome as long lines of potential suitors approach one after the other.

These propositionings take on a more sinister tone when there is an underlying threat or reward. I have lost count of the number of occasions whereby, on the gay scene, sex has been requested, either explicitly or implied, in return for bookings. Some strippers exploit this to the hilt. As has been discussed already, many drag queens book hen shows. I haven't yet met a straight drag queen and many a stripper has 'put out' in return for the hen booking. One drag in particular actually acts as a chauffeur and picks up his chosen strippers to ensure of his 'reward' for that evening.

Similarly, a Midlands drag queen once offered me £50 to suck my cock. I declined and was met with a regaling of other strippers who supposedly had accepted the offer. "Good for them" was my reply. "They work here all the time" was the response. I didn't work there again.

Arson has to be one of the ugliest strippers ever to work the circuit. According to one punter, he has a face like a bag of spanners, is no spring chicken and he is no bronzed Adonis either. His saving grace is that drag queens often refer to him as "the ugly one with the big cock". A few times I have been to gay venues only to hear of his exploits with the venue manager/owner the week before. There was nearly always a veiled implication that "Arson did this upstairs with me, what will you do?" My response of "I'll set your customers alight in the way Arson cannot" was not always warmly received.

With that said, Arson's approach didn't always work either. A venue manager in Cardiff told me of Arson's none too subtle sexual advances towards him. Arson's rubbery features caused a feeling of revulsion, dousing his fiery intentions. From that day forward Arson was banned from the said venue.

Many of these proposals are illicit and not direct. If you respond in kind then bookings will rain forth upon you. For a while there was a gay place in Plymouth that used to hire me on a regular basis. I became friendly with the manager, even staying at his place a couple of times. I would try and arrange a couple of shows in Devon whilst I was down there to ease the petrol burden. When Becky, my shag down there, went loopy one day, I stayed with Marsden. He told me that he had been told (by a drag queen) that I would 'put out' in return for bookings. He very candidly said that was his initial motivation for booking me. Fortunately for me, he assessed my abilities as a stripper ahead of his own sexual motivations with regard to repeat bookings. Some venue managers prefer to abuse their position in this regard.

The number of times I have been the victim of blatant 'heterophobia' has thankfully been relatively small. There is a pretty common feeling of being different and I have seen gay attitudes noticeably cool if they find out they are not my sexual preference. This sort of heterophobia is at least illicit.

I will never forget the time I played a venue in Northampton (at the best of times surely a contender for the weirdest town in Britain). I arrived at the venue very early and not wishing to spend an hour sitting around in the confines of a disabled toilet (my changing room), I went and had a drink of water at the bar. The manager there was initially very welcoming towards me. However, there were several straight girls at the venue and they were more forward on this occasion than their gay counterparts in the initiating conversation stakes. "Are you gay or straight?" is usually the first question that people ask and this night was no exception. I am typically cagey on the answer – "If I told you that I'd have to kill you" – but evasive tactics only go so far. The rumour I was straight spread around like wildfire. The manager stepped outside and his attitude towards me had to be retrieved from the arctic circle. Seeing this, I deliberately hung around afterwards to chat to the girls (and there were enough of them on that night). His angry fire burnt long and bright.

The very same man was to attempt to launch an anti-homophobic charity less than a year later. A worthy cause, but one better represented by someone less prejudicial, I would argue. I have argued with my great friend Uniboy about this very issue on many occasions. Apparently it has been commented on (on the gay scene) that I have been known to talk to women in gay clubs. Of course, I can only do this if the clubs let them in. That is, women also make up the custom of the said clubs. If they are open minded enough to let 'fish' (a gay term for women) into the establishments then surely it must be OK for people to talk to them as well? I hate prejudice in all its forms. However, it always feels doubly barbed when the prejudice comes from a minority group whose mission has been to eliminate prejudicial attitudes in the first place.

I'm a stripper and proud of the fact. Being polite and courteous should be part of the job. Selling my body (for sex) and pretending to be something I am not, isn't. I have a lot of gay friends who accept me for who I am just as I accept them. Some still fancy me and that's great! If sexual discrimination laws applied to the stripping industry, however, I'd be a millionaire by now and that's just plain wrong.

Chapter 17

The Steroid Issue

Another typically asked question I receive is "Do you take steroids?" The answer is no, but the majority of strippers do partake in this pastime. As a sprinter I carefully weighed up the option that was performance enhancing drugs. I concluded that drugs would propel me to a sub 47 second 400m. However, there isn't much money to be earned from that. I'd have spent more money on 'gear' than I would have won in prize money. I would have been risking my long term health and all for a few medals and trophies.

When I started competing in powerlifting, drugs seemed pointless for different reasons. I actually managed to win a British title in one of the powerlifts. However, this is better than it sounds. Powerlifting suffers from the same multi-faceted governance as boxing. I was but one of many 'British' title holders. However, I decided to use my new found national champion status to seek lottery funding. I did, after all, have an offer to compete in the world championships. The downside was that I would have to pay my own flight and accommodation. Also, I was fobbed off and pissed about by the lottery funders. I knew track athletes who were ranked 30th in the country in their event, yet they were receiving over £1000 funding per year.

As national number one in my event it seems I was entitled to nothing. Athletes who are recommended by a board of selectors, who have a chairman with the precursor 'sir' to his name, seemed to get funding. Road warriors do not. I quit the sport soon afterwards, disillusioned about the lack of reward for the amount of effort required.

For the record, I once tried a two-week course of Dianabol whilst I was in Dubai. D-bol, as it is better known, is a mass steroid. I was bored with life and training out there and had always been curious as to the possible effects. Arnold Schwarzenegger used to have 20 for breakfast and a sprinter would typically take eight per day. I took a baby dosage of four per day with a host of oestrogen blockers. One of the side effects of testosterone-based steroids is the water retention and the aromatisation of oestrogens (the female hormone). This can lead to side effects known as 'bitch-tits', where men can get flabby breasts and can even begin to lactate. There was little danger of this in my case. A course should usually last two months, not two weeks. My dosage was very low and my paranoia ensured I was taking other substances to minimise any potential side effects. Some of my reading was suggesting that what I was doing wouldn't work at all.

Some supposed learned scholars postulate that steroids don't have any direct effect on performance at all. Let me assure you from personal experience that this is complete nonsense! Even taking my baby dosage I gained muscle mass in a couple of weeks that would have taken me several months of injury free training in a gym. My recovery rate from sessions was incredible and the strength gains were remarkable. I had essentially plateaued from natural training and my mind boggled as to what might happen if I actually took a proper course of steroids over a sustained period. Still, I saw no point in continuing their usage. It is easy to see how they could become addictive. I felt like the incredible hulk whilst I was 'juicing' and I almost felt as if I could take a bullet head-on. Yet logically there was no real reason to continue. I didn't need that feeling of invincibility to live my life. It might have felt nice, but by continuing I would have been risking my health simply to feed my ego. That obviously wasn't worth it.

It would have been worth it if I thought that by taking drugs, they could earn me a living through sport. Unfortunately I lacked the elite genetics in one sport and there was no money to be earned in the other. Similarly, I lacked the genetics in terms of pure size to earn a living in strongman. Although pound-for-pound I am strong enough to compete, I would need to double my weight. Steroids could probably help add about 40-50% to my current weight, but doubling it may be a problem.

Also, I should clarify here. Taking drugs in sport isn't really cheating. It is simply doing what everybody else is doing. If you don't take drugs in sport you won't make the elite level. If you doubt this, you are naïve. If you have researched it and still don't believe it then you are an idiot (or a liar)! Bodybuilders take stick for not being true sportsmen. Yet those guys are the consummate professionals that every athlete should look up to. They set their alarm to eat (even in the middle of the night), weigh their meals, train extremely hard, train smart (scientifically) and use their bodies as guinea pigs by pumping it full of copious amount of drugs. The benefit of their self-experimentation then tends to trickle down to other sports. Sprinters take mass steroids during winter training and ripping agents in preparation for the summer season. Cyclists take EPO which enables the body to produce more red blood cells. Powerlifters take steroids that increase strength without weight gain (eg Oxandralone). Boxers take diuretics to make the weight. Snooker players take beta blockers to calm their nerves. Drug use is rife at every level.

Drug tests are fairly easily bypassed by those experienced in the methods. Urine testing is widespread and relatively primitive. Athletes have been known to inject a clean syringe of urine directly into their bladder so that they piss out a 'clean' sample, thereby fooling the testers. The drug developers are usually always a step ahead of the testers. If universal blood testing was brought in tomorrow, a lot of athletes would be caught with immediate effect. However, sport authorities know this and will therefore not allow it. If all their top athletes were removed from the sport their sponsors would leave with them. Positive drug tests are therefore routinely covered up and buried. There have been numerous cases of this happening. Under a carpet somewhere, there exists a lot of high profile names that have failed drug tests.

Stripping has no such testing procedure. A stripper's performance is subjective and not quantitatively measured. There is no formal competition with winners and losers so theoretically there is no edge to be gained by juicing. However, we have discussed already how the majority of strippers worship an egotistical god with low self-esteem. Steroids are being used by insecure gym goers the world over who have no intention of ever competing in a sport. Strippers have to go and parade themselves on a stage for others' viewing pleasure. Frequently the equation reads as LSE + HE = SA. Or, low self esteem + high ego = steroid abuse.

A major part of assessing a stripper as a total package has to be assessed on how his body looks. The reality is that when mixed with a decent training programme and a good diet, steroids will obviously enhance this (taken correctly). Therefore, there is a tangible benefit to their usage.

I have heard the moral high ground taken so many times in sport. Supposedly people don't want to see athletes risking their health just so we can see them perform better. Bollocks! The reality is that if the Olympic 100m was won in 10.3 nobody would watch because we are now used to seeing it won in 9.8. Similarly, people want to see strippers with fantastic bodies. The average punter doesn't care if that stripper is juicing and therefore risking his health. It doesn't affect them so what do they care?

I have had this very argument with a drag queen friend. He takes the view that strippers using steroids doesn't matter, it is merely a point of personal preference. Whilst I see his point I'm not quite as lenient. As in sport, if you have one juicer raising the bar of performance it puts the pressure on the other performers to also raise their game. As most sportsmen will already be at their natural peak from a dedicated diet and training programme, the only option to improve is through supplementation. If you can't beat them naturally – you join them.

Don't get me wrong, the percentage of juicers in stripping is not as high as elite sport, but it isn't far behind. The fact that it exists puts pressure on those that don't routinely inject themselves to join the bandwagon. I remember once a couple of punters openly advocated I should start using steroids to get bigger like one of the other guys. I agreed but only on the basis that they pay my medical bills should any complications result. Strangely, they didn't agree to that condition.

Chapter 18

The Truth About the Girls...

The most common assumption about male strippers is that they can and have shagged for England (or their native country). We are all Casanovas with so many notches on our bedposts that we need several beds to accommodate the notches. When I tell men that I have only just met what I do for a living, I usually get a nudge and a wink.

Have I slept with a lot of women? Yes. Do I sleep with a new one every show? No. Do women throw themselves at me because of my stripper status? No. Do I wish they would? Well, of course. Are there women who deliberately seek to bed the stripper. Yes. Are they common? No. Is there any profession where women sling themselves at men because of what they do? In my opinion, relatively yes. In absolute terms, not really. The minge benefits of a stripper can probably compete with almost any profession. However, the sexual statistics purported by the proponents of selected professions are wildly exaggerated. Those naïve enough to fall for the BS simply don't understand the female sexual psyche.

All the opinions that follow have been formed from studious observations by a male stripper working in the lighter side of the sex industry. Allow me to paint a picture...

I once did a show at a gay club in Cyprus. I was there for a few days and was fortunate enough to befriend the barman, Andreas (Andy) Harris. He very kindly drove me around some of the island sights and we spent a wonderful day getting to know each other, talking very candidly. As we were diving into a rock pool he came out with one of the most profound statements anybody has ever said to me: "Nick, you are unlike anyone I have ever met. You ARE a gay man – you're just trapped in a straight man's body."

Now, Andy had already told me he fancied me, but he understood my sexual preference and there the matter was left. That is, until my last night in the club when I was making advances on a gorgeous lesbian (Jo from London). She made it pretty clear that it was a case of girls only for her. Andy hadn't ever been part of the conversation. He simply came wandering up to me and said, "You know how it feels now."

He knew that Jo was my type from our previous conversations. He also knew I would make a move and he knew I had no chance. We both burst out laughing.

I have since adopted his "gay man trapped in a straight man's body" line. Gay men usually challenge me to explain this as I am not gay. Straight men just proclaim that I am gay. Allow me to clarify what Andy meant.

Essentially, I have many of the values of a gay man. I tend to think more like a gay man than a straight man, but it just so happens that I prefer to fuck women to men.

It is my contention that at the core there is actually very little difference between gay men and straight men. The only real difference is their preference for either pussy or cock. However, there is a world of difference in the images that both groups portray. Gay Man tends to project a much truer image of himself, at least those gay men that have successfully come out and are happy about who they are. Sure, there are many gay men who are deeply unhappy about who they are because family/friends are exerting social pressure on them to be something that they are not. Thankfully the societal trend shows a liberalising of views and attitudes and this is far less prevalent today than it used to be. However, it still exists. There are also those gay men who feel the need to project an image of themselves that conforms to a stereotype. No doubt many of these damaged individuals are rebelling against their upbringing that repressed their true nature. Thus, they portray what they are to an exaggerated extreme. Put simply, men don't talk with an effeminate voice naturally. This is put on – in some cases to an extreme. They don't naturally, by way of birth, wave their wrists around limply to make a point. This behaviour is learnt to emphasise a stereotype they feel they belong to.

Gay Man is not well represented by these groups. In my experience the majority of gay men can't stand the 'queenie' types. To quote one of them: "If I wanted something effeminate, I'd sleep with a woman. I want my men to act like men."

In other words, Gay Man is perfectly 'normal'. He has the same interests, eats the same food, plays the same sports, etc as Straight Man. Most gay men do not look like the lost member of the Village People or as if they belong in the Blue Oyster Bar from *Police Academy*. Essentially the only difference is that Gay Man likes to fraternise sexually with his own kind.

This difference in the sexual prey of our two groups of men produces wildly different attitudes, outlooks and behaviours. Each camp has to produce and conform to behavioural norms that are consistent with snaring their very different prey. Cheetahs have very different hunting targets and tactics to lions. So it is with Straight Man and Gay Man.

In my opinion, gay men are far more liberal and open mined when compared to their straight counterparts. This is largely due to the prey that they stalk. Gay Man is hunting quarry that thinks like himself. He therefore understands how the opposition thinks and feels. He is therefore in a perfect position to execute a successful strategy. Gay Man nearly always nets a catch when he goes hunting.

By contrast, Straight Man is in a world of perpetual bewilderment. He doesn't understand his quarry at all. Like the cheetah and the lion he has developed strategies for ensnaring his victim. But usually it will take at least a dozen hunting attempts in order to successfully sink the claws into the victim. Even then, the quarry behaves so strangely, not conforming to his laws of logical behaviour, that frequently the prey slithers from his grasp. Straight

Man has learned that his prey is particularly vulnerable if he sprays alcohol in large quantities at it first. This seems to inhibit the ability of the prey item to slip from his grasp when ensnared.

Gay Man has a tendency to assume (incorrectly) that Straight Man is as successful a hunter as he is. This is because Gay Man often has a special friend who is the quarry of Straight Man. In order to fit in with Gay Man, the straight quarry has a tendency to talk, and only talk, like a gay man (the fag hag). Gay Man has limited hunting skills because his prey is easily caught and therefore assumes the talk to be correct from the straight quarry. However, the reality is something far removed.

In this new technological age, Gay Man now finds that he can find prey virtually anywhere. Internet forums such as Gaydar mean that Gay Man can arrange a meeting with a stranger within an hour an hour of logging on. Gay men have met in 'cruising areas' for decades. These often masquerade as public parks (eg Hampstead Heath) or public toilets. Many gay venues have 'dark rooms'. The sole purpose of these areas is so that people can fumble, grope and have 'zipless fucks' in the dark.

Sex is so easy for Gay Man to come by. There are also the frequently organised gay orgies. My good friend casually commented that his record (to date) is having had sex with 17 different men in the same evening. To qualify, that is only the ones that fucked him. He doesn't count him fucking them, blow jobs, hand jobs, etc!

Straight Man by contrast cannot even begin to dream of such a bounty. Straight Man would like to be just like his gay counterpart, but his quarry will simply not allow it. If Straight Man could have sex with 17 different women in an evening he most certainly would. His chances, however, are slim. Furthermore, Slim was last seen leaving town in the 1960s. In fact, the opposite is true.

Getting laid for Straight Man is an event, something to be celebrated. Once he has successfully found the back of the net, Straight Man all too willingly sets up camp with his new partner and builds a den. Although this is not really in the nature of Straight Man, he fears the reprisals if he doesn't. After all, it may have taken him months of hard work to get into her knickers. He has showered her with gifts, wined and dined her extensively and finally he has achieved his aim. He wants to ensure that her fountain will continue to flow. Therefore, he succumbs to her whims and begins a campaign of willful denial and deceit so that access isn't denied to the fruits. This usually begins with stories that he has eyes for no other women but her. Angelina Jolie becomes an ugly sluttish whore who should be stoned to death for her outrageous comments and behaviour. Straight Man is essentially a conformist against his will.

Soon Straight Man will marry. He will sign a piece of paper pledging allegiance. He agrees because the opportunities seem bleak. Gay Man by contrast is having so much sex that eventually he tires of it and longs for marriage! However, he struggles to find it in his world because everyone is so promiscuous. Gay Man then begins to suffer strange desires, wanting to be straight. He does this without full knowledge. If he could transform into the body of Straight Man for a day, most would probably rescind their initial interest.

I know many a gay man who would argue that he would prefer to be straight. The main argument is that it is difficult to settle down. However, very few straight men would desire to be gay. Partly, this is due to social stigma (regretfully still) and ignorance. The 'backs to the wall' attitude, although dying, is still present. Those with that attitude, in my experience, are usually in the closet anyway.

If we take away the stigma and lack of knowledge, many a straight man would probably take my fictional gender bender pill to swap sexuality. Most straight guys I know live out a tempestuous relationship with their female partners. All relationships are based on compromise, but straight ones more so than most.

Someone once said that "life sucks and the wife doesn't anymore". I would argue that men and women are diametrically opposed creatures. Take sex out of the equation and the two parties would have a minimum of interaction. If women could hear their husbands/boyfriends talk about them when they weren't there, they would dump them straight away! "My boyfriend is different," she protests. Well, I've yet to meet a woman who says her boyfriend isn't different! They can't all be different. The gullible females fell for the hunter's deceptive ploy. In order to remove the knickers he told her what she wanted to hear. The chances are he didn't mean a word of it!

I often lament on how much easier things would be if I was gay. I would be much more in tune with my quarry, both mentally and sexually. Alas, I am what I am and that's not going to change. It has always struck me as a wicked irony, that men will pay me good money to actually give me a massage, whereas I have to browbeat every woman I have ever known intimately into performing the task.

As a whole, men are more creatures of logic compared to women being creatures of emotion. This isn't to say that men bottle up feelings and can't talk about issues. On the contrary my friends and I discuss every subject to the minutia. I have found women can rarely do this because of their distorted view of reality (eg my boyfriend is different). They also seem to struggle more when explaining themselves in purely logical terms.

This is why the myth that strippers get laid every show is false. It fails to take into account the illogical behaviour of the opposite sex! A good friend of mine, another Andy, says that I have taken the whole act of getting laid and redefined it. I have apparently turned it into a social study and art form. I would concede to being partially guilty to this charge. Another friend, Kenneth, says that I see sex as a sport. I'm guilty as charged and proud. Sport is great. It is an outlet for energy, it's competitive and it releases pleasurable endorphins. Sex is the same.

Our typical stripper who hunts pussy on a ladies' night has a simple strategy. Firstly, locate the biggest slag in the room. Secondly, ensure that she has drunk copious amounts of alcohol. Thirdly, attempt to remove her knickers in the toilets/changing area. Looks are irrelevant. Any hole is a goal.

This is no doubt an effective strategy if the aim of the exercise is to ejaculate into a vagina. However, for me at least, this is a little shallow. For a start, drunks are a big no-no. I don't want to wake up in the morning next to someone who can't remember my name let alone what we did the night before! I get off on the fact that she is getting off on the fact that what we are doing is stimulating. If she can barely prevent her eyes rolling into her skull then the whole experience isn't one to behold. Call me picky.

Also, my taste in women is more selective. I have always been a sucker for dark or red-haired women with blue/green eyes. Black girls are excepted on the eyes and, yes, I'm prejudiced against blondes. Thus, in any given room there are only a few possible targets as the hair/eye combination is a rarity.

I like to talk to a girl before we fuck. Intelligence is a huge aphrodisiac for me. However, I find to my continual dismay that women are wired completely differently to men. They are not driven in the same way. Most are incredibly insecure (even the successful career women) and rarely ever make the first move. Also women on the whole don't enjoy sex in the same way that men do. Furthermore, this isn't purely because they have had poor experiences with poor lovers. They are simply not driven to satisfy their desires to the same extent. It's almost as if sex is something they endure along the way to getting married and having kids. I have met so many women who have had unsatisfied sex lives. Yet, instead of doing something about it, they have endured!! I find this bizarre in the extreme.

I have long contended that there is a fundamental difference in thinking when the eyes of opposing sexes lock in initial attraction. On a subconscious level he is thinking, "She's nice, I wonder what she looks like naked." She is thinking, "He's nice, I wonder if he would make a good father to my child." I appreciate that the female population will by now be preparing wooden effigies of my image to burn at the stake. However, if I am wrong, why is it that women who have openly flirted with me for an entire evening suddenly and inexplicably turn on me when I inform them that I have had a vasectomy? It is as if I have just murdered their unborn child! When they were flirting, was I a potential good fuck first and a potential father second? This is highly unlikely, as I am still a good fuck when firing blanks, but I am no longer a potential father. The real cynics would say that I can no longer be trapped by pregnancy and therefore there is no marriage, no maintenance, etc.

Gay Man regularly fucks and doesn't even know the name of the other guy (both are stone cold sober). By contrast, this is extremely rare for Straight Man (unless one or the other parties are off their heads).

A whole ritual is usually to be adhered to for Straight Man to get laid. A mate of mine was recently meeting women from internet forums hoping for a quick shag. The profiles were usually quite suggestive. They would meet for lunch with a view to seeing how things progressed. His hit rate was negligible and after 20 lunches he had paid 20 bills! Only one of the 20 had offered to share the bill with him. What happened to equality? Does it only work one way?

The reason Straight Man will often endure an incompatible relationship is because he fears the inconvenience of finding a replacement. It may take him six months or more of wining and dining! I have watched mates of mine endure constant paranoia from their girlfriends who cling to their every move. Some of them are even told when they are allowed out! I don't know why they don't go and get a surgeon to surgically join them together. Under intense interrogation, the very same mates have no answer and are frequently quite sheepish in their defence. Eventually they admit that she spreads her legs in return for a few dollars and a bit of attention. I don't get it either! Any man in this position needs to go the gym and learn to bench press his oppressor's thumb!

I can't pretend that I understand women. However, I have learnt to predict their traits and behaviours. If I encounter one that plays games in a professional manner I rarely engage. I simply go and seek one that is more genuine. This means that because I am choosy, I probably get laid less than I could. Being a stripper carries with it a certain celebrity status. Certainly, this is influential and makes women more attracted to you than if you were simply a bloke walking down the street.

The behaviour of women on ladies' nights has always been a bit of mystery to me. Ladies' nights, it could be argued, are easier to play for a stripper than the gay nights. However, I have always thought the reverse. Gay audiences certainly can be more intimidating. They don't shout, they don't scream and this could be perceived as disliking the performance. To a performer used to a raucous audience, this can be unnerving as well as a confidence challenge. More likely, however, is that they are critically appraising your performance. If they like you there is a genuine appreciation which manifests itself in a more subtle manner. This subtlety has led many a stripper to proclaim that they don't like gay audiences. PP O' Rourke has been rejected by many a gay crowd because he has alienated his audience completely with his stand-offish closeted homophobia. A regular gay booker in Cambridge complained how PP O' Rourke would insist on being let in the back door, paid up front and then leave immediately after his performance. He wouldn't interact with his audience and refused to let anybody on stage. He famously once introduced himself to Uniboy with the line "Hi, I'm PP O Rourke, I'm straight". He was booked again by the Cambridge guy for a second go. The modus operandi was repeated and the audience turned their backs on him! Thankfully there wasn't to be a third chance. PP O'Rourke now conveniently claims that he doesn't like the gay scene anymore, so he doesn't work it. Similarly, so does Nevergayray. Only a week ago as I write, I worked with him on a ladies' night. I was on first and left to go to a second show. A week later I was having a threesome with two young ladies from the said ladies' night. They informed me that Nevergayray had been asked whether he played the gay scene.

"No, I leave that to people like Nick, I find it tacky."!!!

"That's strange, the other guy said all you strippers play the gay scene," retorted Simone.

"Not me," said Nevergayray, puffing out his chest.

"I'm sure he said you played the gay scene as well. Me and my mate are shagging him next week, we'll ask him again," said Simone, leaving Nevergayray flat footed.

Nevergayray has played every gay venue under the sun! In a well known gay venue in Blackpool, he had nailed his poster to the wall. A cheeky chap of a Northern stripper called AJ had written on it: 'Nice body, but do you have a cock?' Nevergayray obviously returned to the said venue because the next time I was there he had retorted, "You don't need a cock with a body like mine." Once he came off the steroids he began to shrink rapidly back to his normal size losing approximately 40lbs. His cock remained unchanged.

The last poster I saw of myself in Northern climbs had 'I love AJ' tattooed on my arm. Working with AJ and his Real Monty group was a pleasure. Again, my Northern brethren were much easier to get along with than their Southern counterparts.

A good stripper should be able to play either audience and adapt to any circumstance. However, I find the female audience somewhat perplexing at times. From a distance they are much easier to play than their gay counterparts. When a stripper arrives at a venue, the drag queen may have already started a show. The women will typically scream as you enter the room. I'm a total stranger who hasn't done anything, yet I am lauded as something special. I find this odd, as before giving my appreciation I would like to be impressed first. However, this is logical thinking and ladies' nights are not logical.

I have met many a stripper who has bitched that the women haven't screamed enough for them (even though my eardrums have burst). Screaming inflates egos and if future screams don't reach the desired level, stripper hissy fits can result.

Some strippers are not what the name implies. They have been initiated into a troupe such as the Bell Ends or the Aphrodite Occasion. These guys rarely strip beyond a g-string and are served up a screaming audience in a large venue, protected by their other troupe members. When they get brave and perform a ladies' night out on the solo circuit with a few rough, demanding birds who shout "OY, YUL BRYNNER – GET YOUR FUCKING COCK OUT" (as they did with Timberland – who is ageing and bald), egos can get a little bruised. With that said, I have noticed a trend on ladies' nights where the women are noticeably attracted to older men. On the gay scene it is the complete opposite, the meat has to be very tender for most of them. 'Chickens', as they are termed (youngsters), are generally the preferred flavour. A high proportion of women, however, seem to prefer their meat grizzled and burnt.

At nearly every ladies' night I am approached by a forty-something afterwards who opens with "I couldn't watch you... you reminded me of my son". I doubt if there are anywhere near as many dads out there who would worry about watching a stripper who was the same age as their daughter! Yet, female sexuality somehow seems to forbid them bedding a considerably younger man. Some of the approaching forty-ish brigade are even more put out when I tell them I am nearly old enough to be their son's dad, and that I have just aged well. I usually have to produce my driving license before they believe me.

Incidentally, whilst we are on the subject, there are also a few other myths that need to be put right concerning ladies' nights. Lots of women go for men who are a lot older. The same does not occur in reverse. A proportion of these women assume that age equals wealth and go away disappointed. However, others board the bus and go for a ride. I've watched it occur many a time with a perplexed look on my face.

Size does matter. The bigger the cock, the more they want to feel, touch and play with it. Uniboy seems to get his cock sucked on stage nearly every show. The smaller straight boys usually watch on with envious eyes.

Similarly, I have heard more than enough women claim that they don't find male bodybuilders attractive. From what I have seen, there is also more than enough that do find them attractive. The more steroids the man takes, the more appealing he seems to become to his female audience.

Anyway, I digress. I have never really gone around with a decibel counter. Some ladies' nights have women that scream louder than others. It is the competitive, snidey nature of these women that I have never understood. I have watched and observed on numerous occasions as the mood changes from one of adoration to hate when certain individuals don't get their own way and then mobilise a force against the stripper.

I have never really felt threatened when stripping – ever. Twice in gay venues morons wanted to pick fights. The first, I just whispered in his ear "you and me, outside in twenty minutes". He was gone by the time I came out looking for him. The other, I flung halfway across the room and he was disposed of by the doormen. Morons like this are thankfully rare.

Nothing like this has ever happened on a ladies' night with audience members, but things can sometimes become uncomfortable. Intimidating is too strong a word, but I have watched people turn very quickly in their outlook. The desire to leave a place where you no longer feel welcome is a strong one. Principally, this turn in feeling is borne out as a result of rejection.

In the gay venues, people are generally very nice and courteous. Those that come up and speak to you are usually complimentary and curious with many questions. They are genuinely interested and pleased to make your acquaintance. I have no doubt many of them want to get into my knickers. I am sure I will have my fair share of detractors, but these people keep that opinion to themselves. The gay audience work more on the principle that if you have nothing nice to say, don't say it all.

The female audience don't subscribe to this view. Male strippers are there to be used and abused if necessary. Some people come over just to be nasty. In some cases this nastiness is just a poor attempt at a chat-up line. For example "you're full of yourself, you are... you think you're it, don't ya". However, all that will do is raise the heckles of most people. In my getting-laid-is-an-art-form world I can take an instant dislike to a woman and want to fuck her... very hard (provided she is attractive).

As a people-watcher, I will regularly emerge after a performance, go and stand at the bar and begin watching. The approaches will then begin. Sometimes women will approach with genuinely nice comments. Sometimes they approach just to be bitchy. As a general rule, the games have begun!

I defy anyone to successfully demonstrate to me that women, as a species, are genuinely sexual creatures. The ones I gravitate towards are 'honorary blokes'. That is, they think and act with male traits. However, the species as a whole does not operate like this. They would much rather make love than have sex. I'm an exhibitionist and embrace the concept of public sex. Live porn is so much better than a fake movie. Gay men have practiced such methods for decades. However, the term 'dogging' is largely a media creation. For the uninitiated, dogging is supposedly where straight couples go and have sex in secluded public areas whilst others watch their antics. Women, however, rarely partake. I am a dogger. I like to be watched having sex. I get turned on even more watching other people get turned on by watching me.

Yet, in over three years of searching, I have never seen another couple having sex in public. It took me ages to find a girl willing to try it and when we did we were treated like gods. I would get out of the car and people would come over and shake my hand! One hard-core dogger even said that was the best thing he'd seen in eight years and the first time he'd seen a couple at it in a long time. Other doggers may exist but they are not in danger of becoming extinct after a prosperous period. Their numbers were never great in the first place. Women, being less sexual than men, generally reject this sort of sexual behaviour. Love making is not conducive with rough sex in a car park whilst people shout encouragement from the sidelines! Personally, their encouragement just acts as confirmation that we are doing the right kind of 'missionary' work. When something is that good, why keep it to yourself. Share the experience.

Anyway, I'm standing watching at the bar, the women come over and begin their spiels with their many motives. I'm generally good at reading situations. I can usually tell if somebody is attracted to me or not (typically the ones I don't want are attracted to me and the ones I want are not – or is that me being paranoid?). If the signals are good I will reciprocate, but I am not really one for prolonged games. I will usually make it clear that if they seek a boyfriend for love making then I am not he. However, if they fancy a romp in the hay, then maybe we could go and find the nearest barnyard.

This attitude is often met with a look of horror and disgust (oh to be gay!). The look of horror is even worse if they have been asking questions about how much money I earn. Those that open with "are you going to buy me a drink then" are met with "your round first".

I have played the game a few times, but generally only when it has become like a contest. The instances of sober women actually responding to my direct line of questioning are negligible and this is with the benefit of 'celebrity' status. The gay venues have their 'fag hags'. These women who hang around gay men are often my preferred quarry. They tend to have adopted some of the gay values. One night whilst standing at a bar watching, I was approached by a girl in a Swansea gay venue. "Your performance made me hot," she sang at me in a lovely Welsh whisper. As an opening salvo they don't get much better than that! I quickly did my Terminator thing. That is, whereby I scan her up and down analysing hair colour, eyes, figure, etc. My internal data processor will then give a result. A couple of seconds later the words MATCH, MATCH, MATCH were flashing in my head. The grungy, petite rock chick before me with black hair and green eyes needed a good seeing to.

Ten minutes later we had descended to my changing area and were rutting on the floor like a pair of wild animals. This was an excellent result, yet despite that audacious opening, it nearly didn't happen! After some initial questioning, it had been established that the young lady was a student in a nearby halls of residence. Naturally, I suggested a quick car ride to her room was in order. She refuted this, despite clearly wanting to get naked.

I have always tried to respect the venue I have been in by not fucking its customers on the premises. This is even more important in a gay venue. My role is to sell a fantasy and fucking the female customers is a sure-fire way to destroy that fantasy. On this occasion I let my morals slip and sneaked her downstairs, because it was clearly a case of now or never and I thought now was better than never.

The question, however, must be, why was it a now or never situation? Basically, the female of the species seems to lack pride in her sexuality compared to the male who usually revels in it. She couldn't or didn't want to be seen to be preying on a man (sexually). She was happy to be seen receiving attention from the said man (ego/self-esteem issues) but didn't want to be seen to actually have sexual urges and desires that she purged with the said man. Other females would then also see her actions and begin a counter-offensive against her based on subterfuge. After all, the said man would not be paying them the desired attention, so it is only reasonable that all parties are castigated. A campaign of lie and rumour could then have to be instigated.

I have seen this situation a thousand times before and decided I wanted to get laid. She did too, but in order to make it acceptable we had to do it illicitly (albeit on a carpeted pub floor in the cordoned-off downstairs bar). The irony of all this, is that Miss Swansea was about as forward as they come.

That example repeats itself in many different guises time and time again. Another night I had a mate with me in a gay venue. It was a Saturday night at the White Swan in London, always a good mixed night. He was heavily on the pull, I was tired at the end of long evening having already done three shows.

At the end of the show he came up to me with a girl in tow who instantly began shouting my praises in the most awful of Essex accents. My Terminator assessment returned an open verdict. After I had been praised like a god I managed to sidestep her and continue my tour of the packed venue. My phone rang.

"I've got that bird in the car, she wants you. Hurry up before she changes her mind; we can go back to mine." He clearly wanted to fuck this girl, but she had eyes only for the celebrity and he wasn't into sharing anyway. I had pulled a girl when I with him once before. We only had one car and when she got in it and saw him, she simply said, "I've never had two men before..." His eyes nearly popped out of his head and I had to hold him in to prevent him from exiting the moving vehicle.

On this occasion, as an open verdict had been returned, I was willing to be dutiful and do the deed for him. Indeed, I told him to leave his bedroom door open and then maybe he could get a good eyeful. As it turned out the girl worked for the police (not our favourite public workers due to their reluctance to catch murderers, muggers and rapists, but a dogged determination to root out doggers, gays and motorists). The spare mattress was laid out on his living room floor and he retreated to his room (leaving the door open).

My god-like powers of celebrity were clearly waning by the time we got back to his. She was far less keen to get in my knickers than she had been in the club. Perversely, having been set the challenge of getting into hers, my interest was rising and now she had less clothes on, I could also now see a fantastic pair of tits that had been otherwise obscured.

What ensued was an all too common occurrence. I scored the goal eventually, but it took me all night to get there. She was willing, but reluctant at the same time. Some people get turned on by someone playing hard to get. I just get bored and irritated. In this instance we were playing a game, however, and I had to try and show my mate the wares.

When we finally crossed the line of no return, in the dim half light of a rapidly approaching summer's morning, she suddenly became conscious of his potential to watch.

"He could be watching," she said anxiously.

"Don't be silly," I said as I rode her from behind whilst waving to him, who was eagerly but surreptitiously watching from his lair.

I am used to having sex in public and usually get turned on by it. Yet this situation felt strange. Having sex in front of a really close mate, knowing he wanted to be where I was, left me with a slightly empty feeling.

In the full light of morning when my mate rejoined us in the living room, the police girl tried to deny anything ever occurred! Before I could even react, he had pounced on her obvious mendaciousness.

"What are you talking about? I could hear it all from my room!" he said with incredulousness.

"No you didn't," came back the spoilt brat reply.

"I heard you say 'Fuck Me, Fuck Me' " (which she did).

I drove her home and she said she wanted to meet again. I actually thought this might be a good idea. She had the potential to fuck well if she didn't feel so inhibited. However, when I called her again a couple of days later her mood had changed considerably. She'd seen my website and had noticed I was writing a book. She now had a good mind to get the police around to confiscate the book! Obviously, I told her to be my guest. Did I understand this behaviour? Of course not.

There will be those out there who will claim that this sort of behaviour from the women I encounter is because they fall into a certain demographic grouping or category. I refute this completely. Firstly, I have pulled more women in gay clubs than on hen nights. The demographic grouping in those is more varied and widespread. Furthermore, I perform at a large number of private parties and their demographic covers the whole spectrum. It has been levelled at me that ladies' nights have more of a 'council estate crowd'. As a whole this is true and the 90% rule applies (ie 90% of a given population conform to a behavioural norm). However, I could hardly be called a good analyst and researcher if all my test subjects were from the same demographic. They are not.

Another night my quarry was a newly qualified medical doctor. She had an extremely posh accent and my tactics had to reflect the prey. I even broke one of my own rules and took her out to dinner! Over dinner she assured me that she never slept with anybody on the first date and that there was no way that would change. She repeated this a few times. We also got into a discussion of the location of Mt Kilimanjaro. For the uninitiated, it's actually in Tanzania. She was most insistent that it was in Kenya. We settled the disagreement with a bet. If it was in Kenya, I would do anything she asked me to. If it was in Tanzania, she had to strip for me.

A little later, back at her place, her faced turned ashen as she stared blankly at her computer screen, informing her that Kilimanjaro is in Tanzania.

"Where would you like me," I asked with a certain degree of smugness.

She protested and persuaded me to strip first to show her how it's done. I obliged and then began to help her undress.

"You still can't fuck me," she snapped.

"I know," I said as I removed her bra and began nuzzling a nipple.

Eventually, after a long campaign I removed her knickers and began rubbing my erect phallus up and down gently against her clit.

"You're going to have to stop that," she gasped.

"Why?" I asked triumphantly.

"Because otherwise you're going to have to fuck me," she squeaked.

In the morning I woke alone, but to my dismay the Arctic Circle had descended on the room. Icicles hung from the ceiling and snow had fallen on the bed. I could see my breath in the air. The good doctor wanted to usher me from her room as quickly as was humanly possible. At least it might then warm up a bit.

She was intelligent in an academic way, but in all other ways I found her just as backward as many that had gone before her. She was paranoid what her friends might think of the stripper staying the night and what this said about her. I had also persuaded her to renege on her own promise to herself. I was hardly running away, I asked to see her again. She assured me yes, but I knew she meant no.

At a later date I asked her to explain her actions to me in a logical way, so that I might understand her behaviour from her perspective, as opposed to my extrapolated interpretation. She refused and only agreed to speak to me after I told her I was writing about it and wanted her opinions so she could put her version of events. It turns out that apparently it didn't look good for her to be seen with a stripper and "it wouldn't be possible to take me home to her parents". Daddy wouldn't approve (allegedly). What must she have been thinking about when she had a stripper sticking out of her? Who said prejudice is on the way out?

She wasn't the last 'posh bird' or the last doctor I was to get into. Another 'posh bird' told me that we couldn't see each other again because "daddy didn't approve" and the doctor was another one-night thing. I remember discussing with her the nature of my last encounter with a doctor.

"I'll only sleep with you if you promise not to go schizophrenic on me the morning," I said.

"I promise," she said reassuringly.

I woke up to a different woman and made a quick exit fearing for my life. I received an apologetic text later on in the day saying that I must now think all female doctors are complete lunatics. I replied with a simple "yes".

There can be no doubt that sex is a very emotive issue for women. Their male counterparts engage in a physical act, whereas the female often goes on a spiritual journey when sharing her bodily fluids.

Women still have sexual urges and physical needs that have to be met. Their desire and will to satisfy them however, is considerably dampened. I have observed on numerous occasions where women have wanted to get down and dirty (with me), yet their conscience hasn't allowed them to. Their body language and even their language has been all systems go. Yet, they don't want to be seen as 'easy' or a 'slag' in front of their mates. By contrast, Straight Man would receive a round of applause from his mates. The term slag is just a euphemism for somebody who has a good sex life.

Instead, Straight Woman receives jealous looks and snide remarks from her 'mates'. If friends can't be happy for you then surely they can't really be friends. I've slept with women from many different backgrounds and social groupings. A common thread is their lack of genuinely close friendships. They seem to have many superficial friendships but a lack of people that they could rely on to walk through fire for them should they need it. Their female friends typically carry pangs of jealousy and exhibit an air of pretentious rivalry. Their alleged male friends simply want to fuck them (the straight ones). Often they have no idea of this and refute this when they are told.

I firmly believe that men and women can't be friends without the sex getting in the way. They are completely different species with differing interests, motives and priorities. The exception to this is if both parties find each other mutually unattractive or sex occurs and therefore that barrier is removed. A friendship can then blossom. Even then, however, the friendship that occurs between man and woman is very different to that that occurs between the same sex. The friendship is usually born out of a shared experience rather than common interest.

For the record, I do have female friends – they are just relatively few in number. I've had sex with nearly all of my female friends; we got it out of the way early. One in particular saw my website and targeted me from afar (America in fact). She was angling for a shag whilst she was visiting London. However, given everything I've had to say about female sexuality you probably won't be too surprised to hear that she was a female stripper and therefore slightly more forward than most!

If women could observe their boyfriends in the company of their friends I'm sure that they would dump their boyfriends immediately. Sorry to break this to you girls, but every part of your anatomy, what you got up to in your most intimate moments and the amount of noise you make at the height of your pleasure have probably been shared in minute detail with his mates. Of course he told you he's isn't like all those other men. He has to if he wants to keep fucking you – doesn't he?

The number of times I have been direct and blunt with women and it has actually been successful are very small in number. Even the power of celebrity rarely overcomes the insecurity and inhibitions of the female of the species. However, there are exceptions.

I was once playing a gay venue in Exeter. It was a Tuesday night and I had driven all that way just for the one show. The show went well and I had numerous gay approaches afterwards. They turned away one after the other having crashed and burned in a ball of flames. As soon as the fire has been doused another one was there trying his luck.

At the very end of the evening I was approaching the organiser to bid him farewell when I was approached by a gorgeous giggly girl. She had short brown hair, piercing blue eyes and a cracking pair of mammaries. My terminator sense was screaming 'MATCH, MATCH, MATCH' at maximum volume.

"Hello," I said.

"Hello," came back the delayed reply.

She looked starstruck, and had clearly been infected with stripper celebrity.

"I was just leaving," I said.

"Where do you live?"

"Near London."

"You're driving all the way back there now," she said incredulously.

"Of course not," I said.

"Where are you staying then?"

"Your place of course," I proclaimed as triumphantly as I could muster.

She giggled some more and after a brief hesitation said, "OK."

I grabbed her by the hand and began to lead her out of the club before she changed her mind.

The steady stream of gays who had crashed and burned stared at us with open mouths as we left. One of them uttered "bitch" under his breath as we passed.

We got back to hers and soon got naked. She was perfect and her pussy tasted so sweet. I could have dined on it all night. The gays were trying to call her demanding to know what she was up to with the stripper. We took a picture on her mobile of her sucking my cock and texted it to the perpetrators. A reply was instantly returned with one word – "BITCH".

Rebecca was divine and she came across well. She was working a job in a bar to rent her tiny little bedsit. She was no benefit junkie living off the state, which endeared me to her even more. Her long legs had been used on a billboard campaign and she seemed to have a lot more going for her besides. When I set off for home she assured me I was welcome to come and stay with her if I was ever working in the area again. I made a strong mental note to do that.

So it was that six months later I had arranged a trio of shows on successive days across Devon. I picked Rebecca up en route to Plymouth and found it difficult to keep my hands off her. We arrived at the gay venue in Plymouth and Becky duly helped me prepare for the show with her luscious lips and mouth. Afterwards we had a game of pool and she commented what a good weekend she thought it would be.

Back at her place the sex games began and what ensued was perhaps the most memorable sexual encounter I have had to date. She tied my hands behind my back and then got quite forceful with me. Grabbing my hair, she forced me to eat her out for quite some time. Finally, she rode me until I screamed.

What a tragedy it was that I again awoke to a different person. Having shown so much potential the night before, I thought I was going to be in for a weekend to remember. I was, but not the type I had hoped for.

I seem to have a habit of getting girls to do things in the bedroom that they haven't done before. My confidence seems to rub off on them in the heat of the moment. When on the ecstasy train, they step out of their comfort zone and whilst I'm holding their hand they're fine with it. In the morning, however, they are full of sobered-up thoughts and regrets about the kinky depraved stuff they did the night before. Obviously it's not possible that they made a conscious decision to go with their rabid desires. Oh no, I made them do it, of course. I am a man and therefore evil.

I interrogated Rebecca as to her change of behaviour but to no avail. Her rationality gene had been used up for the rest of the year and irrational, emotional female behaviour ensued. The rest of the weekend was a miserable affair as I sought to root out the broken part in her, so that I could fix it take us back to the way it was. My female mechanic skills failed me. I was a little smitten with her. On the last show of the tour, a couple of other offers were given from willing females. On another night I'd have taken up the offer. On that night I instead traipsed off to have a final attempt at fixing the Rebecca express. Needless to say, I drove off into the night and with my repair attempt having failed, I have never seen her again.

The line I used to pull Rebecca worked again one night in Blackpool. Charlotte was slightly more resistant about allowing me to sleep at her place and needed reassuring that I liked redheads. In the end it was a good night, although she did throw me out early in the morning because she feared her dad wouldn't approve of her bringing home a stripper. I have never seen her again either. One part of me is disappointed at that, the other thinks that it is probably a good thing. The memory of our night is good; if I saw her again and any irrational demons emerged, it would spoil the image.

Sex is a game which men have learnt to play. Women, however, set the rules. I like to compete and play the sport. Yet I can't stand the games that have to be played just to get to the start line. Rarely are these games bypassed, even for strippers. I wish I lived in an era where women had overcome their insecurities, didn't need constant reassurance about their looks and actually took the initiative. I don't want to always have to make the first move or be the dominant driving force in bed all the time. Women that lie there and wait to be fucked bore me. I wish I lived in a world where the women were sexual predators. A world where the women fucked my brains out and then didn't ask me to overly respect them in the morning. Politeness is given, respect is earned.

I wish I lived in a world where women could be honest and less deceitful about their sexuality. So many talk up their sexual exploits in an attempt to gain attention and make men want to sleep with them. In reality, they would never do half of what they claim. I abhor bullshit on all levels. If someone tells me they bench press twice their bodyweight, I know this to be extremely unlikely. I challenge them to do it. They never can. If an attractive girl tell me she likes rough sex over the bonnet of a car with a random stranger, I tell her lets go. There is always an excuse.

Gay men often assume that women have the same sexuality of men. They don't know any different, after all. They are forever telling me how their female friend is a man-eater. I then have to explain to them that their female friend is exaggerating her exploits to conform to the norm of the group of gay men with whom she hangs out. It is true that 'fag hags' have adopted more of the gay sexual norms than her non-fag hag counterparts. This is why I like them. However, only one of these man-eaters has met the challenge I have laid down. She got a little freaked at some of the kinky stuff I wanted to introduce, but we did meet and fuck on the basis of a phone call and a description. When I was next passing that way, however, she had mentally collapsed and was worried men were using her. Why didn't she use them? Sex was off the menu.

Threesomes rarely ever work. The girls just get jealous over one another. Of course this doesn't stop me trying and the jealousy occurs to varying degrees. One night in particular the jealousy went off the scale, supposedly between best friends. Two teenagers wanted to point score with the stripper. Both were quite immature mentally and perhaps wary about driving off with a stranger. There was nowhere we could go that was comfortable so we ended up in my car in a dark field. Their gay friend was left in the front as I climbed into the back.

"Suck his cock, I want to see you suck his cock," he barked excitedly in his camp effeminate voice.

It wasn't long before all three of us were naked in the back seat. I was in the middle, my middle finger from each hand in respective vaginas.

"So who wants to go first?" I asked inquisitively.

"I will," snapped the brunette.

"You slut," replied the redhead.

"Bitch."

"Slut."

"Bitch."

"Slut."

"Calm down," I said, my fingers now removed from the warring vaginas with my hands in a parting calming gesture. "You can go first if you like, there is plenty to go around," I said to the now pouting redhead.

"Bitch."

"Slut."

"Bitch."

"Slut."

"Suck his cock," said the forgotten gay boy.

My little head told me to ignore what was coming out of the mouth of the silly hags and fuck them anyway, but my big head couldn't stand their bickering any longer. I ordered them to put their clothes back on and drove them home. I was gutted at their stupidity and the style in which they just ruined what should have been a very good time.

Perhaps it was just as well. Someone later told me they were only 15. Legally, should I ask for ID before getting naked? They looked about 21 and were drinking alcohol. Still, many a man has been strung up by society for less.

Perhaps the nature of the sex game is best illustrated by an incident that happened in a club in Greece. I was performing in a gay club over a series of nights. On the first night, I got chatting to a Greek beauty who clearly had the hots for me. The feeling was mutual. However, as is usual, against my will, we had already begun the opening moves of the sex game. I would have been happy to brutally fuck her there and then on the dance floor. Despite some animalistic urges that concurred with my view, she couldn't be seen to act in such a manner in front of her friends. Nor could she allow me to think that she had animalistic urges. That is, she couldn't for one minute allow me to think she was a 'slag'.

Thus, we chatted, flirted, she stroked her hair every second minute, you get the picture. I steered the conversation around so that I could play one of my ace cards. I engineered a situation whereby she said I must be gay.

"How could I prove you wrong on that?" I said, with as much innocence as I could muster.

"What you mean?" she enquired in her broken Greco-English.

"Well, what could I do to you that a gay man wouldn't do to you?" I qualified.

She countered my line of attack by basically stating that gay men were whores who would park their bike in any hole that would act as a garage, even if the garage belonged to a woman.

"I agree, but gay men don't eat pussy," I said triumphantly. Talking of pussy eating was my favourite way of getting rid of the attentions of overly amorous gays. It had an unusual effect on them. Similar to the effects of kryptonite on superman, pussy munching caused gays to wither and die at the thought. It is something that a true gay man can't even contemplate let alone perform. Every fag hag knows this.

"You are gay, you would not do this," she said invitingly.

I immediately got on my knees and attempted simulated oral sex with her pussy, causing her to recoil in a mixture of embarrassment, horror and unrequited lust. I persuaded her that the women's toilets would be empty, we were after all surrounded by gays. This was my error in the sex game. I had accelerated things too quickly.

We went to the empty women's toilets. We kissed, I played with her tits and then began to make my way down. I removed the jeans and set to work on the knickers, my tongue at the ready to rasp like a snake's. However, this 110lb beauty had suddenly acquired the grip of Svend Karlsen. Her knickers steadfastedly refused to fall.

"I believe you, you're not gay," she shrieked.

"I know," came the muffled reply as I tried in vain to yank the knickers down whilst simultaneously attempting to insert my tongue.

"I can't now – my friends wonder where I am."

Despite my best efforts, I was defeated on the night. Nothing I could say or do would make her change her mind. This particular game decreed that her vagina was sacred on the first night.

We swapped numbers and the next day I was invited to the beach. Realising I was in the middle of a stupid game, I declined. I had to make her think I didn't care. Later that night I was taken to a local beach bar by my hosts. One of them informed me that my quarry, I assumed by pure coincidence, had walked into the opposite end of the bar. I looked up and she was staring straight at me. I waved but did not walk over. My gay hosts did not understand my apparent rudeness. They thought I was on a sticky wicket with this girl. I remained quietly confident. After about half an hour I wandered over to say hello.

"Why did you not come over," she said, more than a little miffed by my flippant approach.

I made my excuses about respectability to my hosts and enquired about what she was up to later. She invited me to the beach the next day. I countered by inviting her back to the club, as the next day was to be my last night.

The next day she called again, inviting me to the beach. I again declined, citing time pressure over pre-arranged engagements and re-issued my invite to the club. She said she might be there.

Sure enough, she came into the club just as I was going on stage. I came straight out and asked if she still thought I was gay.

"Yes, you are gay."

"Are you going to let me prove you wrong this time?"

"How?"

"Up there," I gesticulated towards the women's toilets.

"OK," she said coyly.

I wandered up first. Last time I had to wait five minutes so that her friends would not be suspicious. This time she followed about five seconds later. I picked her up and carried her over to the sinks where I sat her down. After pulling down her jeans, I literally tore the knickers from her body (the elastic snapped). This was hardly a marathon sex session, hard and fast was the order of the day. I turned her round, bent her over the sink and entered her from behind. She kept glancing across and watched our rampant animalism in the mirror. Normally, I won't have sex in the actual venues, but my hosts had actively encouraged me after hearing the story of my glorious failure a couple of nights before.

Afterwards we went back downstairs and there was an uncomfortable 15 minutes where we pretended to be interested in each other over a drink (beyond the sexual attraction). She made her excuses and left the club shortly afterwards, having achieved what she set out to achieve by her visit. I found her simulated interest most amusing and in stark contrast to many of her British counterparts. It actually felt nice to be wanted purely for my body and not for my 'celebrity' or my money. It was just a shame she didn't have the confidence to follow it through on the first night.

The game we played is typical. I would much prefer it if women would have the confidence to go with their urges. For me, there is no thrill in the chase and chivalry is dead. We live in an age of equality and men shouldn't always have to make the first move. If women still crave chivalry then its supporters must realise that they will never be equals. If sex is something women offer in return for jewellery then there is definitely a weaker sex.

Modern society leads us to believe that women have broken their domestic cycle. They've kicked down the kitchen door, burnt their aprons and become sexual predators. It's a nice media created image but not one that the majority of women have embraced. Equality is on offer, but it isn't one that women have yet grasped with both hands. The sex game will probably always act as a good barometer of this.

There is no doubt that since I started stripping, my overall impression of women as a species has dropped. The level of nastiness they often show to complete strangers will never cease to amaze me.

I should qualify here. I'm not talking about career criminals who set out to cause deliberate harm, but everyday people. Conversely, the way women scream because I walk into a venue (as a complete stranger) carrying nothing more than a bag also astounds me. Those very same screamers can turn faster than a world rally car. A couple of incidents exemplify this.

I was performing in Wimbledon one night. Three particularly exuberant women were at the front, one of whom was definitely my type. On completing the show and stalking my quarry, it was clear that my intended target was way too drunk to be entertaining. I talked to her redheaded friend for five minutes before bidding them farewell and getting in my car to go home. I suggested that she take her friend home as she was in a wobbly state.

I awoke next morning to a desperate message from my friend, Andy. Andy had organised the show the night before and had received a phone call at 4 am from the police. They were looking for a 'Mr Sexecute' as he was the leading suspect in a missing person enquiry. I phoned the police to hand myself in and explained to them that they were the victim of a lie perpetrated by evil women. Their missing person was likely asleep in a ditch somewhere recovering from the previous night's alcohol.

Rather than look after their stricken friend and take her home, the other two had clearly lost her somewhere, as they too had fallen into a drunken stupor. Realising that one was missing they blamed their loss on an innocent man who they had met briefly for a few minutes that evening. I told the police that they were haranguing an innocent man and that the girls were formally wasting police time. Unfortunately this didn't seem to go down too well with the police. The argument culminated in me having to tell them to fuck off and call back when the girl had woken up.

To be fair to the police in this instance, someone called back from a non-withheld number about an hour later and apologised. The girl had turned up, still drunk. However, nobody was to be charged for wasting police time and the innocent man never received an apology from his accusers.

Another night I did a hen night with a stripper called Flax. I was driving us both and he persuaded me to go back with a few ladies to their house. He was convinced he was going to fuck one of them. I was happy to be dutiful and wait whilst he did what he had to do. The ladies seemed very enamoured with our presence for the first 30 minutes or so. I remember giving Flax a hurry up sign as I had an early start the next day. Then the jealous husband returned home. Not wanting to be involved in a police domestic incident and not wanting to get involved in a fight over something that didn't happen, we left by the other door. There is no doubt in my mind that the whole thing was a deliberate set-up. I don't think the plan had run its full course. That was for the husband to find her in bed with the stripper. She would have still felt attractive and the husband would have felt terribly slighted. The term 'nasty' does not do her actions justice.

It may seem like I have spent the whole time playing down the easy sex element of being a stripper. Female sexuality does not by and large lend itself to casual sexual encounters after only a brief meeting of eyes. Gay Man can have sex with a multitude of strangers in a manner that Straight Man can only fantasise about. Yet the male stripper can easily outperform his typical straight rival in this area. I need to clarify this. Drunken romps simply do not count. If she can't remember what you did the night before then shame on you both.

Sexecute has had his fair share of casual fucks with those allured in by his 'celebrity' persona. At a house party he was once penned into a bathroom by the Asian host, who got naked whilst her guests suspected nothing downstairs. Another Asian host once followed him outside and coitus was performed on the bonnet of a car in the middle of the country outside a stately home.

The hens (those about to wed) are nearly always well behaved when the stripper arrives. After all, the mother-in-law is often watching. However, sometimes the mother-in-law is not present and egged on by their friends, who think the husband to be is not good for them, the hens can get carried away very occasionally. I have been sucked dry by women who are to wed imminently. They take the final fling before a lifetime of domesticity, quite literally. Another night I was hired by three female students who were all blow job virgins. I ended up being their blow job coach as they took it in turns whilst I sat on a chair in the middle of the room.

Yet another night, I was dragged by my cock from the centre of the room by the wife of the (male) booker, upstairs to the bedroom. Whilst I was performing in their living room she was having a good nosh on my equipment underneath a big cape. At the time, I remember thinking 'her husband shouldn't really see this, this is not good'. However, I had nothing to worry about. The booker encouraged me to fuck his wife whilst he watched. The only proviso was that I had to be quick so the guests didn't get suspicious downstairs!

However, such occurrences are rare. Despite countless numbers of discussions with women about my ultimate fantasy I have still not got anywhere near acting it out. Some have talked the talk, none have got anywhere near walking the walk. I am still waiting to be gang raped by five lascivious ladies. Four will be required to hold down each limb whilst another rides on top. Of course, they will then rotate. Short of paying for it, the chances of it becoming reality seem slim. If I was gay, I could execute this ideal within a few hours of any given start time.

I have already mentioned that women do sometimes offer cash in return for sex. In nearly every situation the offer isn't genuine. By making the offer, in her eyes, I should play the game and then counter the offer by saying I'll do it for free. In essence it is typically a pick-up line used by those lacking confidence. Only on one occasion has a purveyor of that line followed through and only on one occasion therefore have I acted as a gigolo. Even on this particular occasion the lines were blurred. I was officially procured to perform a "private show for one", but it was obvious, to me at least, what was going to happen.

To be honest, I found the whole thing quite uncomfortable. Not because being hired for sex was in any way unnerving or degrading; on the contrary, it was quite empowering. My doubts arose because of the nature of female sexuality (again). I was not being hired as a fuck machine (which would have made it a lot easier). Instead, the booker was looking for companionship more than sex. She was recently divorced. Although she knew what she was doing and the service I was offering, there was a lingering hope that maybe I could offer more. Although I tried to be as sensitive to her needs as I could be, I simply wasn't going to turn into a replacement for her husband. She knew it and I knew it. Therefore, the experience was emotive and difficult. Throughout the whole thing I had nagging doubts about whether this was actually good for her. Should I be taking money off her whilst causing her emotions to play up? I know gigolos aren't meant to think like this but people have feelings and I don't like hurting those of the innocent. This is what it felt like I was doing.

The whole male escort for women industry is practically non existent. I have never met a woman who would admit to paying for sex or who frankly would get turned on by the experience. Women prefer to be loved before they are fucked and the premise of hiring an escort is the other way around. A high percentage (of the admittedly limited percentage of women) of those that would hire a male escort just for the sex probably lack Hollywood babe looks. The job satisfaction derived from the act, for the gigolo, may be limited. I have spoken to one male escort who I believe was genuine and he said work was virtually non-existent. I have spoken to others who have said work was plentiful. These dreamers all earned about £8000/week but strangely drove around in cars that didn't work. These escorts could all run the 100 meters in under ten seconds. As I hope you appreciate by now it is sometimes difficult to differentiate between a liar and a twat.

To sum up this chapter on the fairer sex, I quite damningly will state that I simply wish I was gay. I feel trapped between a rock and a hard place (no pun intended). Nearly every gay man who hears this simply says "be gay then". That, of course, is ridiculous. That would be like me saying to them "be straight then and suffer less prejudice". Few gay men can actually understand my reasoning and logic for wanting to be gay because they are simply not attracted to women.

Those that have tried women in an earlier life often sympathise with me somewhat. Those that have never slept with women simply don't understand and think women operate in the same way (mentally) as men do. Their naivety is astounding.

By contrast, when I tell women that I want to be gay, they think I am gay but in the closet. When I explain my logic they think I am a woman hater/chauvinist. This just makes me want to be gay even more.

Don't completely misunderstand me – I have met some women who are good in bed. The downside is that those that could fuck competitively are all stark raving bonkers – I mean seriously unhinged. This isn't necessarily their fault. It is almost certainly a by-product of their upbringing. Whilst I believe that a certain amount of behaviour is genetic and predetermined, the majority of it is learnt and therefore a result of our environmental upbringing. Unfortunately for me, those that have been able to really make me moan in bed have also made me scream out of it. Their behaviours have included compulsive lying, self-harming, manic depression and threatened suicide. Some of these women have never worked a day in their life (benefit fiends), others have high-powered jobs. Some suffered abuse as children, others did not. All, however, did seem to suffer deep levels of anxiety based on feelings of inadequacy and insecurity.

They fucked like demons, but were impossible to live with. By contrast, those that you would want to live with fucked to love rather than loved to fuck.

EPILOGUE

What has Sexecute done for Nick? Has Sexecute been good for Nick? These are questions I wrestle with on a constant basis. Becoming a stripper has been the best and worst thing that has ever happened to me. When I stepped onto the stage for the first time I was at a pretty low ebb. I had little time for the country I was living in or its fallacious alleged democratic ways. I wasn't interested in polishing up my social skills to fit in with the British hierarchical system. By and large the British still seem to be a strange mix of fear, laziness and dullness – nobody wants to do or say anything that might upset somebody else. Orwellian predictions seem all too close to fruition for my liking. I often compare modern day Britain to the final days of the Roman empire. This once great land seems to be disintegrating and burning around us. Murders, muggers and rapists ply their trade with gay abandon whilst the fat cats grow ever more rotund on their plunderings. The man in the middle is getting burnt, but still he says thank you. I guess I'm destined to be an émigré.

I left Britain once, but it was Sexecute that lured me back. He offered something that was the antithesis to the plundering that was rampant around me – freedom, fun, frolics and the achievement of a lifetime ambition. On one level Sexecute has delivered all that and more. He has certainly allowed me to recover my lost teenage youth years (a period that never happened for me). He acts as a pussy magnet, does wonders for one's ego and masquerades me as a professional athlete. In fact, most men would pay to be in Sexecute's shoes. The great thing is I get paid to be this fantastic road warrior!

Being recognised and pointed out by semi-strangers can be highly addictive, but in reality it is overrated. Sexecute is really a front for a glamorised lifestyle, that for the most part should be consigned to the annals of myth and legend. In reality, Sexecute probably earns less than you do. Your pay check is almost certainly more secure and your working environment probably more salubrious. With plaudits also comes the jealousy and abuse. When did somebody last pour acid all over your car just because of what you do for a living? In essence, Sexecute is a front for a maverick man who simply can't fit in with modern mainstream society and didn't reach the heights he set for himself. Like a loser's reach, mine was too slow and short to hit the peaks. Sexecute is essentially a failed (some would say unlucky) athlete. Having run the 100m in 11.2 and possessing relative body strength that is considered elite, I possessed the raw materials that should have enabled me to eke out a living playing a team sport. Alas, the opportunity never presented itself and I'm destined to remain bitter and twisted about it forevermore. Sexecute is a substitute for that athlete I never became.

I constantly ask myself why are we so anaesthetised to all the lies? Why do people fall into the mortgage/kids trap? Why do people get raped at work all day and then say thank you? Am I the only one that can see the emperor has no clothes on?

Sexecute delivers me from this great evil. I still occasionally wake up from nightmares where I am back working for a large corporate company. I know I'm not alone, my friend and ex boss has the very same nightmares. He's dropped out of society too.

Ultimately, it was my fear of leading a 'normal' life mixed in with a dose of fortune that led to Sexecute's creation. Zoe, my long term girlfriend at the time of Sexecute's birth, always knew that 'normality' was my greatest fear. She used to lament frequently on how I was perhaps never destined to be happy. I have never been overly materialistic, nor have I sought fame. Yet even modest incomes do not come about without paying some homage to normality (for those of us born outside the establishment). She knew this was my greatest fear; my solution was Sexecute and ultimately this is what parted us.

Even the pussy magnet aspect to Sexecute's character is over-rated. Girls often want Sexecute to want them. Some want to shag him. Other still want him for their boyfriend. However, well over 99% of them want him to give up what he was created for within a week. Sexecute therefore struggles to find a girlfriend who can accept him for what he is. Zoe did accept me and him, yet still he broke us apart.

Ironically, as I write this today, another Sexecute girlfriend decided that this lifestyle was too much for her. I met Sylvie as I began writing this manuscript. A great 15 months ensued only for her to end it all like a car crash. She was here yesterday and gone today. She delivered a hammer blow e-mail designed to test even the coping mechanisms of Sexecute. Her ilk are rare. She was a gorgeous 22-year-old mixed race beauty, who was into exhibitionistic public sex. She liked it rough and was willing to experiment. Of course, she had the customary profile of having suffered abuse as a child.

Alas, even she found it too trying to cope with the lifestyle of her stripper boyfriend. She preferred to slink off with a new man. One with no hair, a beach ball physique and a dangerous drug habit. Apparently, he offered 'normality' and 'stability' – something a stripper does not. If I sound bitter, it's because I am. It's hard to take when you are told that you are a wonderful man who has enriched someone's life, but "I can't cope with your job". Sorry and take care just doesn't take the sting out of the barb. How fitting she should deliver the coup de grace as I write the epilogue.

Whenever I perform at a club I sometimes suffer flashbacks. If the DJ is playing Whitney Houston's I Wanna Dance with Somebody, or Lionel Ritchie's Dancing on the Ceiling, they send a cold shiver down my spine. I can't remember why exactly, but I associate both those tracks with my lonely, girlfriend-less teenage years. Sexecute is the eraser of these thoughts.

However, things have come full circle. When you lose, you do so alone. I was starting to love Sylvie but now I feel like a right idiot. I again stand alone, without womanly love for support. Whitney and Lionel taunt me from the sidelines.

The vast majority of men when pressed will admit that it is not in their nature to be monogamous. If it is put on a plate for them and nobody will ever find out, they will dine heartily. In my pre-Sexecute years, I had friends who could never understand my loyalty to one woman. I always replied that I didn't put myself in the situations where temptation arose. The wheel has now come full circle. Now they have kids and don't frequent bars, nightclubs, etc. I have to go into them for a living and attempt to stimulate the clientele. It is hardly conducive to a quiet married life in the country. Many strippers are indeed married. I have not met many that are faithful.

Sexecute drove a wedge between Zoe and Nick. Nick always had the demons, but Sexecute has a habit of letting them out of the box. I sometimes feel resentful against Sexecute for this. I feel he destroyed the relationship with the girl I love. Essentially, due to the nature of his work, he is also virtually unlovable to a woman.

Sexecute ages quickly. He won't live into his hundreds. When he is dead and gone I hope I don't resent my acquaintance with him.

* * *

Nick Molloy and his alter ego Sexecute can be contacted via his website www.malestripper.org